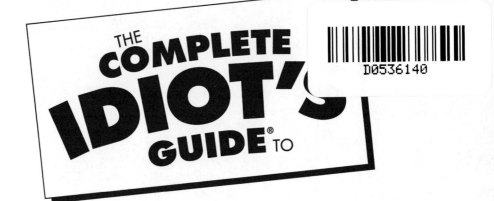

THE
COMPLETE
IDIOT'S
GUIDE® TO

The Great
Depression

by H. Paul Jeffers

ALPHA

A member of Penguin Group (USA) Inc.

To my parents, Tom and Margaret Jeffers, who somehow raised five kids during the Depression.

ALPHA BOOKS

Published by the Penguin Group

Penguin Group (USA) Inc., 375 Hudson Street, New York, New York 10014, USA

Penguin Group (Canada), 90 Eglinton Avenue East, Suite 700, Toronto, Ontario M4P 2Y3, Canada (a division of Pearson Penguin Canada Inc.)

Penguin Books Ltd., 80 Strand, London WC2R 0RL, England

Penguin Ireland, 25 St. Stephen's Green, Dublin 2, Ireland (a division of Penguin Books Ltd.)

Penguin Group (Australia), 250 Camberwell Road, Camberwell, Victoria 3124, Australia (a division of Pearson Australia Group Pty. Ltd.)

Penguin Books India Pvt. Ltd., 11 Community Centre, Panchsheel Park, New Delhi—110 017, India

Penguin Group (NZ), 67 Apollo Drive, Rosedale, North Shore, Auckland 1311, New Zealand (a division of Pearson New Zealand Ltd.)

Penguin Books (South Africa) (Pty.) Ltd., 24 Sturdee Avenue, Rosebank, Johannesburg 2196, South Africa

Penguin Books Ltd., Registered Offices: 80 Strand, London WC2R 0RL, England

International Standard Book Number: 978-0-02-864289-5
Library of Congress Catalog Card Number: 2001097260

12 11 10 09   8 7 6 5 4 3 2

Interpretation of the printing code: The rightmost number of the first series of numbers is the year of the book's printing; the rightmost number of the second series of numbers is the number of the book's printing. For example, a printing code of 02-1 shows that the first printing occurred in 2002.

Printed in the United States of America

Note: This publication contains the opinions and ideas of its author. It is intended to provide helpful and informative material on the subject matter covered. It is sold with the understanding that the author and publisher are not engaged in rendering professional services in the book. If the reader requires personal assistance or advice, a competent professional should be consulted.

The author and publisher specifically disclaim any responsibility for any liability, loss, or risk, personal or otherwise, which is incurred as a consequence, directly or indirectly, of the use and application of any of the contents of this book.

Publisher: *Marie Butler-Knight*
Product Manager: *Phil Kitchel*
Managing Editor: *Jennifer Chisholm*
Acquisitions Editor: *Gary Goldstein*
Development Editor: *Deborah S. Romaine*
Senior Production Editor: *Christy Wagner*

Copy Editor: *Drew Patty*
Illustrator: *Chris Eliopolous*
Cover/Book Designer: *Trina Wurst*
Indexer: *Angie Bess*
Layout/Proofreading: *Cheryl Lynch, Michelle Mitchell, Nancy Wagner*

Contents at a Glance

Contents

Foreword

The "Roaring Twenties" were a time of prosperity, optimism, and frivolity. Young women known as "flappers" shocked older generations by abandoning corsets, cutting their hair short, and wearing short skirts. They even smoked! Both men and women visited speakeasies and drank "hooch." No longer were cars only for the elite, now young and old alike were able to cruise around town in Model Ts. Evenings were spent listening to the Grand Ol' Opry and Irving Berlin songs on the radio. Ordinary investors assumed they would make huge profits by buying stocks on margin.

Then one Tuesday everything changed. The stock market crashed, and the economy began to fail. Without warning, millions of people lost both their jobs and their homes. Banks foreclosed on farms, sending farmers fleeing to the West only to find persecution and few jobs. With one in four workers unemployed, families were forced to turn to bread and soup lines to keep from starving. The Great Depression, the longest and most devastating economic depression in modern history, had begun.

The Great Depression lasted 12 long years. That's one eighth of the entire twentieth century. It was an unprecedented time in history—never before had a recession or depression lasted for such a long duration. Though President Herbert Hoover knew the problem was serious, he tried but failed to end the depression. No one knew how to stop the plummeting economy, yet the people of the United States knew they wanted change. When Franklin D. Roosevelt promised a "New Deal" that would help the "forgotten man," they elected him the thirty-second president of the United States.

With the New Deal, Roosevelt attempted to solve the problems of the Great Depression by putting people to work and protecting their money. The New Deal has left a lasting legacy on the United States. Programs that we now take for granted such as the FDIC, Social Security, and minimum wage were created to help stem the Great Depression and to protect workers during the 1930s. The Civilian Conservation Corps and the Works Progress Administration built bridges, parks, and roads across the United States— infrastructure we still use today.

How much do you really know about the Great Depression? Our ideas of the Great Depression often come from novels and movies such as John Steinbeck's *The Grapes of Wrath,* or from historic, black-and-white photographs of the era taken by Dorthea Lange and others. Although these books, movies, and photographs help us understand the personal effect of the Great Depression, they fail to tell us how or why it happened. How bad was the Great Depression? What went wrong? How did it end? Could it happen again? The book in your hands will answer these questions.

If you have an interest in learning about the Great Depression, you'll find this book indispensable. Its easy-to-read format and engaging content will guide you through this unique period of history. *The Complete Idiot's Guide to the Great Depression* clearly gives readers the who, what, when, and why of this unparalleled economic crisis.

Jennifer Rosenberg

Jennifer Rosenberg is the About.com Guide to Twentieth Century History. Her site at history1900s.about.com contains her writings about the century. In her spare time, she enjoys reading about the past and traveling to historic places.

Introduction

When the men who convened in Philadelphia in 1787 to draft a constitution for the United States of America finished their work, a worried citizen asked Benjamin Franklin, "What have you given us?"

"A Republic," said Franklin, "if you can keep it."

Hardly anyone in the world at that time believed that America's "experiment" in democracy based on free enterprise and capitalism could possibly succeed. With disturbing regularity in succeeding years, predictions of demise seemed on the verge of coming true as the economy experienced downturns that ranged in severity from mild and brief "recessions" to "panics" that resulted in prolonged "depressions." They happened in 1819, 1837, 1857, 1883, 1907, and 1921.

But none of these proved as profound and insidious as that of 1929 through 1941. Except for the Civil War, no event had a greater immediate effect on individual Americans, or a more lasting one on the character of the nation. *The Complete Idiot's Guide to the Great Depression* will give you in brief form a history of those momentous years when many wondered if the United States had, at last, failed.

How This Book Is Organized

Part 1, "Splat!" takes you through the "Roaring Twenties," when the seeds were planted for the crash of the economy that occurred in 1929. You will read of the attempts of the administration of President Herbert Hoover to deal with the crisis, and how the country spiraled into the worst economic depression of all time.

Part 2, "What's the Deal?" recounts the efforts of President Franklin D. Roosevelt and his "brain trust" of advisors to end the effects of the Depression through massive government programs known as "the New Deal."

Part 3, "This Land Is Your Land" (the title of a popular song), looks at the impact of the Depression on individuals and American society as a whole during FDR's first term (1933–1937).

Part 4, "Crackpots and Monsters," presents the many alternative plans for "recovery" offered by some American leaders, including those who advocated the overthrow of the U.S. government or its redesign on the pattern of dictatorships in Germany, Italy, and the Soviet Union. You will also read about the rise of a criminal element that sought to profit from the Depression.

Part 5, "Better Tomorrows," recalls the movies, radio shows, and other ways by which ordinary Americans coped with hardships imposed by unemployment. You will learn what it was like living day to day with no money and not much hope. A feature of the 1930s is world's fairs in Chicago, New York, and San Francisco. You will also learn how, after two terms in office, FDR and his New Deal still struggled to find a way to end the Depression and to keep the United States from being drawn into a world war.

Extras

Sprinkled throughout the story of the Great Depression you will find boxes that provide additional tidbits of information and trivia:

 **Talk of the Time**
These boxes give definitions of terms commonly used during the time of the Great Depression.

 **Timeline**
These boxes provide information about important dates and events.

 Facts and Figures
These boxes give interesting facts and figures about events and circumstances of the Great Depression.

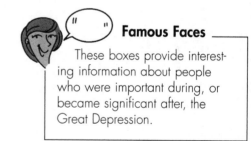 **Famous Faces**
These boxes provide interesting information about people who were important during, or became significant after, the Great Depression.

Acknowledgments

This book would not have happened without the encouragement and confidence in my ability to write it of Jake Elwell, Gary Goldstein, Sid Goldstein (no relation), Elaine Rose Ruderman, and Gail Eveland Hebert.

Appreciation is also expressed to AP Wide/World Photos for use of the photographs in this book.

Trademarks

All terms mentioned in this book that are known to be or are suspected of being trademarks or service marks have been appropriately capitalized. Alpha Books and Pearson Education, Inc., cannot attest to the accuracy of this information. Use of a term in this book should not be regarded as affecting the validity of any trademark or service mark.

Part 1

Splat!

This section describes social, cultural, economic, and political conditions of the years after World War I that planted the seeds for the Great Depression.

These years were the "Roaring Twenties" and "Jazz Age." It was a period marked by a general prosperity, "anything goes" behavior, bootleg booze, speakeasies, "flappers" dancing the "Charleston," Ford Model T "flivvers," ordinary people buying things on the installment plan, and the wealthy getting into the booming stock market.

Ain't We Got Fun!

In This Chapter

- ◆ The return of the doughboys from the Great War
- ◆ Peace, prosperity, and Prohibition
- ◆ Materialism on the installment plan
- ◆ Maldistribution of wealth
- ◆ A stock market boom

In the last half of 1918, of those U.S. troops who saw action in the "Great War" (it wasn't called the First World War until the start of the Second), more than 100,000 "doughboys" of the Allied Expeditionary Force were killed. During the entire four years of the war, 42,000 Americans who had invested in wartime industries became millionaires. When "the boys" came home, they expected to participate in a prosperity that appeared limitless and open to all. They would soon discover they were mistaken.

How Are You Going to Keep 'Em Down on the Farm?

When American troops sailed off to Europe in 1918 to the jaunty Irving Berlin song "Over There," they believed they were going to "make the world safe for democracy." This was "the war to end all wars." Soldiers, however, were not the only American contribution to the war. Along with troops went dollars. Between 1914 and 1918, the United States gave $11 billion in loans to Allied nations. As a result of these loans, at the end of the war the United States replaced Great Britain as the world's creditor nation.

Even before the United States got into the fighting in 1918, American industries were reaping huge profits by selling the Allied powers everything they needed to carry on the war. This meant plenty of jobs at good wages for U.S. factory workers.

Timeline

The 16th "Income Tax" Amendment was first proposed in 1909, but it was not adopted by the states until February 25, 1913. This amendment allowed Congress to impose taxes on incomes, from whatever source.

Huge profits were also harvested by farmers. A bushel of wheat that cost 91 cents in 1910 sold for $2 in 1918. Eager to cash in on the prosperity, people with money began buying up agricultural land, thereby inflating its value. Those who were already farmers joined in the frenzy by taking out mortgages on their farms to buy more land. This kind of debt shot from $3.2 billion in 1910 to $8.4 billion in 1920. The annual interest rose from $203 million to $574 million.

The economy discovered by the returning doughboy appeared to be very healthy. But if he looked closer, he saw that although wages had risen while he was away, so had the cost of living. Prices were up for food, rent, and clothing. Taxes were also higher. This was primarily the result of a federal income tax amendment, the 16th, to the U.S. Constitution.

Inflation was also bad in the post-war period. A common joke asserted that a man who did not have a dollar to his name was 50 cents better off than a man who had a buck in his wallet. A quart of milk went from 9 cents in 1914 to 42 cents in 1919. The prices of steak and eggs had almost doubled.

But wages also had gone up during the war, off-setting the rise in prices. With so many jobs available in industries and the country prospering, and because millions of young men from farms and small towns had gone overseas and gotten a taste of the world in cities such as London and Paris, a popular post-war song asked, "How are you going to keep 'em down on the farm after they've seen *Paree?*"

Bull by the Tail

Although some economists had feared that returning troops would not easily find jobs, by the spring of 1919 the anxiety proved unfounded. With wheels of industry turning day and night, and business experiencing a boom, the horizon looked bright. The word for it was *prosperity*.

Nowhere did the good times and the future look better than on Wall Street. The business of stock trading was so brisk that the clerks who did the paperwork complained they could barely keep up with the buying and selling. The term was (and is) "bull market." When the values of stocks are going down, it's a "bear market."

One day in May 1919 the "bullish" trading set an all-time record of 1½ million shares in one day. By the end of the year there would be only 145 days when activity did not go over a million. Stock prices soared. This bullish trading continued, but much of the buying was "on margin," a system in which only a portion of the price was paid immediately in cash.

Facts and Figures

Between February and May 1919, a share of U.S. Steel went from 90 to 104½. General Motors rose from 130 to 191. Almost every kind of industry experienced similar rises in its stock value.

Good-Bye, John Barleycorn

One American industry not participating in the economic boom was the liquor trade. For the first time in U.S. history, a legal business was targeted for extinction.

Making and drinking liquor had been a major part of American life long before the colonies declared independence from England. When soldiers landed in England before being shipped to the fighting fields of France, they discovered that they liked scotch whiskey. Common in the pubs of London and other towns and cities, the drink had been rare in the United States, where the favored hard stuff was bourbon and rye, commonly called *John Barleycorn*.

Talk of the Time

John Barleycorn was a euphemism for whiskey distilled from corn. It was a term coined by the leaders of the "Temperance Movement" along with "Demon Rum."

Troops in France who had been lucky enough to wangle a pass to spend a weekend in Paris were able to wash away cares with fine French wine and champagne. But after their return to the States, they faced a future in which alcoholic beverages would be prohibited by the 18th Amendment to the U.S. Constitution.

Passed by Congress in late 1917 and ratified within seven weeks of the end of the World War, the amendment banned the distilling and sale of alcoholic drinks and gave the following decade a name: "Prohibition." Demand for the ban came primarily from organized groups, most of them led by women. They exerted pressure on state legislatures, as well as on Congress. By 1917 most states already had enacted prohibitory laws, so they were prepared to accept the 18th Amendment.

Opponents of Prohibition were known as "wets." They contended that there was no way that the ban could ever be enforced. They also warned that if Americans couldn't get a drink legally, they would get one illegally. The controversy over Prohibition would continue for the next 14 years. During that time, supplying liquor to thirsty Americans would be taken over by gangsters in a thriving business called "bootlegging."

Good-Bye Wilson, Hello Harding

Woodrow Wilson was the president of the United States during the war. A Democrat, he was a former college professor who had tried to keep the United States out of the conflict. When the war ended, he was the central figure in promoting American membership in the League of Nations. His hopes, however, were dashed by a Republican-dominated Senate. Perhaps as a result of this rejection, he suffered a stroke that left him partially paralyzed for the remainder of his term.

To succeed Wilson as candidate for president in 1920, Democrats nominated the governor of Ohio, James M. Cox. His running mate was Wilson's Assistant Secretary of the Navy, Franklin Delano Roosevelt. Republicans chose U.S. Senator Warren Gamaliel Harding of Ohio. Their vice presidential choice was the governor of Massachusetts, Calvin Coolidge.

During one of the dullest campaigns in U.S. history, Harding promised war-weary Americans a return to "normalcy." It was a winning slogan. Harding and Coolidge were sworn into office on March 4, 1921. They were to preside over a decade that history would remember as the "Roaring Twenties."

Silver Linings

In 1920, a composer of popular songs wrote a tune that captured the mood of the country. Jerome Kern's song urged Americans to always look for the silver lining and try to find the sunny side of life. For the majority of Kern's countrymen, the sun seemed to be shining everywhere. The whole country seemed to be taking part in a frenzied determination to blot out the horrors of the war and get on with enjoying the peace and prosperity that had been secured by the blood of so many young men that they were given a name: "the Lost Generation."

This Side of Paradise

In 1917 21-year-old F. Scott Fitzgerald had dropped out of Princeton University to enlist in the Army. He'd served as aide de camp to Brigadier General John Ryan but had not gone overseas. A civilian again in 1920, he published a largely autobiographical novel.

Titled *This Side of Paradise*, it served as a rallying cry for rebellious, alienated youth. It enshrined the author in history as the embodiment of the 1920s.

Famous Faces _____

Among the novelists who rose to fame in the 1920s, and the books that carried them, were Sinclair Lewis, *Main Street;* Sherwood Anderson, *Winesburg, Ohio;* James Branch Cabell, *Jurgen;* Edith Wharton, *The Age of Innocence;* Booth Tarkington, *The Magnificent Ambersons;* and Willa Cather, *My Antonia.*

The central character of *This Side of Paradise*, Amory Blaine, was, Fitzgerald wrote, a "romantic egotist." Amory saw himself as a "slicker." Fitzgerald defined a slicker as someone who had a clever sense of social values, dressed well, got into activities in which he could "shine," and went to college as a means of showing "in a worldly way" that he was "successful." Amory felt that modern life no longer changed century by century but year to year and 10 times faster. But it wasn't enough. "My idea," he declared, "is that we've got to go much faster."

Torches of Freedom

The older generation reading F. Scott Fitzgerald discovered to its shock and horror that the youth of the nation, and especially young women, apparently intended to live by a totally different moral code. Their social creed took the form of liberal sexuality in "petting parties" and casual kissing. They danced to jazz, zoomed about in racy cars, drank excessively, donned open galoshes that flapped when they walked or danced (giving the language of the 1920s the word "flappers"), and openly smoked cigarettes.

In 1919 American women marked a milestone in a long struggle for equality with men with the ratification of the 19th Amendment. When it took effect in 1920, they gained the right to vote. Many women also interpreted their new status as liberation from other strictures. The result was the appearance of a figure that historians labeled "the New Woman."

Women who went to the polls for the first time and helped elect Harding president also quickly claimed equal footing with men in all other aspects of life. It was this "new woman" who appeared on the pages of *This Side of Paradise*. She wore her hair and skirts short, ate three-o'clock-after-dance suppers, and danced in a way that appalled the older generation.

Timeline _____

Officially ratified on August 26, 1920, the "Woman Suffrage" amendment, the 19th Amendment, decreed: "The right of citizens of the United States to vote shall not be denied or abridged by the United States or by any state on account of sex."

But nothing signified the arrival of the liberated woman more than her passion for cigarettes. So many joined their boyfriends and husbands in lighting up that they contributed to a booming cigarette industry. Per capita consumption of cigarettes zoomed from 426 in 1919 to 700 in 1925 and kept on rising. The sales of cigarettes jumped 8 percent in one year (1920–1921) to more than 52 billion. This rising demand required rapid expansion of production by the three major makers, R. J. Reynolds, American Tobacco Company, and L&M (Liggett and Myers).

The head of American Tobacco, George Washington Hill, knew a good thing when he saw it. He is credited with popularizing smoking in public by women. He achieved this by a combination of advertising and psychology. To obtain an analysis of women's motivation in taking up cigarettes, Hill hired a psychiatrist, A. A. Brill. He not only explained why women smoked, but he also gave a portrait of the New Woman. Brill said, "Some women regard cigarettes as symbols of freedom. More women now do the same work as men do. Many women bear no children; those who do bear have fewer children. Feminine traits are masked. Cigarettes, which are equated with men, become torches of freedom."

Birth of the PR Man

If one person can be credited for significantly contributing to the boom years of the 1920s, it would have to be Edward Bernays. An advertising executive, he invented "public relations." Among his successes, in addition to selling Lucky Strike cigarettes to women, was the softening of the image of multimillionaire John D. Rockefeller by suggesting during the depths of the Great Depression that America's richest man give out dimes.

Another pioneer in massaging public opinion and affecting sales of industries turning out consumer goods was Albert D. Lasker. An advertising man based in Chicago, he represented Pepsodent toothpaste, Kleenex, Palmolive beauty soap, the Radio Corporation of America (RCA), Sunkist oranges, and the Republican Party.

Bernays, Lasker, and others rank as important figures in the 1920s because they provided, through public relations and advertising, an impetus among ordinary Americans to spend their wages on all things, both necessities and luxuries. Bernays, Lasker, and the other PR and ad men told the public that they deserved these things as a reward for their sacrifices during the Great War and their hard work after it ended.

If people couldn't afford their hearts' desires, they could get everything they wanted right here and now with a small "down payment" and easy terms for paying off the rest.

Facts and Figures

The most popular smokes during the 1920s were Lucky Strike (American Tobacco), Camel (Reynolds), and Chesterfield (L&M).

Buy Now, Pay Later

Since the beginning of the American experiment in democracy and capitalism, Americans had followed the advice of old Ben Franklin in his *Poor Richard's Almanac*: "A penny saved is a penny earned." But in the 1920s, thanks in great measure to alluring ads for enticing products, *Poor Richard's* counsel was tossed overboard. To make the idea of buying on credit appetizing, clever ad men came up with a sweetener called "buying on the installment plan."

In a time of silver linings, money in your pocket, and seemingly boundless prosperity, the old notion of saving for a rainy day was as out of date as the waltz was to a flapper puffing away on a cigarette while dancing the Charleston. But why should a manufacturer go along with installment buying? The answer was found in the basic reality of capitalism known as supply and demand.

Throughout the 1920s the two got out of balance. American manufacturers were churning out so much in the way of consumer goods that people's demands weren't keeping up with the supply of goods in overstocked warehouses. This abundance was the result of an astonishing increase in the productivity of workers.

In the 1920s the output per worker in American industry lept by nearly two-thirds. But this happened at a time when wages were not keeping up. Take-home pay in the same 10 years rose by only 8 percent. Consequently, the manufacturers were making enormous profits. This was great, so long as workers bought what was being made. Hence the appeal of the installment plan in moving products from shelves and off the sales floors.

Suddenly, the average American was able to buy washing machines, electric irons, refrigerators, new furniture, vacuum cleaners, and the two most desired products: radios and automobiles.

Out of Thin Air

In the age of television, cellular phones, wireless computers, and thousands of radio stations offering every kind of program, it may seem amusing to you that sending words and music through the air could have been thought of as miraculous. But if you had been around in the 1920s and had a few spare dollars to "put down" to buy something that was essential to your happiness, you would have bought a radio. Then you would have sat beside it (and stared at it) for hours, just as we do today with TV.

When radio burst onto the scene in 1920, having one in your home became a national craze that no subsequent new product matched in rapidity and breadth of sales in so short a time, including TVs, computers, and microwave ovens. Two years after they went on the market, annual sales totaled $60,000,000 (in 1920s money). By the end of the decade, the sum was $842,548,000 (an increase of 1,400 percent). Following the stock market crash of 1929 and throughout the 12 years of the Great Depression, radio proved to be (as you will read later) the most important means of entertainment, news, and information.

The idea that a radio could become "a household utility in the same sense as the piano and phonograph" was first proposed in 1916 by a young, former shortwave operator for the Marconi Company. His name was David Sarnoff. On April 14, 1912, he had been at his Marconi "wireless" atop the Wanamaker department store on lower Broadway in New York City when the ocean liner *Titanic* radioed that it had hit an iceberg and was sinking. In 1916 he suggested to the head of the Marconi Company in the United States, Edward J. Nally, that a receiver could be designed "in the form of a simple 'Radio Music Box'" that could be "placed in the parlor or living room." Music on the radio would then stimulate sales of phonographs and records to play on them. Sarnoff said that the radios could sell for $75.

The result of this proposal was the formation of RCA, with sales of RCA radios in 1922 exceeding Sarnoff's forecast for the first year ($7,500,000). In 1922 RCA sales tallied $11,000,000. In that year the number of radio stations jumped from 8 in January to 76 in July. By the end of 1922 there were 500 stations. At the end of the decade, radio spanned the country. The day after a broadcast of a popular program, listeners talked to one another about it with the same excitement as viewers of *The Sopranos* in 2001.

The only product for sale that surpassed radio in enthusiasm and a desire to own was the one being turned out with breathtaking speed and quantity by Henry Ford.

Timeline ———
The first movie with a sound-track, *Phonofilm*, was shown by inventor Lee De Forest at New York's Rivoli Theater in April 1923.

Timeline ———
On July 2, 1921, at Boyle's Thirty Acres in Jersey City, New Jersey, Sarnoff ran the equipment for a blow-by-blow account of a prize fight between U.S. heavyweight champion Jack "the Manassa Mauler" Dempsey and French champion Georges Carpentier. (Dempsey won with a fourth-round knockout.) This was radio's first important broadcast.

Fordissmus and the Flivver

Henry Ford did not invent the automobile. He made a car in a way that the average person could afford to buy it. In doing so, he joined a very small roster of individuals in all of history who transformed the world of their time. With an idea and an initial investment of $28,000, he introduced the most important technological innovation since the dawn of the Industrial Revolution. "Machinery," said Henry Ford, "is the new Messiah."

By perfecting a system of building automobiles on an assembly line, starting in 1908 with the Model T (known by those who drove them as Flivvers), he literally put Americans on the road. Never mind that at first there were no roads, unless you thought a rutted, often muddy wagon path was a road. Someone came up with a word for the assembly line: "Fordissmus." It meant efficient, mass produced, and *cheap*.

Ford cars were a driving force (pardon the pun) behind many of the industries that put money in the pockets of hundreds of thousands of workers who produced steel, nickel, lead, leather, glass, and rubber. (Ford used only Firestone tires until 2001, when problems with shredding treads caused numerous accidents.) Other beneficiaries of Ford's success included the petroleum industry, hotels (and a convenient new roadside hostelry called the motel), textile makers, and construction firms who rushed to build the roads that an increasing number of Americans wanted to drive on in their Flivvers.

In Massachusetts in 1922 for example, 223,112 automobiles were registered. The number would grow steadily. One of the effects of the car in Massachusetts and elsewhere was a steady decrease in usage of public transportation, especially interurban and suburban lines. To help meet the costs of road-building and maintenance, Massachusetts and other states began installing tollbooths on the busiest roadways. During the 1920s more than a billion bucks were spent on road and highway construction with another $400,000,000 on streets in cities and towns.

Automobility also made it easier for people to pick up and move from rural areas into cities. This migration sparked a building boom in apartment houses and urban homes, along with expansions of city-based factories to hire a growing labor force. Between 1920 and 1928 the construction business grew by 50 percent or around $5 billion.

The question in the 1920s was no longer "How are you going to keep 'em down on the farm after they've seen Paree?" It was: How far could you go in your Flivver without getting a flat tire or a breakdown? By every measure, Americans had begun a love affair with the car that nine decades later showed no sign of cooling off.

Seeds of Trouble

In 1921 the song-writing team of Richard A. Whiting (music) and Gus Kahn and Raymond B. Egan (words) turned out a ditty with a title that summed up the country's prevailing gay mood by asking, "Ain't We Got Fun?" But anyone who really listened to the lyrics of the smash-hit number found that the words revealed a nation that was fooling itself.

"Ain't We Got Fun?" was about a couple who were behind in their rent, ducking bill collectors, in debt to the grocer and butcher, and expecting a visit from "Mister Stork." The husband in the song talked about "not much money," yet asked his bride, "Ain't we got fun?" The songwriters then put a finger on just what was wrong with the country. The father-to-be noted that there was nothing surer than "the rich get rich and the poor get children." Another version of the line said that while the rich got richer, the poor got poorer.

Economists and sociologists referred to this as "maldistribution of wealth." Historians of the 1920s cite the phenomenon as the chief cause of the Great Depression. A study of the 1920s by the Brookings Institution (America's Capacity to Consume) found that 1/10 of 1 percent of American families (24,000) had an income equal to that of the bottom 42 percent (11½ million). The survey noted that despite the apparent prosperity, "income was being distributed with increasing inequality."

Maldistribution of wealth meant that if you were at the low end of the economic ladder, your cash went for necessities. Whatever remained went to paying off the stuff that you bought on the installment plan. In most instances there would be nothing left for savings. If you were rich, you had plenty of money to buy luxury items and to "take a plunge" into the stock market.

Reasons for the Wall Street Boom

Two words: productivity and profits. The first was father to the second. As noted, American workers in the post-war years proved very productive. But while they were toiling so effectively, they were earning low wages. This combination of increased output and minimal labor costs went straight to corporate bottom lines in the form of profits for investors.

Two more words: demand and supply. As noted, U.S. industries were turning out products so fast at low labor costs and with such abundance that workers with limited funds were encouraged to buy goods now and pay for them later. This served to increase demand, encouraging more production, thereby adding to the profits. Throughout the 1920s corporate profits rose 62 percent. Dividends to stockholders went up 65 percent.

So what could be wrong in all of this? Think about it! You have underpaid workers turning out goods in record amounts that they can only afford to buy on credit. This enormous output at bargain labor costs creates wealth for people who already have far more than enough money, thereby widening the income gap.

In a country founded on the principle that everyone has the right to try to get rich, what's wrong with that? Nothing, as long as people keep on buying the things that industry turns out.

Now ask yourself this: If you were around in the 1920s and had to work for a living, how many radios, washers, refrigerators, phonographs, and automobiles would you need, especially if the ones you had still weren't paid for?

Probably, if you had been around to hop on the merry-go-round of the Roaring Twenties, you would have thought that you'd found the silver lining. You'd enjoy your radio, tool around town in your Model T, drop in for an illicit cocktail at your neighborhood speakeasy, and join everybody else in the joint in asking the musical question, "Ain't We Got Fun?"

Americans Look Back and Ahead

One of the lessons learned from the history of the United States is that in the years immediately following a war people would rather look ahead than back. After the Revolutionary War, they had no interest in raining revenge on people who hadn't supported the break with England. Instead, Americans turned their attention to inventing a new kind of country. Following the Civil War, the nation looked to expanding into the West.

When the Armistice was declared on November 11, 1918, ending "the war to end all wars," the United States found itself not only the most powerful nation in the world, but also a nation facing the future with unbounded optimism. But this did not mean that Americans forgot about the more than four million men who'd served in the armed forces, nor the men who'd been killed.

Yet there was another chilling statistic to be considered. In the year before the United States entered war, the national death rate from "strong drink" stood at 5.2 per 100,000. This fact, plus a long campaign to ban alcoholic beverages, provided a strong argument for those who pushed through the 18th Amendment to begin the era of Prohibition. In the first year of the ban (1920), "drys" pointed with self-satisfaction to the fact that the death rate from use of strong drink had dropped to 1 in 100,000.

Facts and Figures

If you were "an average American" in 1920, your disposable income went up 9 percent. But if you were in the top 1 percent in income, the money you had available to spend went up 75 percent.

Famous Faces

Future *Monday Night Football* commentator Howard Cossell was born in Winston-Salem, North Carolina, on March 25, 1920.

The Road to Prosperity

The strength of the post-war economy was noted in statistics of the automotive industry. In 1920, more than 300,000 American-made cars had been exported, an increase from the pre-war year of 1917 of more than 200,000. If one needed proof that Americans were in love with cars, he found it in the more than 10 million autos that were registered in the year 1920. (In 1917 the figure was a little less than 5,000,000.) America's two leading export products were cotton and cars, followed by wheat, gasoline, and tobacco.

Overall American exports in 1920 totaled $8.4 billion, the bulk of which went to foreign countries. By 1927, as a result of increased tariffs (a major factor in bringing on the Depression), those numbers were cut in half. Prosperous America led the world in the number of telephones, up from 11.7 million in 1917 to 14.3 million in 1922, or about 14 times as many phones as there were in Great Britain.

As to the population of a prosperous and forward-looking country, in 1920 there were 105,710,620 men, women, and children counted in the census. The estimated population by the year 1928 was put at 200 million. The percentage of Americans living in urban areas was 51.4 percent, up from 45.8 in 1910, which indicated a movement of people from farms to towns and cities that would escalate through the decade of the 1920s. Of the 6.3 million living on farms in 1920, a little more than half were in the South.

Life expectancy in 1920 for men living in cities was 51.65 years. The life span of a city woman was 54.87. For black men it was 40.45 years and for black women, 38.45.

How to Keep from Growing Old

With so many Americans getting behind the steering wheel of a car in the 1920s, the magazine of the American Mutual Insurance Company gave these tips on how to avoid reaching old age:

- Always pass the car ahead on curves and turns.
- Demand half the road—the middle half.
- A few shots of booze will enable you to make your car do real stunts. For permanent results, quaff long and deeply of the flowing bowl before taking to the road.
- Always speed.

The Least You Need to Know

- After World War I, the United States economy was booming, but there was a dangerous maldistribution of wealth.
- President Harding was elected on a pledge to return the country to "normalcy."
- Despite the banning of sales of alcoholic drinks, Americans continued to imbibe in speakeasies and at home.
- Americans bought cars and radios on "the installment plan" and stocks on a credit system called "margin."

Who Says You Can't Buy Happiness?

In This Chapter

- ◆ The trouble with Harding
- ◆ Coolidge: "The business of America is business"
- ◆ Two books: *Main Street* and *Middletown*
- ◆ The way to get rich without working
- ◆ Henry Ford and the great car race

When Warren G. Harding became president in March 1921 with a pledge to return the country to "normalcy," the United States was beginning an era of technological innovation, social upheaval, and a booming economy. Americans were optimistic that America's future was bright. Only after Harding unexpectedly died in 1923 did they learn his administration was riddled with crooked men.

Pleased that the new president, Calvin Coolidge, declared "the business of America is business," the country continued merrily along on the highway to happiness. Huge profits were being made by three groups: investors in Wall Street, land speculators, and a new breed of entrepreneurs defying Prohibition by bootlegging liquor. To keep up with competition, Henry Ford brought out the Model A, and Americans went crazy over it.

A Great Guy to Play Poker with on Saturday Night

Warren G. Harding had gotten elected while campaigning without leaving the front porch of his house in Marion, Ohio. A former newspaperman who had been the governor of Ohio and a U.S. senator, he was a likeable guy who enjoyed a game of poker with his cronies. Learning that he'd won the election, he wisecracked, "I feel like a man who goes in on a pair of eights and comes out with aces full."

His campaign pledge had been a promise to return the country to "normalcy." What he meant was a 180-degree turn from the policies of his predecessor. President Woodrow Wilson had wanted the United States to join a League of Nations and play an important role in world affairs. Harding called for "America first."

In a 1920 speech in Boston, he'd said, "America's need is not heroics but healing; not nostrums but normalcy; not revolution but restoration, not surgery but serenity."

As one observer noted, Harding struck a sympathetic chord. After the Great War, the people were physically and spiritually worn out. What most wanted were peace, quiet, and healing. They desired nothing more than to get on with their lives and enjoy the fruits of prosperity. If ever a president was just the right man for the times, a majority of voters had decided, it was Harding.

What the people didn't know was that their affable president had brought into the government a bunch of cronies who were eager to feed at the public trough. These men, who hoped to line their pockets, became known as "the Ohio Gang." Between 1921 and 1923, they gave the country its most corrupt administration since the scandals under President Ulysses Grant.

Whether Harding knew about the pillaging that was going on under his nose is an open question. Before anyone could ask him, he fell ill while on a trip to the West. He died under mysterious circumstances in San Francisco on August 2, 1923. The official cause was a heart attack brought on by a meal of tainted crab. A lot of people thought he had realized that the jig was up and had committed suicide to avoid having to answer for scandals, such as the *Teapot Dome*. Some people suspected he'd been murdered.

Quiet Man in a Roaring Country

The only president born on July 4 (1872), Calvin Coolidge is also the only one who took the oath of office from his father. (He was a storekeeper and notary public.) It was administered shortly after midnight on August 3, 1923, in Plymouth Notch, Vermont, in the house where Coolidge had been born. When the ceremony was over, the thirtieth president of the United States went back to bed.

In one of history's ironies, a man who clung to traditional New England morality and who had earned the nickname "Silent Cal," suddenly was president of a country in which the old ways were being tossed out in a frenzied pursuit of bootleg booze, sexual freedom, buy now, pay later consumption, and ways of striking it rich without working.

"A Puritan in Babylon"

When the most distinguished journalist of the 1920s, William Allen White, wrote a biography of Coolidge, the title he gave it was *A Puritan in Babylon*. It would be hard, if not impossible, to coin a phrase that better summed up both a president and his time in office.

The new president quickly became famous for not saying much. And when he did speak, he made his point succinctly. On the subject of the men involved in the Harding scandals: "Let the guilty be punished." To a woman who said she'd made a bet that she could get him to say three words, he replied, "You lose." On what he saw as the main purpose of the nation which he now headed: "The business of America is business."

Being Young in Babylon

As you've read, manners and morals were changing so quickly in the mid-1920s that what one person defined as normal, another found shocking, quite immoral, and decidedly un-American. All you had to do was look at the behavior of the younger generation to see that things weren't like they'd been when Cal Coolidge was a kid in Vermont. The editors of *Literary Digest* were so alarmed that they convened a symposium on the subject "Is the Younger Generation in Peril?"

Talk of the Time

Teapot Dome was an area of land in Wyoming that resembled a teapot. It was one of two federal oil reserves set aside for use by the Navy. The other was Elk Hills, California. They were secretly leased to private oil companies by a Harding crony, Interior Secretary Albert Fall, in return for bribes.

Famous Faces

Born in 1868 in Emporia, Kansas, William Allen White bought the local newspaper, *The Emporia Gazette*, in 1895 and made it into one of the most influential papers in the cause of "progressive" government. In 1923 his editorial on the subject of freedom of expression ("To an Anxious Friend") won a Pulitzer Prize.

Talk of the Time

Arguably the most influential periodical of its time, **Literary Digest** was a precursor of magazines such as *Time*, *Newsweek*, and others by dealing with current affairs and often conducting public opinion polls.

An explanation of what was going on with the younger generation had been put into words in an article on the subject in *Atlantic Monthly* in 1920 by John F. Carter. It was a reaction to what the older generation had left them. He wrote, "They give us [a world], knocked to pieces, leaky, red-hot, threatening to blow up; and then they are surprised that we don't accept it."

A Walk Down "Main Street"

In the year that Carter offered Americans his analysis of why the youth of the country were acting peculiarly, and as William Allen White's *Emporia Gazette* editorials were being avidly read across the country, another writer published a novel in which the veneer of American society was ruthlessly peeled away. It showed that young people felt suffocated, helpless, and unhappy.

The author of this scathing portrayal of life in the small towns of America, titled *Main Street*, was Sinclair Lewis. Born in Sauk Centre, Minnesota, in 1885, he was a Yale graduate who'd written for such popular magazines as *Cosmopolitan* and *Saturday Evening Post*. His second novel, *Main Street*, was set in a fictional small town (Gopher Prairie, Minnesota). Through the main character, a young woman named Carol Kennicott, Lewis satirized the narrowness and provincialism of middle America.

Its "Main Street," he said with a sharp tongue planted in cheek, "is the climax of civilization." Carol Kennicott was married to a doctor named Milford. Settling in Gopher Prairie, she hoped to reform the place, only to feel the sting of narrow-mindedness and the unimaginative nature of the residents.

The book not only appealed to the restless youth of the post-war generation, but it earned Lewis the Nobel Prize for Literature, the first given to an American. Lewis remained a critic of American "hypocrisy" throughout the 1920s with the novels *Babbitt* (1922), *Arrowsmith* (1925), *Elmer Gantry* (1927), and *Dodsworth* (1929). All these works are regarded as classics and provide a window to the decade.

A Couple of Visitors to Middletown

As Calvin Coolidge presided in the White House, there existed no more typical small town in the United States of America than Muncie, Indiana. Consequently, one day in 1924 there arrived in the community a pair of sociological researchers, Robert S. and Helen Merrell Lynd. For the next 18 months they gathered data and conducted interviews. Disguising the name of the town, they published their findings in 1929 with the title *Middletown: A Study in Modern American Culture*.

The work stands as a classic of American scholarship and perhaps the most detailed and thoughtful portrait ever presented of life in an American community. In it they described changes in lives of "average" people since the 1890s. Among their revelations was that the pace of change was faster among a "business class" than in the "working class."

The Rich Are Different

One of the most famous quotations to come of the years of the Great Depression involved two of the era's greatest writers, F. Scott Fitzgerald and Ernest Hemingway. "The rich are different from us," said Fitzgerald.

"Yes," Hemingway replied. "They have more money."

This was a truth the Lynds found in Middletown's two classes. The groups were alike in a desire to accumulate all the things that prosperity made available, either paid for in cash by the well-to-do or on the installment plan by the "working class" whose women were urged by advertisements to make their lives easier by buying now and paying later.

Between May and October 1923, the people of Middletown bought more than 1,000 irons, 709 vacuum cleaners, 463 toasters, 371 washing machines, 144 electric heaters, 18 refrigerators, 3 electric ranges, and 1,173 electric hair curlers.

"It is in part by compelling advertising couched in terms of certain women's values," the Lynds wrote, "that use certain of women's values is being so widely diffused."

What the ads for these products offered the people of Middletown and towns all over the country, was found in a newspaper ad by the local electric company: "Time for sale! Will you buy? Where can you buy back a single yesterday? Nowhere, of course. Yet, right in your city, you can purchase tomorrows. Time for youth and beauty. Time for club work, for church and community activities. Time for books and plays and concerts. Time for home and children."

A Few Significant Statistics

◆ In 1924, 99 percent of Middletown (Muncie) homes had electricity.

◆ Total wage earners in Indiana: 1,127,032. Of these, 941,647 were men and 185,385 were women.

◆ The population of the United States (counted in the 1920 census) was 105,710,620. Men: 53,900,431. Women: 51,810,189.

◆ Types of work in order of numbers employed: manufacturing, agriculture, trade, paid domestics, clerical, transportation, professional services, mining, and public service.

- Women's jobs in order of numbers employed: clerks, telephone operators, lawyers and judges, education, and welfare workers.

- Of the more than four and a half million persons engaged in gainful employment, the racial/national breakdown in order was whites born in the United States, whites foreign born or of mixed parentage, foreign-born whites, blacks (listed as Negroes), Native Americans, Chinese, and Japanese.

- Workers who were between 10 and 15 years of age (both sexes, totaled nationally): 2,641,260.

- Number of farms: 6,448,343. Acreage: 503,073,007. Value of all farm property: $77,924,100,333.

- Examples in pounds of what the average family ate in a year: beef, 66.1; pork, 40.5; chicken, 23.4; fish, 31.4; milk and milk products, 324; eggs (dozens), 61.2; wheat bread, 397.7; sugar, 147.5; apples (pecks), 17; potatoes, 709; and coffee, 39.3. Telephones in the United States in 1922: 14,347,395.

The World According to Mellon

On December 4, 1924, Coolidge's man in charge of the Treasury Department, Andrew Mellon, who happened to be one the richest men in America, brightened every heart on Wall Street. "Taxation," he declared in his annual report, "should not be used as a field for socialistic experiment, or as a club to punish success." (Half a century later, President Ronald Reagan would tell Congress, "The taxing power must not be used to regulate the economy or bring about social change.")

In designing the Revenue Act of 1924, Mellon saw to it that the titans of industry would not have to worry about being punished. Under the legislation, people with an annual income of a million dollars saw their taxes cut from $600,000 to less than $200,000. The reduction for small taxpayers was not as generous, further adding to the economic pinch that spurred buying of things they wanted or needed but could afford only on credit.

Of concern to Mellon was the unsettling fact that in 1921 and in 1923 there had been business recessions. The main cause of the first had been a sudden deflation. It was triggered by increased productivity which produced the glut of goods that, in turn, led to the innovation of installment-plan buying. But the remedy was not sustained, resulting in another dip in 1923. Unemployment was a nagging problem. In 1924, the Lynds found that 62 percent of workers in Muncie had been temporarily laid off. They also found that members of the "business class" believed being out of work was the workers' own fault. A wife of a prominent businessman told the Lynds that "anyone who really tries can get work of some kind."

While the Lynds noted the working class of Muncie suffered from a continuing uncertainty about having and holding a job, they did not find a loss of confidence in the notion that times would get better. Workers showed that optimism by buying the goods rolling off the country's assembly lines.

In the Coolidge mid-years of the decade, per capita disposable income for all Americans was rising modestly. But if you were in the top 1 percent on the income ladder, the money you had on hand was going up faster. With the Coolidge/Mellon tax cuts, you had even more. What to do with it? Invest and get more!

Facts and Figures

One of the factors contributing to people being laid off was the introduction of new machinery because industries required fewer workers. The jobless rate during the Coolidge years would range from 5.2 to 13 percent.

Come on in, the Water's Fine

Under the heading "The Bull Markets" in the 1925 edition of *The World Almanac*, a financial and economic review of the preceding year noted an "outburst" in stock-trading activity had "gone into such solid ground" that it not only represented a feeling of elation but also a coming "epochal business and financial expansion."

This enthusiasm for what lay ahead economically was demonstrated in November 1924 when voters gave Calvin Coolidge the presidency in his own right. He easily defeated Democrat John W. Davis and the Progressive Party candidate, Senator Robert La Follette of Wisconsin. Coolidge's tally was two million more votes than his opponents' votes combined.

Approval of the election outcome by stock buyers was expressed in 21 million-share days between election day and December 3, 1924. To put this in perspective, in all of 1923 there had been only 86 million-share days, and in 1921 there had been only 21. Compared to shares of Dow Jones Industrials traded per day in the year 2001, which routinely totaled hundreds of millions, these figures for the first half of the 1920s seem paltry. But back then they were a very big deal.

Facts and Figures

The total number of shares traded on the New York Stock Exchange in 1923 was 237,276,927. Today the number often exceeds a half-billion shares in a day.

How to Get Rich Without Working

If you think that the vigor with which stocks were being traded showed a desire by investors to own a piece of a prosperous or a promising company, you're wrong. Most buyers were more interested in finding stocks that they expected to go up in value so that they could sell them for a nifty profit.

The popular term for this was (and still is) "making a killing on Wall Street." Stodgy economists call it "speculation." Historians looking into causes of the Great Depression cite the practice as one of the reasons for the bursting of the prosperity bubble in the autumn of 1929.

Here's How It Worked

Suppose you belonged to the "business class" that was defined by the Lynds in their study of "Middletown." You've got plenty of money to buy goodies being churned out by thriving industries, and you have lots of left-over cash to put into the stock market. Before the 1920s, the customary way for you to buy stocks was to look for a solid firm that over time would pay healthy dividends. But times had changed, and now you are like Amory Blaine in *This Side of Paradise*. You want everything to go faster, including getting a quick return on the money you put into stocks.

What you want to get in on is one of the quickly rising stocks of industries that are making the highly demanded consumer goods that are easily available on credit. But you're too impatient to hold on to your shares and collect dividends. Because the value of your shares is going up every day, the thing to do is to keep your eye on the quotations and unload your stocks at a point that will give you a sweet profit.

Great! But suppose that you have your eye on several such stocks, only you don't have enough dough to buy them all. Never mind! You can do what the would-be buyer of a washing machine did when he didn't have the full purchase price. You buy on credit. In the field of consumer products, that's the installment plan. When you acquire stocks that way, you're "buying on margin."

Timeline _____

In 1925 the highest federal income tax rate was 25 percent.

For 10 percent down and using the stock as collateral for a loan of the remaining 90 percent, you're in business. Buy a bunch of stocks on margin, watch them shoot up in value, sell them at a profit. Repay your margin debt.

Do it again and again.

Nothing to Worry About

Although the fever for margin-buying was increasing as Calvin Coolidge took his second presidential oath of office on March 4, 1925, this time in front of a huge throng at the U.S. Capitol, the *World Almanac* economic analyst found no cause for concern. He wrote, "The most impressive and reassuring feature of the current rise in securities and the great volume of transactions is that their financial requirements have imposed no burdens on the banks through loan expansion."

 **Facts and Figures**

If you bought General Electric stock at the end of 1923 at 196 you could have sold it at its 1924 high point of 281. General Motors went from 15 in 1923 to a 1924 high of 62½.

Statistics showed that the majority of stock buyers were paying cash or its equivalent to buy shares. The increase in margin-buying was well within bounds. "Before sounding an alarm," wrote the *World Almanac* analyst, "even the more cautious commentators may safely await the hoisting of the danger signal 'Watch your step' when bank loans raise the red semaphore."

So in 1925, everything was, in the popular phrase when things are going well, "hunky dory."

If you wanted reassurance that the direction was still up, you could take a look at the automobile business. As noted, the value of General Motors stock almost tripled in 1924. The reason for GM's lusty growth was its most popular car, the Chevrolet. It was selling briskly at prices ranging between $510 and $765. It offered a belt-driven generator, cam-operated oil pump, and new and improved brakes. Soon it was leaving Henry Ford's Model T in a cloud of dust.

But there were other makes competing with the Model T. The mid-1920s saw the debut on America's roads of the Plymouth, De Soto, Viking, Pontiac, LaSalle, Marquette, Graham, Cord, Roosevelt, and American Austin. When Ford produced the Model T, it was available only in black. But the cars of Ford's competitors were coming off assembly lines in a rainbow of hues. This burst of color was made possible by the invention of pyroxylin, a chemical that made possible a vast variety of finishes.

 Facts and Figures

In the mid-1920s there were 387,760 miles of paved and 2,941,294 miles of unpaved roads. In 1924 there were 11,466 automobile fatalities.

All these developments in the auto industry, as you will soon read, sent Mr. Ford and his engineers hurrying back to their drawing boards at Ford Motor Company's headquarters, located at River Rouge, Michigan.

A Bootlegger Named Gatsby

The only enterprise doing better business than cars and the stock market in the USA of "Silent Cal" Coolidge was the peddling of booze. When Prohibition came in, the head of the federal agency put in charge of enforcing it, Commissioner John F. Kramer, vowed, "This law will be obeyed in cities large and small, and in villages, and where it is not obeyed it will be enforced." He also pledged that liquor would not be "manufactured nor sold nor given away nor hauled in anything on the surface of the earth or under the earth or in the air."

He was, of course, as anyone who's ever watched an episode of the TV show *The Untouchables* knows, as wrong as he could be. He was answered with the greatest demonstration of law-defiance in the history of the country. The 100-percent proof that banning John Barleycorn had come a crapper was a language suddenly brimming with new words: speakeasy, rum-runner, blotto, hooch, cocktail, high ball, and bathtub gin.

Prohibition was so widely and openly defied that America's most famous humorist since Mark Twain, a guy with an Oklahoma twang and aw-shucks manner by the name of Will Rogers, got howls of laughter when he cracked, "Prohibition is better than having no liquor at all."

Whether Americans were buying huge console radios on the installment plan or stocks on margin, they either personally had the acquaintance of, or knew about, a colorful and often mysterious character in the business of quenching one's thirst for a drink with a little kick in it—a bootlegger.

In 1925 the author whose *This Side of Paradise* informed an older generation that its children were engaging in petting parties and other shocking behavior, published his second novel. *The Great Gatsby* introduced readers to Jay Gatsby. He lived on Long Island and threw lavish parties. Hundreds of guests came and went like moths. The novel's narrator, Nick Carraway, heard rumors that Gatsby was the son of the German emperor, a spy in the war, or possibly a fugitive killer.

He was, in fact, a bootlegger. A figure right in step with his times, he was a man who believed in the green light and "the orgiastic future" that can be grasped if "we will run faster." Writing of one character, Fitzgerald captured the essence of the Roaring Twenties: "Her voice is full of money."

Suddenly in Love with Lindy

On May 20, 1927, there was no way of knowing how many millions of Americans lifted an illicit drink in a toast and held their breaths, as a daring, handsome young aviator, Charles Lindbergh, took off in a very small airplane named *Spirit of St. Louis* from Roosevelt Field, Long Island. His destination was Paris, France. His goal was to win a prize for becoming the first person to cross the Atlantic alone, or as everyone learned to say, "solo."

Charles A. Lindbergh poses with his plane Spirit of St. Louis *in this 1927 photo.*

(AP Photo)

When he made it, he was a hero called "Lucky Lindy." The "ticker-tape parade" he was given through a blizzard of streaming paper in the *"canyon of heroes"* became the measure against which the size and success of all the succeeding parades for later heroes would be measured.

Henry Does It Again

Six months after America went ga-ga over Lindy, Henry Ford got back into the auto race. On December 2, 1927, the Ford Motor Company joyously and eagerly rolled out the Model A.

Talk of the Time

The **canyon of heroes** is a mile-or-so-long stretch of Broadway in lower Manhattan that goes from the tip of the island (The Battery) to City Hall. Alas, in the era of computers ticker tape is no longer available for tossing down, and windows of many of the new skyscrapers in the area can't be opened.

The only thing Ford could have done to make the appearance of the new car a more spectacular event would have been to put Lucky Lindy at the wheel. *The New York Herald Tribune* estimated that a million people flocked to Ford's Manhattan headquarters to look at it.

In following weeks, thousands of orders were placed for a car that was available in almost every color you could think of. And you eventually had your choice of styles. There were three kinds of roadsters, three coupes, phaetons, cabriolets, victorias, and six sedans. By 1929 the Model A had pulled ahead of the Chevy in sales. They sold for under $500, but if you didn't have it, you could buy one on credit.

Famous Faces

Singer Rosemary Clooney was born in Maysville, Kentucky, on May 23, 1928.

When Sinclair Lewis published *Main Street* in 1920, a character in the novel gazed at a Model T and said, "That this Ford might stand in front of the Bon Ton Store, Hannibal invaded Rome and Erasmus wrote in the Oxford cloisters."

Seven years later, the people of *Main Street* and the Lynds' Middletown who loved their Model A's eagerly took to the road as never before.

Highways to Heaven

Suddenly, the American landscape bloomed with "filling stations" where a person could get free road maps, "tourist rest stops" in the form of clusters of cabins, camping sites, and places to pull off the road to have a meal or snack. A "motorist" found himself and his family enticed to stop for a moment at diners and other eateries. Many of them featured a new kind of "roadside architecture" in which hot dog stands were in the shape of a giant frankfurter on a bun. Others were built like windmills, lighthouses, giraffes, and whales.

If you wanted to, and you had the time and money, you could make your way to U.S. Highway 6, Route 66, and Route 30 (the Lincoln Highway) and head to the West Coast. Like the rest of the country, California was enjoying the booming economy. Good wages brought a growing labor force. Industrial output soared. And real estate values zoomed upward.

Not since the Gold Rush of 1849 had "the Golden State" seen such an influx of outsiders. As unrestrained prosperity reached giddy heights, high-pressure boosters and promoters went all out to portray California as Heaven on Earth. In 1924, the country's most popular singer, Al Jolson, made a record of a song (written with Bud De Silva and Joseph Meyer) with the alluring message that when the wintry winds were blowing and the snow started to fall, the place to go was where a frown was mighty hard to find. It was "California Here I Come."

The only place more appealing than California and Wall Street to Americans who had an itch to speculate, was another state with abundant sunshine and plenty of land for sale at bargain prices: Florida. The result was rampant real estate sales and development in such places as Miami, Coral Gables, Boca Raton, and Palm Beach. But the phenomenon didn't last. It would go bust along with the rest of the country in October 1929 when the fun and games of the Roaring Twenties came to a crashing halt.

The Air Hero as Pitch Man

On December 10, 1927, seven months after Lucky Lindy winged his way into history and American hearts, he arrived in Washington, D.C., to receive plaudits from the Congress. Members of the House and Senate voted to award him with a commendation that was intended as a citation for valor in warfare, the Congressional Medal of Honor. Two days later, Lindbergh was again piloting the *Spirit of St. Louis*, this time to Mexico. Joined by his mother, Evangeline, who flew down to Mexico City from Detroit in a plane belonging to Henry Ford, Lindbergh was the guest of the president of Mexico. Using a Mexican-built plane, he took the chief executive for his flight. Back on the ground, Lindy saw his first bullfight.

Returning to Washington in March of 1928 to receive the Medal of Honor from President Coolidge in a White House ceremony, Lindy gave plane rides over the nation's capital to a pair of senators and 42 representatives and their families. His purpose was to make the lawmakers "air minded" in the hope that they would vote to fund military air services and to support the development of civilian flying. To drive home the need for the United States to lead the way in aviation, he spoke before the military committees of both houses of Congress to urge higher pay for officers and enlisted men in the Army Air Corps.

The Saga of Submarine S-4

One week after Lindbergh was voted the Congressional Medal of Honor for heroism in flying solo across the Atlantic, an undersea drama began off Provincetown, Massachusetts, that would keep Americans praying for five suspenseful days. On December 17, 1927, as the U.S. Navy submarine *S-4*, with 40 men on board, was surfacing, it was rammed by the U.S. Coast Guard destroyer *Paulding*. It was on patrol in search of rum-running boats and ships.

The *Paulding* suffered heavy damage to her hull but made it back to port under tow. The *S-4* quickly sank 101 feet to the bottom off the tip of Cape Cod. As news of the collision was flashed from Massachusetts, it seemed as if every activity in the whole country came to a halt as people awaited the latest report.

Famous Faces

"Jolie," as Al Jolson was often called, was the biggest star in 1920s show business. Famous for performing in black face, his real name was Asa Yoelson. In 1927 he was the star of the first "talking" movie, *The Jazz Singer*.

When Navy divers reached the sub, they heard taps on the hull. In Morse code, the tapping signaled that six sailors were alive but that their supply of air was rapidly dwindling. Although air was forced into the sub, the tapping stopped on the fourth day.

Recovery of bodies began on January 4, 1928. When all were located, the death toll was 5 officers, 34 enlisted men, and a civilian observer. After an investigation, a Navy board of inquiry ruled on February 21, 1928, that the skippers of both ships "are jointly responsible for the collision."

On March 17, the *S-4* was raised and towed to Boston. Examination of the interior showed that after the collision, everyone in the sub had escaped drowning by getting into watertight compartments. They'd died because of deadly gasses and exhaustion of their air.

At the time of the loss of the *S-4* the United States had only four fleet submarines of over 1,000 tons each, capable of speeds of 20 knots, and equipped with 3-inch guns. Britain had two subs of the same class. Japan had four. Because of restrictions imposed by the treaty that ended World War I, Germany was allowed none. But by the end of the Great Depression in 1941, submarines of the new German navy that were built by the Nazi regime would be prowling the sea lanes of the North Atlantic in "wolf packs."

As of October 1, 1928, the U.S. Navy had 18 battleships and 3 aircraft carriers. On the day that would mark the end of the Great Depression, December 7, 1941, every battle-ship in the Pacific Fleet would be caught and destroyed at their berths by Japanese bombers at Pearl Harbor. While the Navy's three carriers were at sea, also untouched in the Japanese sneak attack were three subs. But in 1928 if you had been around to declare that the airplanes being championed by Lindbergh, aircraft carriers, and submarines would carry the United States to victory over Japan and bring an end to the age of the battleship, you would have been told to have your head examined.

The Least You Need to Know

◆ Following the death of President Warren G. Harding in 1923, his successor, Calvin Coolidge, promised continued prosperity and declared that "the business of America is business."

♦ Author Sinclair Lewis's novel *Main Street* criticized U.S. society for narrowness of mind and provincialism.

♦ A survey of a "typical" American small town by sociologists Robert S. and Helen Merrell Lynd found people divided into two classes dictated by wealth and defined as "business class" and "working class."

♦ As Charles A. Lindbergh was hailed as a hero for flying the Atlantic alone, auto-maker Henry Ford introduced the Model A.

Wall Street Follies

In This Chapter

- ◆ America continues to enjoy "Coolidge Prosperity"
- ◆ The United States thrives; Europe struggles with debt
- ◆ Coolidge steps down
- ◆ Herbert Hoover elected
- ◆ The stock market crash of 1929

With the economy of the United States booming, average Americans were buying goods on credit, and the rich were borrowing to buy stocks and make a killing on Wall Street. Still struggling to recover from the World War, Europe went further into debt to the United States. But "Coolidge Prosperity" was really an unhealthy maldistribution of wealth in the United States and between the United States and Europe. After Coolidge decided not to run for a re-election in 1928, he was succeeded by Herbert Hoover. When banks began failing at the end of the first year of the new president's term, the rest of the economy tumbled like a row of dominoes. Americans didn't realize it, but the Great Depression had begun.

Verses at the Side of the Road

On December 2, 1927, there came together in one new product a perfect blend of the automobile, improved roads, and advertising. The new item was

Burma-Shave. It was a creamy shaving soap that came in a jar. Instead of having to use a brush to make lather from a cake of soap, a man applied a glob of Burma-Shave with his fingers.

To market it, the manufacturer set up signs along highways. But these were not huge billboards. They were a series of rectangular metal placards (six of them, each 36 × 4 inches) widely spaced along the road. As drivers passed by, they read verses that always ended in the words "Burma-Shave," like these:

Facts and Figures

The first brushless shave cream was English, but it was a poor product. Burma-Shave was invented by a Minnesota insurance man, Clinton Odell, and a friend, Carl Noren, who was a chemist, both of Minneapolis. The idea to try selling it through roadside signs came from one of Odell's sons, Allan.

Your shaving brush
Has had its day
So why not
Shave the modern way
With
Burma-Shave (1929)

You'll love your wife
You'll love her paw
You'll even love
Your mother-in-law
If you use
Burma-Shave (1932)

The signs were popular fixtures of American highways until 1963. They disappeared primarily because of interstate highways and the fact that people drove their cars too fast to read them. To see a Burma-Shave sign today, you'll have to go to the Smithsonian Institute in Washington, D.C.

Ironically, one of the first of the clever marketing devices said:

Shaving Brushes
You'll soon see 'em
On the shelf
In some museum

The clever use of roadside signs by Burma-Shave is mentioned in this history of the Great Depression because the product and its smart use of advertising capsulized what America was like in the late 1920s. In the decade before the Great Depression hit, America seemed to be a country of open roads, limitless horizons, and the-sky's-the-limit optimism that good times were here to stay.

Economists call such a condition "consumer confidence." People who have it see no reason why they shouldn't get what they want by buying on credit. When the phenomenon reaches Wall Street, people who buy stocks are "bullish." In the late 1920s the bullish outlook took the form of buying stocks with borrowed money that would be paid back when the purchased shares were sold.

The term, as noted, was "speculation." Because of it, from early 1928 to September 1929 the average price of industrial stocks measured by the Dow Jones Company rose from 191 to 381. For example: If you wanted to buy a stock for $85, you put down $10 of your money and borrowed the rest ($75) from your broker. If the stock went up in the next year to $420 (as RCA did), and you sold it at that price (minus 5 percent to the broker), you had a profit of 3,400 percent. Nice!

There was so much of this borrowing going on that by September 1929 brokers had loaned speculators more than $7 billion. The reason a lot of money was available for such loans by brokers was a reduction in the interest rate at which banks could borrow money. In 1927 the Federal Reserve Board (the national bank) cut the rate at which it lent to banks by half a point, lowering the rate to 3.5 percent. The reduction was made in part because of a change in the international money situation.

As noted earlier, as a result of U.S. loans to European allies in the World War, the United States had replaced Great Britain as the world's creditor nation. About half of this money went to reconstruction. The rest was primarily used to buy food, most of it from the United States. After the war, as Europe rebuilt, the United States extended more help in the form of more loans. This produced—here's that word again—a maldistribution of wealth.

The Problem of the 1920s

To even out this imbalance, Europe needed to sell its goods to the United States. The problem with this was that the United States placed high tariffs on the products that came in from overseas. This often meant that European products were too costly for Americans to buy them: To repay American loans, Europe had to sell its goods in the United States, but the tariffs made them too expensive.

The problem also applied to products that the United States wanted to sell overseas. Europeans, who were unable to sell to America, had no money to buy American products. Another result of this maldistribution of international wealth was a flood of money that foreign investors put into the United States stock market, rather than investing it in European industries.

Facts and Figures

In the late 1920s three fourths of the people earned $2,500 a year or less. They spent almost all of it for the basic necessities. The leftover went to buy the "luxuries" (such as radios and cars) on credit. The top quarter of the earners, who took in more than 55 percent of the national income, did not have to use credit unless they were interested in speculating in the stock market.

Famous Faces

A bomber pilot in Italy in World War I, in 1928 Fiorello La Guardia was a progressive who opposed Prohibition and advocated many social programs for helping the poor and needy that would not become reality until Roosevelt's New Deal programs in the 1930s.

A Warning Voice

One American who did not share the confidence so many Americans felt regarding the free-wheeling, cheap-money economy in 1927 was a New York congressman, Fiorello H. La Guardia. In a speech in the House of Representatives, he said, "Whatever may be said about 'Prosperity' today, and personally I believe it is simply stock-ticker prosperity, the fact remains that we have considerable unemployment."

A Few Words About "Silent Cal"

Speaking of President Calvin Coolidge, the decade's most famous cynic, muckraker-journalist and magazine publisher, H. L. Mencken, would write, "There were no frills while he reigned, but neither were there any headaches." If the 1920s had not been a time of "Coolidge Prosperity," Mencken believed that Coolidge "would have responded to bad times precisely as he responded to good ones; that is, by pulling down the blinds, stretching his legs upon his desk, and snoozing away the lazy afternoons."

Famous Faces

Founder and editor of the opinion magazine *American Mercury*, H. L. Mencken was called "the most powerful personal influence on this whole generation of educated people" by the distinguished columnist Walter Lippmann. Mencken was (in his own words) "against all theologians, professors, editorial-writers, right-thinkers, and reformers." He was opposed to socialists, anarchists, super-patriots, censorship, and Prohibition. If you wanted to sound smart (or if you were), you quoted him.

Quiet Man in a Noisy Time

In a history of the Roaring Twenties titled *Only Yesterday*, Frederick Lewis Allen wrote this about President Calvin Coolidge: "He was not a bold leader, nor did he care to be. He followed no gleam, stormed no redoubt." If you conclude from this that Coolidge was boring, you're right. But he was the man the people wanted. What they desired was to be left alone while they went about the business of America, which, their president declared, was business. To be certain that it flourished, he got taxes cut for everyone, reduced the national debt, and pared the cost of government.

Today, with so much time being spent in Congress battling over the size of the government budget, you may find it difficult to believe that before 1921 there was no federal budget office. It came into being as the "Budget Bureau" in the Treasury Department with passage on June 19, 1921, of the Budget and Accounting Act. The law for the first time required a president to send a budget to Congress that included estimates of receipts and expenditures for the following year. The Act also created a General Accounting Office to carry out audits of government agencies.

President Harding's policies had been friendly to business, and his successor saw no reason not to follow that course. He did it by enthusiastically signing pro-business legislation. And he did it by vetoing measures that he considered bad for business.

Hard Times Down on the Farm

Two of Coolidge's vetoes were of proposed laws to help farmers. They were in a slump that had started after the war and continued through the decade. Coolidge rejected federal assistance on the grounds that government buying of farm products to bolster prices was unsound economic policy because (1) it sanctioned government price-fixing, (2) it was an improper delegation of taxing power, and (3) it would lead to overproduction and to profiteering.

The result was a continuing money squeeze on farmers because of a glut of products. This didn't mean that the farms were harvesting more food than the world needed. The problem was getting a proper price for their produce. These hard times down on the farm were significant because agriculture employed one fourth of the working population of the United States.

Because farmers borrowed money from banks to buy seed and meet the other costs of raising food, the low prices they were getting were insufficient to pay their loans. Farm mortgage debt during the years of Coolidge Prosperity mounted to nearly $10 billion. To make matters worse, American farmers, who had been selling much of their output to the world, found themselves in competition for markets from such agricultural giants as the Soviet Union. Day by day, as manufacturing hummed along nicely and the values of stocks zoomed, the American farmer was fast losing ground—and his shirt.

Dough for the Doughboys

In a burst of patriotism and gratitude to "the boys" who'd gone off to war gaily singing George M. Cohan's "Over There," Congress voted to pay them a bonus. The idea was to compensate them for the difference between their soldiers' pay and what people at home were getting in wages. The measure had been met with a veto by President Harding.

Famous Faces

With the exception of Francis Scott Key ("The Star-Spangled Banner") and Irving Berlin ("God Bless America"), no popular-song writer did more to praise Old Glory and the United States than George M. Cohan in the decades before the first World War ("You're a Grand Old Flag"), and for several years after it. He was not, as Hollywood would have you believe in the James Cagney movie *Yankee Doodle Dandy,* born on the Fourth of July. Cohan was born on July 3 (1878).

When the veterans' bonus came up again, Coolidge also gave it a thumbs-down. But the veto was overridden. Except for officers above the rank of captain, and figured on the basis of $1.25 a day for overseas service and a dollar a day for those who stayed stateside, it set up 20-year endowment policies from which vets could borrow up to one quarter of the value.

However, Coolidge was able to successfully veto a second measure granting a general increase in the pensions of veterans of all America's wars. Later in this book you'll read how these bonus promises planted Coolidge's successor in the middle of one of the most disgraceful acts by the United States government against American citizens.

Ten Words from Silent Cal

With the country basking in the glow of Coolidge Prosperity, no one who was gambling on margin on Wall Street in 1927 would have taken a bet offered by anyone who was crazy enough to wager that Coolidge would not run for a second term in 1928. So imagine the shock and surprise on August 2, when Coolidge announced that he was not going to run for re-election. In keeping with his nickname, Silent Cal did not actually come out and say it. He handed a bunch of reporters who were with him on a vacation in the Black Hills of the Dakotas a slip of paper on which he'd written, "I do not choose to run for President in 1928."

Why did Coolidge decide not to seek re-election? Some writers believed that Coolidge somehow foresaw that the good times were not going to last, so rather than being blamed for a downturn, he preferred to go back to Vermont. A more likely explanation is that after the unexpected death of his son, he had no heart for the presidency. Sixteen-year-old Calvin Jr. died from blood poisoning in 1924 as the result of a foot blister that he got while playing tennis. The senior Coolidge wrote in his autobiography, "When he went, the power and the glory of his presidency went with him."

After Coolidge, Who?

The immediate front-runner for the Republican presidential nomination in 1928 was Coolidge's Secretary of Commerce, Herbert C. Hoover. Born in West Branch, Iowa, on August 10, 1874, Hoover was a graduate in engineering of Stanford University. Between 1897 and 1914, he ran mining operations in Australia, China, and other parts of the globe. During and after the World War, he was put in charge of American relief projects in Europe, earning a deserved reputation as a great humanitarian.

For optimism and confidence in the economy in the late 1920s, no one matched him. During the 1928 presidential campaign, he said, "We in America are nearer to the final triumph over poverty than ever before in the history of any land." Admitting that America had not yet reached that goal, he vowed that "given a chance to go forward with the policies of the last eight years, we shall, with the help of God be in sight of the day when poverty will be banished from the nation."

What a Contrast!

Hoover's opponent was the Democratic governor of New York, Alfred E. (Al) Smith. The two candidates differed on virtually every issue, especially Prohibition. Smith was a "wet." Hoover saw the banning of booze as "a great social and economic experiment, noble in motive and far-reaching in purpose." Hoover had been raised as a Quaker. Al Smith was Roman Catholic. Hoover was a college graduate. Smith dropped out of school as a boy to support his mother after his father died. Smith spent a lifetime in politics. Hoover's first run for office was in 1928.

 Famous Faces _____

After the 1928 election Coolidge returned to the practice of law in Northampton, Vermont. He had little to say about what was going on in the nation. When he was asked if he would ever consider a return to politics, he had an eight-word answer: "Nothing would induce me to take office again." He died of a heart attack on January 5, 1933, at age 60.

Famous Faces

After losing the presidential election of 1928 to Hoover, Al Smith completed his term as New York governor (succeeded by Franklin D. Roosevelt), then became head of the corporation that built the Empire State Building. He made a bid for the Democratic presidential nomination again in 1932 but lost to Roosevelt.

Although Hoover denounced the raising of religion as an issue in the campaign, especially in the South, Smith's Catholicism was a major factor. In the end, "the happy warrior," as Franklin D. Roosevelt had called Smith when nominating him, was unable to overcome Protestant Americans' doubts about the loyalties of a "papist" in the White House. But what really beat Smith was a broad national contentment with the way things were. It wasn't Smith's religion that gave Hoover a landslide win and the largest Electoral College margin since President Grant (444 to 87). Hoover won on the strength of Coolidge Prosperity.

Great Expectations

Because Herbert Hoover had the bad luck to become president when the Prosperity bubble was about to burst, making him the enduring symbol of that dark period, you may be surprised to learn that he entered the White House with a heroic image and a reputation as a miracle worker. Hailing Hoover's post-war relief efforts in Europe, economist John Maynard Keynes declared, "Never was a nobler work of disinterested goodwill carried through with more sincerity and skill, and with less thanks either asked or given."

Hoover's relief work impressed then–Assistant Secretary of the Navy Franklin D. Roosevelt so much that Roosevelt told President Wilson, "I wish that we [the Democratic Party, after Woodrow Wilson's term ended] could make him President. There couldn't be a better one."

Famous Faces

An English economist, John Maynard Keynes was the editor of the influential *Economic Journal*. He blasted punitive reparations imposed on the defeated Germans. His theories on the need to regulate economies would influence the role of government in society more than any economist before or since.

Another later mistaken impression of Hoover is that he was a dyed-in-the-wool conservative like Coolidge. Actually, Hoover in 1928 was seen as a "progressive" in the mold of Theodore Roosevelt. He was on the record in opposition to the "laissez faire" doctrine in which employers "could ride roughshod" over labor. He believed that the problem in the U.S. economic system was an unfair gap in the distribution of income. He didn't say "maldistribution," but that's what he meant. To correct the inequity, he favored taxing the "well-to-do" at higher rates than people who "earned" their money. Unlike Coolidge and the Republican Party leadership, he was not a champion of keeping the government's nose out of how the business of America was conducted.

Obviously, the majority of voters in the 1928 election who gave him seven million more votes than Al Smith looked on Hoover with great expectations. In his inaugural address, he said the goal of his administration would be the "perfection of justice whether in economic or social fields," and "direction of economic progress toward prosperity and the further lessening of poverty."

Singing a Song of Cheer Again

Thanks in large measure to Hoover's upbeat outlook, Americans went around singing a new, hugely popular song by Jack Yellin (words) and Milton Ager (music). With the giddy title "Happy Days Are Here Again," the ditty told Americans that their "cares and troubles are gone," so "sing a song of cheer again." That certainly was true if a person had his money in corporations. In 1929 the top 200 held 49 percent of all corporate wealth, with $81 billion in assets.

This concentration was the result of a wave of mergers and business consolidations. What this meant was that about 2,000 men who sat on the boards of directors of the 200 corporations were in a position to exert control over the lives of everyone in "Middletown" and on Main Street. But if one had the bad luck to be a farmer, the message of "Happy Days Are Here Again" was a bitter joke. Because of the elimination of price supports and a world agricultural glut, the doughboy who had gone back to the farm after the war found himself in a losing battle not only to make ends meet but also to stay afloat. One of the weapons in that struggle was the farm cooperative.

In an effort to help these enterprises, President Hoover signed the Agricultural Market Act in June 1929. It set up a Federal Farm Board to provide a revolving low-interest loan fund of $500 million. The money was intended to encourage cooperatives as a way to stabilize prices by cutting production. The problem with this was that farmers didn't want to take land out of use.

What's Really Going on Here?

On the day before Americans got out their flags and fireworks to celebrate the Fourth of July in 1929, the readers of newspapers' financial pages who were in the stock market found reasons to be content in a report by Moody's Investors Service. It stated that the continuing rises in stock values were justified because they were in line with industrial activity.

But as America's kids ended their summer vacations to head back to school in September, a respected stock market statistician and analyst, Roger Babson, broke into the headlines with a very scary prognostication. At the 16th National Business Conference held in

Massachusetts, he predicted a market crash. He advised "wise investors" to pay up their margin loans and to quit buying on margin. The result was an immediate "break" in stock values in the last hour of trading on Friday, September 6, 1929.

However, Babson's gloom was offset by Yale economics professor Irving Fisher. He bullishly scoffed at Babson's bearishness by assuring investors. He said he saw no recession in the offing. Speculators accepted Fisher's viewpoint. By the end of September, margin buyers were on the cuff with their brokers by another $1.5 billion. On the subject of dispensers of future doom and gloom, *The Wall Street Journal* asked, "Why is it that any ignoramus can talk about Wall Street?"

A man who could never be called an ignoramus was the president of the American Bankers Association (and vice president of First National Bank of Chicago). In a speech to a convention of bankers held on October 2, 1929, in San Francisco, Craig B. Hazelwood declared, "It may be fairly stated that many conservative bankers in this country are gravely alarmed over the mounting volume of credit that is being employed, both by brokers and by individuals."

Two weeks later Professor Fisher again put his two cents in. He saw stocks staying high because of increased earnings. And six days after that, he ventured that stock prices were too low. He opined that quotations hadn't caught up with real values. Joining in this cheery outlook on the same day, the chairman of the National City Bank of New York, Charles E. Mitchell (just back from a two-week tour of Europe), said he saw no signs of a Wall Street Slump. The next day, Wednesday, October 23, 1929, stocks gained sharply, with many issues showing net advances. But in the last hour of trading, the Dow Jones Industrial average dove by 21 points. The loss obliterated all the gains of July and August.

Oh, the Changes a Day Can Bring

On Thursday, October 24, 1929, the stock market's bottom sagged. Because of heavy liquidations, 2.6 million shares were sold in the last hour of trading. The "record decline" wiped out many accounts that had been bought on margin by people who suddenly couldn't cover them. The "paper loss" was $4 billion. Unfazed by what appeared to be a calamity, Professor Fisher was still singing "Happy Days Are Here Again." He assured bankers on that grim Thursday that the "slump" was "only temporary."

On Friday, Wall Street found itself swamped by a 12,894,650-share day. As stock tickers lagged in reporting the downward activity, thousands of investors were being wiped out without knowing it. On Saturday (they traded on Saturdays in 1929), frantic stock brokers sent out letters to clients, warning against "hysterical" selling and urging them to buy.

Come Monday, October 28, the Dow Jones Industrials plummeted more than 38 points, a one-day loss of 13 percent of their values. It was such a disastrous dive that nothing could be done to stop it. And so, on Tuesday, October 29, ever-after enshrined in the annals of Wall Street as "Black Tuesday," as 16.4 million shares were traded, the Dow went down, down, down, and farther down. When the bell rang to close the day, the Industrials were off another 45. The show business newspaper *Variety's* front page said it all: "Wall Street Lays an Egg."

Why did the economy collapse? The short answer is that businesses had turned out more product than they could sell to a population that was over its collective head in debt in a country whose economy had been based on—by now you know what: maldistribution of wealth. No one understood it at the time, but "The Great Depression" was under way.

Leaking Like a Sieve

When President Coolidge delivered his last State of the Union message to Congress on December 4, 1928, he noted that while the Prohibition Amendment had turned the country officially dry in 1920, the federal enforcement bureau was still struggling to prevent violations, especially by smugglers. Despite millions of dollars devoted to stopping the "rum runners," little progress had been achieved in stemming the flow of liquor into the United States from other countries.

One of the easiest places for bootleggers to get the hooch was Canada. Liquor was readily available in government stores to any adult. In 1926 the giant country to the north had raked in almost $2 million from the province of Quebec alone. As of June 30, 1928, the value of hooch streaming across the U.S. border from the land of the Maple Leaf was nearly $25 million.

Tallying the Cost

In an ongoing attempt to put a stopper in this international booze trade, as well as in the brisk business in illegal liquor made in the United States by bootleggers, the U.S. government in the eight years since adoption of the 18th Amendment had spent a staggering $177 million. Of that sum $32 million went to the Coast Guard, but that figure did not include another $37.5 million for additional destroyers of the type that sank the *S-4* submarine.

The head of the Prohibition enforcement unit in the U.S. Justice Department, Mrs. Mabel Walker Willebrandt, noted for the record, "The foreign vessel hovering with supplies of liquor off the coast of the United States continues to be a source of trouble."

One of history's most famous headlines.

A Big Headache

So how was the government doing in the area of prosecutions of the bootleggers? Let's look at the biggest market, New York City. Between 1928 and 1929, there were about 15,000 convictions, with about three quarters of a million dollars collected in fines—a mere drop in the bucket compared to the cost of enforcement. Between 1920 and 1930, federal prohibition agents arrested about 577,000 offenders. Less than two-thirds were convicted. But this was a small fraction of the number of Americans defying the law.

To be fair to law enforcers, the task they had was enormous. In order to make Prohibition effective, they were expected to police more than 18,000 miles of national boundaries. To check the flow of liquor, they would have had to prevent the diversion of 170 million gallons of legal "medicinal" alcohol to manufacturers who made it into booze. American doctors were writing more than 11 million prescriptions to people whose only ailment was a need for a stiff drink. Brewing of booze was going on in an estimated 22 million homes. So much brewing and distilling was going on that someone composed this:

Timeline _____

Seven rivals of gangster Al Capone were rubbed out in a garage in Chicago on St. Valentine's Day 1929.

Mother's in the kitchen
Washing out the jugs;
Sister's in the pantry
Bottling the suds;
Father's in the cellar
Mixing up the hops;
Johnny's on the front porch
Watching for the cops.

If all these acts of defiance could have been caught, and the violators prosecuted, there would not have been enough judges to handle the cases. To avoid paralyzing the entire legal system, courts established "bargain days" on which pending cases were disposed of without a jury by promising light sentences if defendants pleaded guilty. It was a desperate "plea bargain" system that would be embraced in the "war against drugs" from the 1980s to this very day and with as little effect in curing the problem.

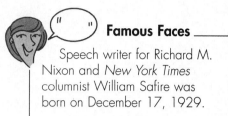

Famous Faces

Speech writer for Richard M. Nixon and *New York Times* columnist William Safire was born on December 17, 1929.

Another Way to Get High

In the two years since Charles A. Lindbergh thrilled the nation with his flight across the Atlantic, and due in large measure to efforts by him and other famous fliers such as World War I "Ace" Eddie Rickenbacker, commercial aviation had been taking off to such an extent that Coolidge declared in his final message to the Congress that progress in civil aviation "is most satisfying."

The national airway system was growing in leaps and bounds. A report by the Commerce Department noted that in 1927 the distance flown on scheduled trips (mostly air mail flights) was nearly six million miles. More than half a million miles had been flown by 8,679 paying passengers. To handle the increasing traffic, there were 352 municipal airports in operation, along with 325 private and commercial facilities. And more than 600 were in the planning stage.

A survey by the Commerce Department found that in the first six months of 1928, there had been 390 accidents in which 153 people were killed and 276 injured. The cause of 43.29 percent of these accidents was pilot error. Engine failures or other mechanical problems were the cause of 22.35 percent. The remainder were attributed to bad weather and nighttime flying.

If going up in an airplane seemed too daring in 1928, the Germans offered an alternative in the form of the *Graf Zeppelin*. It was a huge, hydrogen-filled, "lighter-than-air," passenger-carrying balloon. Under the command of Dr. Hugo Eckener, and with a crew of 18 officers, 15 machinists, 2 stewards, and 20 passengers who'd paid $3,000 per seat, it astonished the world by flying from Germany to the United States in 111 hours and 46 minutes. It then flew from its base at Lakehurst, New Jersey, to Los Angeles in a nonstop, breathtaking, 39 hours and 48 minutes.

The future of zeppelins, known in the United States as dirigibles, seemed so bright that plans for the Empire State Building in the heart of Manhattan included a mooring mast 1,250 feet above West 34th Street. But as you will read later, that rosy prospect went up in flames as another German airship, the *Hindenburg*, exploded while landing at Lakehurst on May 6, 1937.

By then the United States was deep into the Great Depression and Americans could only shake their heads in dismay over the words that Calvin Coolidge had chosen to end his last message to Congress nine years earlier. The president credited with nearly a decade prosperity had said, "Our country has been provided with the resources with which it can enlarge the intellectual, moral, and spiritual life. The issue is in the hands of the people. Our faith in man and God is the justification for the belief in our continuing success."

The Least You Need to Know

- Following the death of President Harding in 1923, the United States enjoyed nearly six years of "Coolidge Prosperity."
- In the 1928 presidential campaign against Democrat Al Smith, Republican Herbert Hoover pledged a continuation of prosperity.
- Most financial experts expressed confidence that the years of economic boom would continue, but others warned of the danger of use of credit by stock buyers.
- On "Black Tuesday," October 29, 1929, the stock market crashed, triggering the Great Depression.

Chapter 4

Hooverville

In This Chapter

♦ The government slowly realizes how bad things are
♦ Bread lines, soup kitchens, and Hoovervilles
♦ The country needs a good laugh
♦ Things Hoover did that were wrong and right

Once the Hoover administration realized that the economy was not having another of its periodic, temporary re-adjustments, the question was how to provide relief to the unemployed. To keep the federal government going, Hoover chose to raise taxes and tariffs on international trade. As unemployment grew, many people were on the verge of starvation. Thousands lived in shantytowns that were called "Hoovervilles." Finally recognizing a need for some kind of direct government aid, Hoover initiated policies and programs that laid a foundation for Franklin D. Roosevelt's New Deal.

Not Your Usual Short Slump

On October 25, 1929 (the day after stocks took a nose dive), the president of the United States gave a speech. In spite of the crashing sound coming from Wall Street, Herbert C. Hoover said, "The fundamental business of this country, that is production and distribution of commodities, is on a sound and prosperous basis."

A couple of weeks later, he was cautioning suddenly broke and out-of-work Americans that any lack of confidence in the economic future or the strength of U.S. business was "foolish."

If there was one word that people chose to describe Hoover's personality, it was "optimistic." Psychologists define such a rosy outlook in trying times as not seeing a glass of water as half-empty, but half-full. People who study techniques of propaganda call it "creating a bandwagon effect." If a president is optimistic, the people will also be upbeat. The politician's term is "jawboning." The hope is that if you say something is so, it will become so.

Hoover wasn't the first public official to jawbone, nor was he the last president to give it a try. As you will read, among the first words out of President Franklin D. Roosevelt's mouth when he took office in 1933 were "The only thing we have to fear is fear itself." When President Gerald R. Ford faced skyrocketing prices in the late 1970s, he believed that Americans could "Whip Inflation Now" by thinking their way out of it. Ford even had a button made with the word "WIN" on it. For Ronald Reagan, the slogan was "It's morning in America." President George Bush (the first) talked about "a thousand points of light."

Timeline

To show confidence in the 1930 economy, citizens of Cincinnati, Ohio, wore large buttons that said: "I'm sold on America. I won't talk depression."

But sooner or later, the people doing the jawboning woke up to the fact that all the happy talk could no longer obscure reality. As historian Robert S. McElvaine noted in a now-classic 1984 book, *The Great Depression*, Hoover faced a "disease" that was too serious "to be cured instantly by an injection of confidence."

During the first two weeks of November 1929, no amount of jawboning could obscure the fact that, as one observer noted, the stock market "continued to act like a rubber ball bounding down statistical stairs."

When in Trouble, Call a Conference

While still showing America a smiling and optimistic face, the President called business leaders to the White House for a series of conferences about the worsening state of affairs. He continued to say that restoring public confidence was vital. In a speech to members of the press who belonged to Washington's Gridiron Club, he justified his jawboning. He said, "Fear, alarm, pessimism, and hesitation swept through the country, which, if unchecked, would have precipitated absolute panic throughout the business world with untold misery in its wake."

As he spoke, quite a lot of Americans were feeling miserable. The crash that ruined industries had cast them out of work. Each day that passed had brought more unemployment. The purpose of Hoover's meetings with the top men of business was to urge them to show confidence in the economy by continuing to invest in their companies and others. And just as important, he asked them not to slash the pay of those who still had jobs. Henry Ford promised Hoover more than that. Rather than cutting wages, he pledged, he would raise Ford employees' wages to seven dollars a day. Heartened by all this, the influential *Kiplinger* newsletter told its subscribers that the businessmen who'd met with Hoover came away predicting that 1930 would be a "good year."

Birth of a Little Bull Market

While Hoover's song of optimism lilted across the country, it seemed as if those who had written Wall Street's obituary had been a trifle hasty. The month of December brought a heartening up-tick. It was called the "Little Bull Market."

As 1929 drew to a close, the president of the New York Stock Exchange, Richard Whitney, was so elated that he invited friends and associates to a big party on the trading floor on December 31 to welcome in the New Year by celebrating the recovery. When the gong signaled the end of the day's trading, a business reporter for *The New York Times* noted "a pandemonium of noise" from happy clerks. "The din," he informed his readers, "could be heard as far away as Broadway."

The celebrating continued well into the spring of 1930. So good did things look that Secretary of Commerce William Doak saw no reason why normal business condition could not be restored "in two or three months."

Birth of a Magazine

A new business magazine joined in the chorus of hurrahs. In the fifth issue (June) of *Fortune* (started by Henry Luce), analyst Merryle Stanley Rukeyser praised Hoover's cheery rhetoric. "I am one of those," he wrote, "who think that the engineer in the White House made a magnificent gesture to stem psychological panic and to demonstrate that the human will could be an effective contributing cause in shaping the co of the business cycle."

What Goes Up Must Come Down

Anyone who believed that the ball that had been bouncing down a statistical staircase had reached the bottom was wrong. A closer look at what was going on in the U.S. economy in 1930's first quarter gave reason to be alarmed. The evidence was found in the statistics of Henry Ford's auto company and all other car makers (34 of them). Sales were way down. So were the profits in the railroad business. Banks also felt embattled. The only industries doing well were those involved in providing entertainment to people who'd been knocked for a loop. They were radio and movies (see Part 5, "Better Tomorrows").

Assessing the truth of 1930 in his book *The Hungry Years*, the historian T. H. Watkins wrote that however stubbornly the nation's sundry leaders tried to defy reality "by sending up increasingly gaseous balloons of optimism," between October 1929 and summer of 1933 the country was falling into the worst recession in history.

Lies, Naked Lies, and Statistics

While Hoover and others were talking up optimism, the statistics of the economy presented a sobering outlook. Since the peak of Coolidge Prosperity, the Gross National Product had gone down by 29 percent. Consumer buying dipped 18 percent. Construction was off by 78 percent. Investment plummeted 98 percent. The rate of unemployment zoomed from 3.2 percent to nearly one fourth of the working population.

One day in December 1930, a Hoover friend by the name of Arthur Woods, who had been put in charge of "the President's Emergency Committee for Employment" (PECE), got a letter from a citizen who saw through all the happy talk. Assailing "a bunch of overley [*sic*] rich, selfish, dumb, ignorant money hogs," he said of the words "Justice for all" in the Pledge of Allegiance to the flag: "What a lie, what a naked lie."

aughing to Keep from Crying

Early in 1931 President Hoover said, "What this country needs is a good big laugh." The way to dispel "a condition of hysteria," he ventured, "was for someone to get off a good ke every ten days."

is led a pair of wiseacre comedians to respond with this bit of dialogue: First comic: iness is improving." Second comic: "Is Hoover dead?"

e line that really drove home the point came from America's most beloved humorist ark Twain. "The United States is the only country in history," cracked Will to go to the poor house in an automobile."

Vaudeville comedian Will Rogers is shown in a publicity photo for the Ziegfeld Follies *of 1922.*

(AP Photo)

Famous Faces _____

Born in 1879 in the Colagah Indian Territory of Oklahoma, Will Rogers shot to fame with his topical, low-key humor in the 1917 *Ziegfeld Follies*. His act was a combination of lariat-twirling and witty asides on current events. When he began making movies (silents and then talkies), Americans took him to their hearts. His two other famous remarks were "All I know is what I read in the papers" and "I never met a man I didn't like."

An Abundance of Jokes

A persistent image of the Great Depression from its start right up to today is that of a stock-market loser jumping out of the window of his office on a high floor or perching on a ledge before taking a header because he'd been wiped out. There were suicides, but the jumpers were not as plentiful as jokes made about them.

In one magazine cartoon, a hotel clerk asked a distraught-looking guest, "Do you want the room for sleeping or jumping?" Another joke had two men taking a death-dive together because they'd held a joint stock account. These were not the kind of jokes that President Hoover was hoping to hear every 10 days. But grim as they were, they never failed to get at least a chuckle.

A Whole Lot of Apples

There are no more telling pictures of the hard times following the collapse of the prosperity of the 1920s than those of out-of-work men selling apples on the streets. The peddlers didn't show up suddenly on their own. When the International Apple Shippers Association found itself with an oversupply, a quick-thinker on the sales staff proposed that the abundance be sold to jobless men on credit. Bought at wholesale prices, they were soon selling for a nickel each on city streets everywhere.

One of the apple sellers was "Apple Annie." She caught the eye of a New York newspaperman by the name of Damon Runyon. Annie was one of the characters who inspired Runyon to publish a collection of stories under the title *Guys and Dolls*. You can see a version of her played by Bette Davis in the 1962 film *A Pocket Full of Miracles*. The guys and dolls of Runyon's yarns were also put into a Broadway musical with that name (1950) and then into a movie musical starring Frank Sinatra and Marlon Brando (1951).

An unemployed apple seller is shown at the height of the Depression in 1935, in midtown Manhattan.

(AP Photo)

Famous Faces _____

Damon Runyon fascinated Americans with hilarious stories about tough guys, tin-horns, gamblers, nightclub singers, chorus girls, and other "Broadway" types, such Harry the Horse, Nathan Detroit, and Nicely Nicely Johnson. What was the appeal of Runyon's characters? One of them, Waldo Winchester (a take-off on gossip columnist Walter Winchell), explained it best: "Many legitimate people are much interested in the doings of tough guys and consider them very romantic." We still do!

How Long Can You Live on Hope?

Remember "Middletown"? In 1930 when the Lynds visited the real town (Muncie, Indiana) to see how folks there were getting along, they learned that one out of four people had lost a job and had not been able to find a new one. Another investigator into small-town America found the situation just as bad in towns in New England. Of Lowell, Massachusetts, writer Louis Adamic wrote that thousands of unemployed "walked around like ghosts or were hiding away in their shacks and small rooms." A labor union official reported that two thirds of the city's textile workers were idle or employed only part-time.

Facts and Figures _____

The jobless rate rose from four million in 1930 to eight million in 1931. In 1932 there were 12 million. But only about one-fourth were getting relief, mostly in the form of food handouts.

The real meaning of not having work was evidenced in places such as barbershops and stores. Many men in Lowell, Massachusetts, had taken to having their hair cut at home. A butcher noted that hardly anyone who came in bought steak. They wanted cheaper cuts, and many asked for bones to use in making soup. A dentist found that steady patients had given up coming in unless they had a toothache, and then they told him to pull the offender, rather than putting out money to try to save it. A dry-goods store owner told Adamic, "I don't know how much longer I can hold out on hope."

A jobless man in New Bedford said that he'd thought about killing himself and his family, but "didn't have the guts." What he had, he said, was hundreds of dollars of debt. "There's nobody I know in town who's ever had any money that I don't owe him some. You don't know what it means to have a wife and kids and no work and no money and be in debt."

Such a Day Will Not Come

So where was Herbert Hoover? The president was in the White House and sticking to his belief in "rugged individualism" and good old American virtues, such as aiding your neighbor and not running to the federal government for help. He was also feeling hurt that he, the man who'd helped feed war-torn Europe, was seen as being indifferent to the plight of Americans who'd had the bad luck to lose their jobs and were fast running out of hope. There's no better way to show his answer to the crisis than to condense parts of a statement that he handed out to the press:

> This is not an issue as to whether people shall go hungry or cold in the United States. It is a question on one hand whether the American people, on one hand, will maintain the spirit of charity and mutual self-help through voluntary giving and the responsibility of local government as distinguished, on the other hand, from appropriations out of the Federal Treasury. I am willing to pledge myself that if the time should ever come that the voluntary agencies of the country, together with the local and State governments, are unable to find resources with which to prevent hunger and suffering in my country, I will ask the aid of every resource of the federal government because I would no more see starvation amongst our countrymen than would any senator or congressman. I have faith in the American people that such a day will not come.

As Hoover saw it, there was no reason for anybody to go hungry. Local and state governments had set up food programs, and such organizations as the Salvation Army were operating soup kitchens and bread lines.

A Salvation Army relief worker tends to a line at a local soup kitchen during the Great Depression. Date and location are unknown.

(AP Photo)

Other charitable groups had created places that their grateful customers called the "Five-and-Dime Depression Restaurant." One could get a lunch that might include an egg, a dish of baked beans, a bowl of soup, a doughnut, and a cup of coffee. Cost: six cents.

A priest of a Lithuanian church in Lawrence, Massachusetts, told Louis Adamic, "I can do so little. Mothers come to me and cry and say they have no money to buy food and shoes for the children, and winter is here. We make collections in the church, and I give them money. One family I know had lived on lentils, nothing but lentils, all this year. They can't afford to buy bread."

Two Ideas, Both Bad

There were things that Hoover was prepared to let the government do. Because so many people weren't working, they were not paying taxes. To keep the federal government's books from going into the red, Hoover sought to raise money through a sales tax and with a hike in import tariffs. The Revenue Act of 1932 was the largest-percentage tax increase in peacetime to that time. Rather than impose a tax at the point of sale, it placed the tax on manufacturers, who then passed it on to consumers as higher prices.

Because American agriculture was struggling to compete with farm products brought in from overseas, the Smoot-Hawley Act of June 1931 raised tariffs from 38 to 49 percent. Its effect was to make matters worse by contributing to a worldwide trade war. Stresses and strains on the global economy worsened when Britain abandoned gold as the underpinning of its money. This led to a rush by foreign investors to hoard gold by converting their U.S. gold-backed dollars to bullion.

Facts and Figures

The Revenue Act of 1932 raised top tax rates from 25 to 63 percent.

Borrowing Time

Despite Hoover's belief that localities and charities could best provide relief to the unemployed, it became clear that not enough was being done. The president found himself being pressured to provide assistance by the federal government. The result was the creation of the Reconstruction Finance Corporation (RFC).

With $500 million made available, the agency provided emergency financing for banks, life insurance companies, building and loan associations, farm mortgage associations, and railroads. Within six months, RFC authorized $1.2 billion in loans to about 5,000 such organizations.

Five months later, the RFC's scope and functions were extended to permit $1½ billion in temporary loans to the states to finance the relief of economic distress through public works projects. At the same time, Congress passed the Federal Home Loan Bank Act. It was a measure proposed by Hoover to create a Home Loan Bank Board. It established banks to offer long-term mortgages in order to encourage home ownership. The law was also intended to reduce home foreclosures.

Broken Promises

You'll recall that when business leaders such as Henry Ford met with President Hoover shortly after the 1929 market crash, they promised not to lower the pay of employees. But in the fall of 1931 as they found their businesses struggling, their pledges went out the window. Wage-slashing that began with the United States Steel Corporation (a 10 percent cut) quickly spread to other manufacturers.

Many individuals and families, who'd been barely managing to keep body and soul together and a roof over their heads, found they could no longer make ends meet. When they weren't able to pay the rent or make the mortgage payments, they were out on the street.

A Shanty in Old Shantytown

No matter how disastrous a situation seems to be, Americans can always count on someone coming up with a ditty for them to sing about it. In 1932 a popular songsmith named Ted Black sat down at his piano with a blank sheet of music composition paper to turn out just such an anthem for the times. It began with a four-line verse about living in a tumbledown shack by an old railroad track. It had a roof so slanty that it touched the ground.

When Black named the song "In a Shanty in Old Shantytown," there were untold thousands of such makeshift dwellings in towns and cities all over the country. While the term "shantytown" was in wide use, the most popular name given to these communities was "Hoovervilles."

In *Just Around the Corner: A Highly Selective History of the Thirties*, Robert Bendiner recalled seeing them along the Hudson River on a stretch of land below the luxury apartment houses of New York City's Riverside Drive. "I daily passed the tarpaper huts of a Hooverville," he wrote, "where scores of families lived the lives of reluctant gypsies."

Such encampments for the homeless sprouted everywhere. Made of whatever materials were handy, they usually appeared in vacant lots or rose as "suburbs" on the outskirts of towns and cities.

In a 1932 photo of a New York City "Hooverville," this crude shack, built of loose boards and flats of boxes, served as a home for unemployed men during the Great Depression.

(AP Photo)

Who Are These Men?

Among the people who were forced to live in Hoovervilles or get their meals in soup kitchens were men who had fought in the World War to "make the world safe for democracy." For doing their duty they'd been promised bonus money. It was supposed to make up the difference between their service pay and wages received by war workers who'd remained civilians. Called the World War Adjustment Act, it became law in 1924 over Coolidge's veto. It delayed full payment for 20 years.

But in 1932, veterans who were broke, many of them living in Hoovervilles, decided that if the government could bail out bankers and businesses, it should come across with the bonus money immediately. To drive home their point, they marched to Washington in the summer of 1932 to appeal to Congress to amend the bonus law. Reminding Americans that in the war they had been known as the "A.E.F" (Allied Expeditionary Force), they called themselves the "B.E.F." (Bonus Expeditionary Force). Some 15,000 veterans, many accompanied by wives and children, set up a "Hooverville" on land on the other side of the Potomac River in Anacostia, Virginia, and a shantytown on the Mall between the Capitol Building and the Washington and Lincoln monuments.

On June 15, 1932, the House of Representatives passed the bill that the vets wanted. It would provide $2.4 billion to pay off the bonus funds that had been promised. But the vets' hopes were dashed when the Senate defeated the measure. Because there were thousands of bonus marchers in the capital with no money to go home, the government provided the necessary funds. Most of the vets left town.

Famous Faces

Serving under General MacArthur as his aides in breaking up the Bonus March and its camps were future World War II heroes Dwight D. Eisenhower and George S. Patton.

Famous Faces

Novelists born in the Hoover years included E. L. Doctorow (January 6, 1931), Toni Morrison (February 18, 1931), Tom Wolfe (March 2, 1931), and John Updike (March 18, 1932).

About 2,000 refused to leave. This resulted in an attempt by the Washington, D.C., police to evict them. In the ensuing clash, two vets and two policemen were killed. But the veterans were still in the capital and their Anacostia encampment.

President Hoover called on Army Chief of Staff General Douglas MacArthur to mobilize soldiers to clear them from the city. He moved to do so on July 28. To the superintendent of the city's police force, he pledged, "We are going to break the back of the B.E.F."

Using tear gas, the troops quickly drove the veterans from city streets and the Capitol Mall. Then, without orders from Hoover to do so, MacArthur sent troops across the Potomac to oust those who remained in Virginia. Attacking with tear gas, they met almost no resistance as they set fire to the huts and shacks.

When it was over, the casualties included an 11-week-old baby, an 8-year-old boy who was partially blinded by tear gas, a vet with a severed ear, another with a bayonet wound, and more than a dozen people who had been gassed. MacArthur justified his actions by saying he'd moved against "a mob" that had been driven by "the essence of revolution."

The American people were shocked. How they felt about Herbert Hoover and his handling of what was now being called "the Depression" would be registered when they went to the polls in November.

An Army in Retreat

As the vets fled from Washington, they found soldiers barring them from crossing bridges into Virginia. As they headed to the Maryland border, state police stopped them with roadblocks. When rain began around four in the morning, the large, milling throng was allowed to enter the state with orders to keep moving.

Two days earlier they had regarded themselves, and thought the country regarded them, as heroes trying to collect a debt long overdue. They had boasted about their months or years of service, their medals, their war wounds, and their patriotism. But the president of the United States had accused them of being outlaws. Others in government said they were "Red" radicals, the dregs of society, and criminals. In a final insult, someone in government had said that most of them weren't veterans at all.

Reporting the routing of the Bonus Army for *The New Republic*, Malcolm Cowley noted, "The veterans were expected to disperse to their homes, but most of them had no homes, and they felt that their only safety lay in sticking together."

Thieves and Plug-Uglies

Somehow a rumor raced through the dejected ranks that the mayor of Johnstown, Pennsylvania, had invited them to the city whose chief claim to fame was that it had been hit by a disastrous flood in 1900 in which 2,000 people had perished. Suddenly in 1932, the small industrial town nestled in the hills of western Pennsylvania found itself facing a new inundation. But this one was a wave of thousands of hungry and homeless fellow Americans.

A panicky editorial writer for the *Johnstown Tribune* warned the town, "In any group of the size of the Bonus Army, made up of men gathered from all parts of the country, without discipline and lacking effective leadership in a crisis, without any attempt on the part of those leaders to check the previous records of the individuals who compose it, there is certain to be a mixture of undesirables—thieves, plug-uglies, and degenerates. The community must protect itself from the criminal fringe of the invaders."

Ex-soldiers, sailors, marines, airmen, and others who'd fought in the war to make the world safe for democracy were now being seen as "invaders." What they couldn't know as they approached their destination and found trucks waiting for them was that the police escorts for the convoy had orders to lead them past Johnstown and to the border, where they would become a problem for Ohio. Some of the men in the Bonus Army were so bitter that they spoke of marching to Washington again, but this time with guns to start a revolution.

After recording this incendiary talk in his reporter's notebook, Cowley wrote in his *New Republic* article, "The Flight of Bonus Army," that "a thousand homeless veterans, or fifty thousand don't make a revolution. No, if any revolution results from the plight of the Bonus Army, it will come from a different source; from the government itself. The army in time of peace, at the national capital, has been used against unarmed citizens. This, with all it threatens in the future, is a revolution itself."

U.S. Senator David A. Reed, a Pennsylvania Republican, said, "I do not often envy other countries their governments, but I say that if this country ever needed a dictator like Benito Mussolini of Italy, it needs one now."

The Least You Need to Know

◆ While President Herbert Hoover searched for ways to deal with the worsening Depression, unemployed Americans were living in shantytowns that they called "Hoovervilles."

◆ Yielding to pressure to provide federal aid to the states in providing relief, Hoover approved a system of loans for funding of public works programs.

◆ Between 1930 and 1931 the unemployment rate doubled, from four to eight million. In 1932 it was 12 million.

◆ When Congress refused to speed up payment of a bonus for World War I veterans, a "Bonus Army" of 15,000 vets gathered in Washington to protest, but the U.S. Army drove them out.

Part  2

What's the Deal?

This section covers the election of President Franklin Delano Roosevelt, his program for national economic recovery in which he promised the nation a "New Deal," and the "Brain Trust" of people he appointed to run it.

During FDR's "first 100 days," Congress passed laws to create so many new federal agencies which were known by their initials that the New Deal seemed like a bowl of alphabet soup. To boost national morale and inform the people about the goals of these new programs, FDR took advantage of the popularity and power of radio with "fireside chats" broadcast from the White House.

5

The Man with Three Names

In This Chapter

- ◆ Hoover is blamed for the continuing Depression
- ◆ Democrats nominate Franklin Delano Roosevelt for president
- ◆ The 1932 election
- ◆ Prohibition ends
- ◆ FDR's inaugural address

With one fourth of the nation's workforce unemployed and with local and state governments, along with private charities, trying to feed, clothe, and house millions of people, the Herbert Hoover administration was blamed for worsening the Depression. During the 1932 presidential election campaign, Franklin Delano Roosevelt promised a New Deal, and Prohibition ended.

Hoover and the Valley of Depression

The plight of millions of Americans, and the problem faced by the president of the United States as he pondered whether to run for re-election in 1932, were summed up in a re-wording of Psalm 23 by one E. J. Sullivan:

> Hoover is my Shepherd, I am in want,
> He maketh me to lie down on park benches,
> He leadeth me by still factories,
> He restoreth my doubt in the Republican Party.

He guided me in the path of the Unemployed for his party's sake,
Yea, though I walk through the alley of soup kitchens,
I am hungry.
I do not fear evil, for thou art against me;
Thy Cabinet and thy Senate, they do discomfort me;
Thou didst prepare a reduction in my wages;
In the presence of my creditors thou anointed my income with taxes,
So my expense overrunneth my income.
Surely, poverty and hard times will follow me
All the days of the Republican administration.
And I shall dwell in a rented house forever.
Amen.

In balancing pluses and minuses of running again, Hoover found many items on the positive side. The Congress had given him the Relief and Construction Act and the Federal Home Loan Bank Act. An international conference in Lausanne, Switzerland, seemed to have eased financial tensions in Europe. The gold drain from the United States was not only stopped, but much of the gold had flowed back. Bank failures had slowed. The stock market was showing signs of improvement. And most of the people had jobs.

On the negative side, the brutal rout of the Bonus Marchers had given his administration a black eye. "Hoovervilles" seemed to be everywhere. Meals for hundreds of thousands of Americans were doled out by bread lines and soup kitchens. Farmers were in such bad financial shape that some of them were resorting to violence. Industry was operating at less than half its level of 1929. The wages of many workers had been slashed.

Even the man who was Calvin Coolidge's Secretary of the Treasury, and was now the U.S. ambassador to Britain, Andrew Mellon, had become a gloom-and-doomer. In a speech in London in the spring, he'd said, "None of us has any means of knowing when and how we shall emerge from the valley of depression in which the world is traveling."

After weighing all of this, Herbert Clark Hoover, thirty-first president of the United States, decided to go for a second term. When the Grand Old Party gathered in Chicago in June, the convention's delegates approved him on the first ballot. The platform called for sharp reduction in government expenditures, balanced budget, high tariffs, keeping the gold standard, restricting immigration, and continuing (but modifying) Prohibition.

Political Ribbing on Broadway

While Herbert Hoover was wrestling with problems of a Depression that was being more and more blamed on him, the state of politics was taking a good-natured beating in the hit Broadway musical of the 1931–1932 season. With songs by George and Ira Gershwin and a book by George S. Kaufman (also the director) and Morrie Ryskind, the story is that of presidential candidate John P. Wintergreen. One of his slogans is "Vote for prosperity and see what you get."

His vice presidential running mate is Alexander Throttlebottom (modeled on Vice President Curtis). When they are elected, no one can remember who the vice president is. Only when taking a tour of the White House does Throttlebottom learn from a guide (who does not know he's talking to the vice president) that the vice president's job is to preside over the Senate.

Filled with satire and jokes that caught the mood of a country that was doubting its political institutions, *Of Thee I Sing* was the first musical to win a Pulitzer Prize. It still ranks as one of Broadway's greatest shows. If you could see a production of the musical today, you'd get a laugh from two story lines that seemed to look ahead in time. The First Lady shares the Oval Office, and there's a move to impeach the president because of a situation during the election campaign involving a beauty contest winner who had expected Wintergreen to marry her.

Famous Faces

Charles Curtis, Hoover's vice president, was part Kaw Indian and was born in Kansas in 1860. A former congressman and U.S. senator, he made a bid for the GOP presidential nomination in 1928. Although Hoover's loyal vice president, he'd opposed using troops against the Bonus March. He died in 1936 at the age of 76.

A Flock of Presidential Wannabes

Although no slate of candidates for office in 1932 was as comical as the team of Wintergreen and Throttlebottom, there was a big field of presidential wannabes. In addition to Herbert Hoover and the Democratic Party's nominee (see the following section), there were:

Presidential Candidate	Party
Verne L. Reynolds	Socialist Labor
Norman Thomas	Socialist
William Z. Foster	Communist
William D. Upshaw	Prohibition
W. H. Harvey	Liberty
Jacob S. Coxey	Farmer-Labor

An Abundance of Democrats

When the Democratic Party's convention was called to order in Chicago on June 27, 1932, the delegates sniffed the sweet smell of victory in the air. They gathered to choose a nominee from an impressive list of contenders. In alphabetical order, they were:

Newton D. Baker, Woodrow Wilson's Secretary of War

Harry F. Byrd, governor of Virginia

James Cox, candidate in 1920

John Nance Garner, Speaker of the House of Representatives

William Murray, governor of Oklahoma

Albert C. Ritchie, governor of Maryland

Franklin D. Roosevelt, governor of New York

Alfred (Al) E. Smith, the 1928 candidate

Owen D. Young, president of General Electric

Observing the delegates and noticing their confidence that they would win in November, Anne O'Hare McCormick of *The New York Times* wrote, "To the Republicans politics is a business, while to the Democrats it is a pleasure. The keynote speaker was Senator Alben W. Barkley of Kentucky. In a very long speech he voiced the belief of many Americans that "the Hoover administration and the policies it has pursued have largely contributed to the disaster which has overtaken ours and the world's affairs."

When all was said and done, and after a lot of bargaining for votes, exhausted Democrats nominated the ticket of Franklin D. Roosevelt and John Nance Garner, whose nickname was Cactus Jack.

To Break Foolish Conditions

In 1932 tradition dictated that the nominee of a political party didn't show up at the convention to accept the honor by making a speech. Roosevelt junked the precedent by flying to Chicago (the first time a presidential candidate traveled by plane). When he spoke, he declared, "Let it from now on be the task of our party to break foolish conditions."

An Unintended Slogan

When Roosevelt and his aides, Raymond Moley and Samuel Rosenman, drafted the acceptance speech to be delivered at the convention, they had no idea that the heart of it would be in three words in the last paragraph. It began, "I pledge you, I pledge myself, to a new deal for the American people."

Seventy years later in an age when political slogans are the result of polling, focus groups, and campaign "war rooms," it's hard to believe that the words "a new deal" were not intended to be the motto for the Roosevelt campaign. But, as historian Nathan Miller noted in *F.D.R.: An Intimate History* (1983), Roosevelt saw no special significance to the words. Only after they appeared in a political cartoon did *New Deal* become "the watchword of a fresh and vibrant political faith."

Talk of the Time

The phrase **New Deal** originated in a 1932 article by Stuart Chase in *The New Republic* titled "A New Deal for America." The phrase was also included in a speech nominating John Nance Garner for vice president. Thirty years earlier, FDR's cousin, Theodore Roosevelt, had promised voters that as president he would give the country "a square deal."

A Pleasant Man Without Qualifications

The enduring impression is that the Democratic Party's nomination of Franklin D. Roosevelt was universally accepted in 1932 as a case of everyone agreeing that he was the right man at the right time. This was by no means the way it was. Before Roosevelt won the nomination, one of the country's most respected political columnists, Walter Lippman, had written that Franklin Roosevelt was "a pleasant man … without any important qualifications for the office."

Journalist Elmer Davis (who would be chosen by FDR at the start of World War II to head the Office of War Information) thought Roosevelt had no political convictions. "You could not quarrel with a single one of his generalities," Davis said. "But what they mean (if anything) is known only to Franklin Roosevelt and God."

The eminent jurist Felix Frankfurter (whom FDR would appoint to the Supreme Court) explained that he was supporting Roosevelt only "because I think the most urgent demand of the hour is to turn Hoover out."

Although the Democratic presidential nominee was governor of New York, and had been James Cox's running mate on the party's losing ticket in 1920, a vast number of potential voters knew little or nothing more about him. He was so unfamiliar to some that they thought that because his name was Roosevelt, he was probably the son of Teddy Roosevelt.

Who Was Franklin Delano Roosevelt?

When Franklin Delano Roosevelt was born at Hyde Park, New York, on January 30, 1882, his 23-year-old cousin Theodore was a member of the Republican Party and in his first term in the Assembly of the New York legislature. During Theodore's presidency, Franklin was at Harvard University and then a law student at Columbia.

Always an admirer of cousin Theodore, Franklin charted a course in politics that seemed deliberately patterned on Theodore's. He served in the New York legislature, then as Assistant Secretary of the Navy in the Wilson years (TR had the post under President McKinley), and as governor of New York.

Two facts about Franklin Delano Roosevelt were not known to many Americans in 1932: (1) His wife Eleanor was also a Roosevelt (she was the daughter of TR's brother Elliott), and (2) Franklin did not have the use of his legs. They were left paralyzed after he was stricken with polio in 1921. That he couldn't walk without being supported by someone on each side of him and that the car he was sometimes photographed driving had special levers to run it would not be known by the general public until after his death in 1945.

U.S. President Franklin D. Roosevelt is greeted by L. P. D. Tilley, Premier of New Brunswick, Canada, on Campobello Island on June 29, 1933. In the car with the president are Mrs. Eleanor Roosevelt, Ambassador Norman Davis, and Franklin Jr., his son.

(AP Photo)

Speaking for the Forgotten Man

An important milestone on Franklin D. Roosevelt's journey to the Democratic presidential nomination was marked on April 7, 1932. It took the form of a coast-to-coast radio address. In the 10-minute broadcast he demanded an economic recovery program that was the reverse of Hoover's policy of helping business in a way that relief would trickle down to the people. Roosevelt proposed a program that "puts faith once more in the *forgotten man* at the bottom of the economic pyramid."

The speech had such a tremendous impact that it immediately made Roosevelt a rallying point for the distressed and dispossessed.

Talk of the Time

The phrase **"forgotten man"** appeared first in an article by William Graham Sumner in 1883. But Sumner's forgotten man referred to a man in the middle class, not one who was poor.

What This Country Needs

One of the most famous comments made by an American politician came during the Wilson years during a speech in the U.S. Senate when Vice President Thomas Marshall was presiding. As the speaker was going on and on about "what this country needs," Marshall said to a clerk, "What this country needs is a good five-cent cigar." The aside was heard by reporters, who published it. The remark was Marshall's only memorable contribution to U.S. history. Despite the possible pitfalls of getting a wisecrack in response, politicians have persisted in saying "what this country needs."

Franklin Roosevelt did so on May 23, 1932. In the commencement address at Oglethorpe University in Atlanta, Georgia, he gave a "what this country needs" preview of what he would do if elected president. Saying that the country needed and demanded bold and persistent experimentation, he warned, "The millions who are in want will not stand by silently forever while the things to satisfy their needs are within easy reach."

A Contest Between Two Philosophies

Declaring that the presidential election was "a contest between two philosophies of government," Hoover warned that Roosevelt's "so-called new deals" would "destroy the very foundations of the American way of life." Roosevelt said to newspaper reporter Anne O'Hare McCormick, "I have looked into the faces of thousands of Americans. They have the frightened look of lost children."

Hoover and the Republican leadership, he said at another time, were "the Four Horsemen of Destruction, Delay, Deceit, Despair." He said the Depression resulted because Hoover's administration had encouraged speculation and overproduction, had attempted to minimize the stock market crash, erroneously charged the cause of the collapse to other nations, and refused to recognize and to correct "the evils at home which it brought forth." It delayed relief and forgot reform.

A long line of jobless and homeless men wait outside to get a free dinner at New York's municipal lodging house in the winter of 1932–1933 during the Great Depression.

(AP Photo)

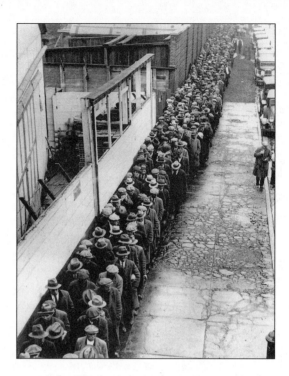

In a speech to the Commonwealth Club of San Francisco, Roosevelt presented quite a different view from Hoover's of the role of the federal government. Because every American has a right to life and a right to make a living, Roosevelt declared, the duty of government was "the maintenance of a balance, within which every individual may find safety if he wishes it; in which every individual may attain such power as his ability permits."

Hoover asserted that the changes proposed by Roosevelt were of the most "profound and penetrating character." If brought about, he warned, "this will not be the America which we have known in the past." The result would be enormous expansion of the federal government and the growth of bureaucracy such as never seen in history. He predicted, "The grass will grow in the streets of a hundred cities, a thousand towns; the weeds will overrun the fields of a million farms."

A Long Wait for Change

The only question was how big Roosevelt's win would be. It was huge: 28,800,000 votes to Hoover's 15,750,000. In the Electoral College it was 472 to 50. Hoover carried six states, all but two in New England. The Roosevelt landslide gave Democrats control of Congress.

But under the Constitution, there was nothing Roosevelt could do to start delivering on his New Deal until March 4, 1933. At the time the Constitution was written and adopted, the period between election and inauguration days, known as "the interregnum," made sense in a country that was primarily agricultural and travel was on foot or horseback. But in the era of the train, airplane, and automobile, and in a nation deep in an economic Depression, those four months saw economic conditions worsen. There was a "lame duck Congress" in which many of its Republican members had been defeated, but still held power, and a president whose policies, and he personally, had been overwhelmingly repudiated.

Catching Up with the Times

To eliminate the long period between the election and the inauguration in future elections, the Constitution was amended in 1933. It moved the Inauguration Day to January 20. It also shifted the date for the convening of the new Congress to January 3. But because of the time needed by states to ratify the 20th Amendment, its purpose in closing the gap in time between a presidential election and taking office would not be realized until the election of 1936.

John Barleycorn Becomes Legal Again

A second constitutional amendment in 1933 (December 21) would become the law of the land much sooner. It repealed the 18th Amendment, which had introduced Prohibition. Proposed on February 20, it was declared ratified 11 months later (December 21, 1933).

While repeal legalized liquor, it did not bring an end to the gangsters who had thrived in the business of bootlegging. The "mob" just went into other, and even more profitable, illicit enterprises (see Part 4, "Crackpots and Monsters").

A Scary Moment in Miami

During the interregnum while Hoover, the lame duck Congress, and an impatient and an increasingly desperate Depression-wracked country marked time in anticipation of the New Deal that had been promised, President-Elect Roosevelt took a break in the work of putting together an administration. In February 1933 he went cruising on millionaire Vincent Astor's yacht. When it docked at Miami, Florida, the tanned and happy-looking soon-to-be president told reporters he hadn't opened his briefcase in 12 days. He then got into a car to go to Bay Front Park for a speech.

He told a huge crowd that the "only fly in the ointment on my trip has been that I put on twelve pounds." As he headed toward a railroad car that was to take him back to New

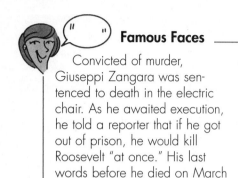

Famous Faces

Convicted of murder, Giuseppi Zangara was sentenced to death in the electric chair. As he awaited execution, he told a reporter that if he got out of prison, he would kill Roosevelt "at once." His last words before he died on March 21, 1933, were, "Adios to the world."

York, he paused to chat with another Miami visitor, the Mayor of Chicago, Frank Cermack. At that moment, shots rang out.

Fired by an unemployed bricklayer named Giuseppi Zangara, the bullets missed Roosevelt. Cermack was hit and died a short time later. Wrestled to the ground, Zangara explained to police, "I want to make it clear I do not hate Mr. Roosevelt personally. I hate all presidents, no matter from what country they come, and I hate all officials and everybody who is rich."

Shocked Americans realized that had a woman spectator not grabbed Zangara's arm as he fired his gun, their next president might have been Cactus Jack Garner.

An Exchange of Notes

Exactly two weeks before Roosevelt was to take the oath of office as president, he was at New York's Hotel Astor in Times Square for an annual satirical show put on by the reporters who covered politics and called themselves "The Inner Circle." While many of the jokes were at the expense of President Hoover, the country's next president also found himself the butt of their humor. Then, just before midnight, a Secret Service agent handed Roosevelt a message from Hoover. Handwritten, the note began, "A most critical situation has arisen in the country of which I feel it is my duty to advise you confidentially."

The "critical situation" was a worsening crisis in which banks were failing at such a rate across the country that frightened depositors were demanding their money. Worried that these "runs" on the banks would become a full-fledged panic, Hoover asked the president-elect's help. He wrote, "The major difficulty is the state of the public mind, for there is a steadily degenerating confidence in the future which has reached the height of general alarm. I am convinced that a very early statement by you upon two or three policies of your Administration would serve greatly to restore confidence and cause a resumption of the march of recovery."

Roosevelt considered the appeal "cheeky." He viewed it as a call from Hoover for Roosevelt to abandon polices he'd advocated in the campaign. He replied to Hoover's note, but not until ten days later. Expressing equal concern about "the gravity of the banking situation," he rejected Hoover's appeal for a statement. The loss of confidence was so "very deep-seated," he said, "that the fire is bound to spread in spite of anything that is done by way of mere statements."

With banks tumbling like dominoes, Roosevelt was not in a mood to do what Hoover had asked and, thereby, put himself in a position of sharing the blame. On March 3, 1933, rebuffed by Roosevelt, with banks shuttered or "on holiday" in a score of states, U.S. gold reserves below the level required by law, and the government of the United States unable to meet its payroll, Herbert Hoover spent his last full day in office. Late that night, he said to an aide in a grim tone, "We are at the end of our rope. There is nothing more we can do."

High Noon at the Capitol

Saturday, March 4, 1933, in Washington, D.C., was cold and gray with a hard northwest wind. In the automobile carrying the day's central figures along Pennsylvania Avenue toward the Capitol, the climate was even chillier. Washington correspondent Arthur Krock would describe the mood as the government changed hands "comparable to that which might be found in a beleaguered capital in wartime." People who looked up at rooftops saw soldiers with machine guns.

Yet the exchange went as planned, and when Franklin D. Roosevelt stood to speak, with his large frame supported by heavy iron leg braces and hands gripping the podium, the shivering crowd before him and a scared nation listening on radios waited anxiously.

> **Timeline**
> The Empire State Building opened on May 1, 1931, with less than a third of its offices rented.

The Gift

Not since Abraham Lincoln's second inaugural—and not again until John F. Kennedy spoke on January 20, 1961—was the spirit of a nation so uplifted. "This is preeminently the time to speak the truth," said the thirty-second president of the United States, "the whole truth, frankly and boldly."

Then: "First of all, let me assert my firm belief that the only thing we have to fear is fear itself—nameless, unreasoning, unjustified terror which paralyzes needed efforts to convert retreat into advance."

And near the end of the speech: "We do not distrust the future of essential democracy. The people of the United States have not failed. In their need they have registered a mandate that they want direct, vigorous action. They have asked for discipline and direction under leadership. They have made me the present instrument of their wishes. In the spirit of that gift I take it."

He'd promised a New Deal. Now he had to deliver it. *Fast.*

The West Wing

When FDR moved into the president's house on March 4, 1933, he found that a ramp to accommodate his wheelchair had been built in a colonnaded, covered walkway between the White House proper and an extension containing offices. Including an oval-shaped one for the president, the addition had been rebuilt after the space (the Executive Office Building) caught fire on Christmas Eve 1929. Seeing opportunity to gain more office facilities in the burned-out structure, Hoover had it rebuilt, but with a redesigned interior to provide better use of space.

The term "west wing" at that time, and for many years after, was no more than a geographical reference. It would become *The West Wing*, and the president's elliptically shaped workplace would be called "The Oval Office," in the era of network TV's evening news programs.

Although Hoover's rebuilding had greatly improved efficiency in the executive wing, when FDR and his New Dealers took over four years later, they found it to be too small and almost obsolete. By the close of FDR's first year, his staff was almost double that of Hoover's. Determined to do something about the space problem, Roosevelt pushed through plans for a major renovation.

Working Space with View

The American people learned of the plans from FDR over the radio in June 1933. Telling them why the work needed to be done, he demonstrated that he had great respect for the White House as a national symbol. He gave his assurance that the old and beloved lines of the White House wouldn't be altered, but added that the necessities of modern government business required "constant reorganization and rebuilding."

The reconstruction began in the third week of August 1934 and took 100 days. When it was done, FDR turned his attention to remodeling the White House grounds. The lawns, driveways, guard posts, the fencing, and gardens that visitors to Washington see today are largely the result of FDR's renovations.

A Place Called Shangri-La

In December 1928 when Calvin Coolidge was looking ahead to leaving the White House and returning to Vermont, the *St. Louis Post-Dispatch* ran an article that he'd written on the subject of being president. Among his observations was a suggestion that there be available to the nation's chief executive "a modest house in the hills somewhere near Washington, to which the Chief Executive might go to rest and escape the summer heat of the capital."

As you no doubt know, just such a retreat exists in the Catoctin Mountains of Maryland, about 75 miles from the White House. Known as Camp David, it was named by President Eisenhower in honor of his grandson, and the name has stuck. But when the rustic collection of cabins and woodsy walkways was created by the U.S. Navy in the early 1930s, Roosevelt called it "Shangri-La." He took the name from a mysterious paradise where no one grew old in James Hilton's best-selling 1932 novel *Lost Horizon*.

As recalled by one of FDR's sons (Elliott), FDR went there almost every weekend. But in the 12 years of the his presidency, his wife Eleanor never set foot on the property. In 1942 when a fleet of B-25 bombers led by Colonel James "Jimmy" Doolittle flew from aircraft carriers to attack the Japanese capital of Tokyo, FDR was asked by White House news reporters where the planes had originated the raid. He replied with a smile and tilt of his head, "They came from Shangri-La."

The Least You Need to Know

♦ Blamed by voters for the Depression, Herbert Hoover lost his bid for re-election in 1932 in a landslide to Governor Franklin D. Roosevelt of New York.

♦ Roosevelt's closest advisors had been his aides as governor.

♦ FDR's program for economic recovery got the name "the New Deal."

♦ With ratification of the 21st Amendment in 1933, the era of "the great experiment" known as Prohibition ended.

Chapter 6

Have These Guys Got Brains!

In This Chapter

- ◆ FDR's "Brain Trust"
- ◆ Banks take a holiday
- ◆ The first 100 days
- ◆ Problems on the farms
- ◆ A fireside chat

As Franklin Roosevelt took the oath of office on March 4, 1933, between 12 and 15 million Americans were out of work, bread lines and soup kitchens were common sights in cities, and farms were going under. But the most pressing problem was that people were rushing to withdraw their money from banks. To stop the panic, the banks are ordered to close for "a holiday."

With a "Brain Trust" assembled to advise him, Roosevelt called the Congress into special session. He demanded passage within 100 days of laws creating federal relief agencies to get people back to work. Action was also needed to keep rebellious farmers from resorting to violence to hold on to their land.

A White House Visitor

Three days before Roosevelt became president, movie theaters all over the country started showing a film about a president. It was made by newspaper magnate William Randolph Hearst's Cosmopolitan Studios. Released by Metro-Goldwyn-Mayer, it starred one of the country's most popular actors, Walter Huston, as President Judson Hammond. He seemed to be Hollywood's version of Herbert Hoover. With the country deep in an economic depression, he did nothing.

Famous Faces

A stage star of the 1920s, Huston had introduced the now-classic "September Song" in the Broadway hit *Knickerbocker Holiday*. He later starred as the grizzled old gold miner with Humphrey Bogart in *The Treasure of Sierra Madre*, directed by his son John. Walter later played the murdered captain of the ship *La Paloma* in John Huston's *The Maltese Falcon*. He is Anjelica Huston's grandfather. If *Gabriel over the White House* shows up on your TV, it may seem dated and far-fetched, but for a means of understanding how much the country wanted a miracle in 1933, don't miss it.

But after he was nearly killed in a car crash, Hammond was visited by the Angel Gabriel. Suddenly, he took a series of steps to help the people, steps that were a remarkable preview of the programs of the New Deal. This was remarkable because the movie had been made before Roosevelt's election. In April 1933 it was one of the top six box-office hits.

Famous Faces

The most powerful newspaper owner in America in the 1930s, William Randolph Hearst was the man on whom Orson Welles patterned the title character in *Citizen Kane*.

While no one claimed that Franklin Delano Roosevelt's program for pulling the nation out of the Depression had come from a Heavenly visitor, neither were the vast majority of Americans prepared to object to whatever action their new president proposed. Nor did they care—or know very much—about the men he'd brought into the government with him.

A Trusty Trio

During the interregnum, Roosevelt's mother had posed the question that was on everyone's mind. "I wonder," Sara Delano Roosevelt had said, "who you will take to Washington."

At that time Roosevelt already had a small group of trusted men who'd advised him as governor of New York. Known as the "Brain Trust," they were drawn from colleges and universities. They were liberals (some said they were "radicals"). Their existence was a secret until a newspaperman revealed it.

Roosevelt had used the informal group as a sounding board for his ideas, but he was open to theirs. In these give-and-takes, said Brain Trust member Raymond Moley, Roosevelt "would listen with rapt attention" as "a student, a cross examiner, and a judge." As FDR prepared to become president, the Brain Trust played a key role in shaping goals of the new administration. But once FDR was in office, the men no longer met as a group.

The three members of the Brain Trust were:

- **Adolph Berle.** Youngest man to receive a Harvard law degree (age 21). Law professor, Columbia University.
- **Raymond Moley.** Ph.D., Columbia, in political science. Expert on criminal justice. Considered himself an enemy of "Wall Street." Collaborated with FDR on the "Forgotten Man" speech.
- **Rexford Guy Tugwell.** Economist. Ph.D., University of Pennsylvania. Economics professor, Columbia.

Facts and Figures

One of FDR's long-time aides, Samuel Rosenman used the term in a derisive way. Then *New York Times* reporter James Kieran picked it up. Both men used the plural "Brains Trust." Over the years it became the singular "Brain Trust."

Roosevelt's "old hands" who were not part of the Brain Trust included the political strategists Louis Howe, James Farley (he would be FDR's postmaster general), Edward House (an advisor to President Wilson who was addressed as Colonel, his military rank in the first World War), and Samuel I. Rosenman. But the closest advisor to the new president was his wife, Eleanor.

Sorry, the Bank Is Closed

Remember the note that President Hoover sent to Roosevelt during a show at the Hotel Astor that asked Roosevelt to say something to help stop the nationwide runs on banks? And you will recall that Roosevelt took his time in answering it, then did nothing? Well, by the time the two grim-faced presidents were riding up Pennsylvania Avenue for FDR's inauguration, some governors had taken the matter into their own hands. They'd ordered the temporary closing of banks in their states.

The closings were called "holidays" and varied from a day in Louisiana and two in New York to eight days in Michigan. As of March 2, 1933, 21 other states had suspended or had drastically reduced banking operations. This was pretty extreme, but since 1930 more than 5,000 banks had been temporarily forced to shut down in the face of panicky depositors who demanded their money.

Facts and Figures

Banks could not just hand over the money. With $3.4 billion on deposit, withdrawals in that amount (which the banks didn't have on hand anyway) would have meant a collapse of the entire economy.

With so many states declaring bank holidays of different lengths, and with the fear of further runs, Roosevelt used the emergency powers of a law that was meant for wartime (the Trading with the Enemy Act of 1917) to issue a proclamation (effective on March 6) that ordered *all* banks to take a "holiday" of four days. The action also suspended transactions by the Federal Reserve, trust companies, credit unions, and building and loans. And it clamped a three-day embargo on exports of gold, silver, and paper money, unless a Treasury Department license was obtained. (Good luck in getting one!)

Did the bank holiday do the trick? Yes. During the first three days after the holiday ended, 4,507 national banks opened their doors and found nobody rushing to take money out. Instead, cash that had been hoarded out was back in. Gold and gold certificates also flowed back into the Treasury and Reserve banks. No longer worried about a banking system collapse, the stock market saw a two-week rise in value of 15 percent.

Would this have happened if FDR had done what Hoover's note had asked? Perhaps. If so, would President Hoover have gotten the credit? Maybe. Did FDR play politics with the banks? You decide.

Streak of Lightning

Excuse the political incorrectness, and the bad taste, but after Roosevelt took the oath of office on Saturday, March 4, 1933, he hit the ground running. Rather than attend an inaugural party for family and friends, he had Eleanor represent him while he worked out the bank holiday proclamation with Treasury Secretary William Woodin, Attorney General Homer Cummings, and Brain Truster Ray Moley. That done, FDR went to bed.

On Sunday, he called for a special session of Congress to begin the following Thursday, March 9. White House correspondent Ernest Lindley said of the outburst of activity in the White House, "It was like a streak of lightning out of a black sky."

Will Rogers came through with, "We have no jobs, no money, we have no banks; and if Roosevelt had burned down the Capitol, we would have said, 'Thank God, he started a fire under something.'"

Putting Out the Fire

The problems facing Roosevelt were stopping the devaluation of the dollar that had occurred since the start of the Depression, getting help to hungry and homeless millions, putting people back to work, reducing mortgage debt, devising reforms of the national financial system, and aiding farmers by controlling surplus crops which drove down prices. When Congress met, it first took up the measure that Roosevelt wanted in order to quell the banking crisis. Representative Bertrand H. Snell told the members, "The house is burning down and the President of the United States says this is the way to put out the fire."

The House vote was unanimous. The U.S. Senate okayed it 73 to 7. At eight o'clock that night, the president signed the New Deal's first law. The Emergency Banking Relief Act would be followed by a period of frantic legislating that would go into the history books as "the first 100 days." Between March 9 and mid-June, Congress also passed and Roosevelt signed the following:

- **Economy Act (March 20).** Designed to balance the federal budget by reducing government salaries, it also reorganized agencies.

- **Beer-Wine Revenue Act (March 22).** Legalized sales of wine, beer, lager beer, ale, and porter of 3.2 percent maximum alcoholic content by weight, or four percent by volume. (This was a prelude to full repeal of Prohibition, discussed later.)

- **Civilian Conservation Corps Reforestation Relief Act (May 31).** Authorized 250,000 jobs for men 18 to 25 in reforestation, road construction, prevention of soil erosion, and national park and flood-control projects under Army supervision.

- **Gold Standard Abandoned.** Aimed at devaluation of the dollar abroad, along with increasing the prices of commodities, silver, and stocks on American exchanges.

- **Federal Emergency Relief Act (May 12).** Created the Federal Emergency Relief Administration (FERA), and it authorized $500 million in grants and a system of matching funds to assist the states in providing relief (food, clothing, and so on).

- **Agricultural Adjustment Act (May 12).** Designed to restore the purchasing power of farmers by eliminating surpluses. (More on the farm situation in the following section.)

- **Tennessee Valley Authority (May 18).** Intended to develop the economic and social well-being of the Tennessee River Valley regions in Tennessee, North Carolina, Kentucky, Virginia, Mississippi, Georgia, and Alabama. Between 1933 and 1944, the TVA would build nine main-river dams and many subsidiary ones, helping to provide electricity to millions of people.

- **Federal Securities Act (May 27).** Compelled full disclosure to investors of information related to new security issues and the registration of offerings with the Federal Trade Commission.

- **National Employment System Act (June 6).** Established the U.S. Employment Service.

- **Home Owners Refinancing Act (June 13).** Set up the Home Owners Loan Corporation to refinance home mortgage debts for nonfarm owners.

- **Banking Act of 1933 (June 16).** Created the FDIC (Federal Deposit Insurance Corporation) to guarantee bank deposits under $5,000.

- **Farm Credit Act (June 16).** Provided for short- and long-term credits for agricultural production and marketing.
- **Emergency Railroad Transportation Act (June 16).** Designed to promote reorganization of carriers and elimination of duplicate services.
- **National Industrial Recovery Act (June 16).** Intended to revive industrial and business activity through the National Recovery Administration (NRA). The president was empowered to set up codes for industries that would exempt them from antitrust laws. Of all the New Deal programs, this one would prove to be the most controversial, ultimately producing a crisis between the White House and the U.S. Supreme Court (discussed later).

President Franklin D. Roosevelt is shown signing a law creating the Tennessee Valley Authority in this May 18, 1933, photo. Roosevelt envisioned "a corporation clothed with the power of the government but possessed of the flexibility and initiative of private enterprise." Others are unidentified.

(AP Photo/TVA)

Famous Faces

A trained social worker, Frances Perkins became a reformer of conditions in "sweatshop" factories in New York. She'd been a protégée of Al Smith and Governor Roosevelt's state industrial commissioner.

Handful of Marauders

Looking back to a time when an astonished nation observed all that was going on in their capital city and Washington's old hands watched with alarm, Raymond Moley recalled that he and the others who'd come into government with FDR felt as if they were "a handful of marauders in hostile territory." They were, indeed, an unusual group. Some were old friends of the president from New York.

The newcomer who attracted most of the attention was Frances Perkins. She made history as the first woman to serve on the Cabinet. Named the first Secretary of Labor when the former Department of Commerce and Labor were split into two departments in 1933, she also made an impression because of her seemingly endless supply of stylish hats.

The Rest of the Roosevelt Cabinet

A mixture of old friends, allies, new faces in FDR's political life, and three Republicans, the other Cabinet members were:

Secretary of State: Cordell Hull

Secretary of the Treasury: William Woodin (Republican)

Attorney General: Homer Cummings

Secretary of Interior: Harold L. Ickes (Republican)

Secretary of War: George H. Dern

Secretary of the Navy: Claude A. Swanson (former senator)

Postmaster General: James Farley

Secretary of Commerce: Daniel C. Roper

Secretary of Agriculture: Henry A. Wallace (Republican)

Roosevelt's Staff

As followers of the news and viewers of the TV show *The West Wing* know, the senior staff of today's president is huge, numbering in the hundreds. But in 1933, they could be counted on one hand. FDR's long-time political strategist, Louis Howe, was his chief secretary. (There was no Chief of Staff, as there is today.) His personal secretary was Marguerite (Missy) Le Hand. Steven Early was press secretary. The secretary in charge of who got in to see the president (appointments) was Marvin McIntyre. Two Brain Trusters were assistant secretaries in departments. Ray Moley went to the State Department, and Rexford Tugwell became an assistant to Agriculture Secretary Wallace.

Keeping the Necessary Balance

When Henry A. Wallace became Secretary of Agriculture, he already knew a great deal about the job. His father had held the post in the Harding and Coolidge administrations. A graduate of Iowa State College, Henry had been editor of a family newspaper, *Wallace's Farmer*. Among his other accomplishments was the development of a high-yield hybrid strain of corn that resulted in major advances in plant genetics.

"When former civilizations have fallen," he said when he took office in March 1933, "there is strong reason for believing that they fell because they could not achieve the necessary balance between city and country."

Uproar on the Fruited Plains

Out in the vast country that "America the Beautiful" called "the fruited plains," farmers were in very serious trouble. In three years, net farm income had sunk by more than a third. Income of the average farmer had fallen nearly by half. Farms were foreclosed because of delinquent mortgages. The situation was so dire that on March 14, 10 days after Roosevelt's inauguration, 200 farmers had stormed the Saline County Courthouse in Wilbur, Nebraska, and held the sheriff hostage to try to keep him from selling a farm.

At the End of Their Rope

On March 24, when a county attorney in Iowa tried to serve an eviction notice, he was also grabbed and held until he agreed to work out a rental agreement with the farmer. Other irate Iowa farmers went so far as attempting to lynch a judge, but thought better of it. They left him without his pants. This attack on a judge prompted the governor to declare martial law and send out the National Guard.

All of this tumult increased pressure for federal action in the form of the farm relief legislation pushed through Congress in the first 100 days. But farmers were not happy about being required to take land out of production and to slaughter livestock on the promise that in doing so they would get better prices. To most of these farmers, such policies made no sense in a country in which people in cities were going hungry.

"Ladies and Gentlemen, the President of the United States"

The first president of the United States to be heard on the radio was Calvin Coolidge. During the election of 1924 as he sought the presidency in his own right, a 26-station coast-to-coast network broadcast one of his campaign speeches. His inaugural address had also been carried by a continental hookup, as were the speeches by his successors, Hoover and Roosevelt.

Because Roosevelt had used radio successfully as governor of New York to explain his policies and solicit public support, he saw its potential after the first days of his administration as both a means of introducing himself as the new president and putting minds at ease about what was happening in Washington, especially regarding the bank holiday.

The way he chose to address the country on radio as president was an innovation. Instead of making a formal speech, he spoke in a folksy manner that left each listener feeling as if the president had been talking to him only, right there in the parlor, or over the backyard fence. Those who tuned in for the March 13, 1933, broadcast had no idea, nor did Roosevelt, that they were hearing the first of 30 such radio addresses over a period of 12 years that would be known as "fireside chats."

Famous Faces

Harry Butcher, a CBS vice president in charge of the network's Washington office, named FDR's radio talks "fireside chats." Butcher later served in World War II as chief press aide to General Dwight D. Eisenhower.

An innovation in the procedure of methods adopted by the American Administration was started by President Franklin D. Roosevelt when he made a 15-minute radio address, on March 13, 1933, explaining to the people of the nation just what he had done in the banking situation. The President gave the cause and effect of the recent banking holiday and told of his plans for bringing conditions back to normal in the immediate future.

(AP Photo)

The place chosen in the White House for the fireside chats was not the president's office, as is the custom for TV addresses today. FDR spoke from the Diplomatic Reception Room. With his script in a black loose-leaf binder, he entered 15 minutes before going on the air. Waiting in the room were presidential aides, radio technicians, newspaper reporters, movie newsreel cameramen with equipment and lights, and the special "White House announcer."

Employed by NBC, he was Carleton E. Smith. He established the tradition of the chief executive not being introduced by name, but with the words, "Ladies and gentlemen, the president of the United States."

After All This, What Changed?

You may think that with all the confident talking and passing of laws that the economic ball which had been going down for so long would be bouncing back up. But FDR biographer and historian of the New Deal, Arthur Schlesinger Jr., found that the program of recovery that was enacted in 1933 "made no basic changes in the American economy." Some improvement was detected, but not much.

Industrial production was up dramatically, but it had fallen so low that any upturn would have seemed impressive. The measure of economic recovery is the unemployment rate, and in that category the figures remained dismal. Bread lines were just as long, soup kitchens as busy, apple-sellers as numerous, the rebellious mood on farms hadn't cooled, prices weren't rising, aimless men were as prevalent as before the 100 days, and winter was coming.

Juggling Money

The agency created to handle the dispensing of federal funds for emergency relief (FERA) was headed by Harry Hopkins. Worrying about the fate of the unemployed and homeless in the cold months, he recognized that there was no way that programs of the first 100 days could be functioning in time to help. What was needed, he advised Roosevelt, was an immediate program that would give jobs to four million people.

With Congress adjourned for the year, there was no way to obtain the estimated $400 million cost and no guarantee that Congress would approve it anyway. Consequently, Roosevelt decided to get the money Hopkins needed by switching funds from the Public Works Administration to a new agency to be called the Civilian Works Administration. This juggling act was accomplished by executive order on November 8.

A week later, Hopkins promised to have four million people in government-created work by Christmas. He missed the date, but by January 8, 1934, more than that number were in the program (4.3 million). As the year progressed, the total would be nearly 20 million. As you will read in the next chapter, not all these jobs were the kind that a person could make a career of in the long run—or probably want to. But as Hopkins once said to an aide, "People don't eat in the long run. They eat every day."

The Sound of Popping Corks

As of seven o'clock in the evening (Washington, D.C., time) on December 5, 1933, FDR signed a proclamation by which any American old enough to have a drink with full-strength alcohol in it, and who could afford to buy one, was able to do so legally. This was made a reality because an hour and a half earlier, Utah became the last state (36 of 48) needed to ratify the 21st Amendment and repeal the 18th.

Perhaps some of the people who offered a toast to the freedom to have a drink thought back over the 13 years, 10 months, and 18 days since Prohibition had shut off the taps to remember that in 1919 they and their countrymen had been at the top of the world. They lived in the richest nation in the world. America had been so rich then, in fact, no one ever dreamed that one day it would go bust, that one out of every four Americans would be looking to the government for their next meal, and that at the end of 1933 there would be 30 million Americans whose families had no regular source of income.

"My Gosh, It's Mrs. Roosevelt"

While Franklin D. Roosevelt worked long and hard to be elected president, then plunged into the job with unbounded energy, his wife was a reluctant First Lady. Eleanor Roosevelt confessed to her very close friend Lorena Hickock, "I have never wanted to be a President's wife."

A niece of President Theodore Roosevelt, she'd been painfully shy as a girl and acutely aware of her prominent teeth, awkwardness in movement, and squeaky and sing-song speech. But when Franklin was stricken with polio, she had been forced to emerge from her cocoon to campaign for Democrats when her husband couldn't. When she became First Lady, she continued to be outspoken by holding regular press conferences in the White House. Indeed, her first one took place before FDR's initial meeting with newsmen in the Oval Office.

Open only to women, Mrs. Roosevelt's press conferences had one rule. There must be no questions about politics or policy. Often knitting as the women reporters posed questions, she spoke in a voice described as "gentle, soft, cultured." In addition to these question-and-answer sessions, she began her own radio show, for which she got the standard pay of radio stars ($500 a minute), wrote for magazines, lectured twice a year for a fee of $1,000 per talk, and wrote a syndicated newspaper column, "My Day." In 1937 she published an autobiography titled *This Is My Story*.

Regarded politically as even more liberal than FDR, she cast aside the First Lady's traditional role as the White House's hostess and traveled all over the country to observe the effects of the New Deal, then report back to FDR. In the first year of the administration, she traveled so much (an estimated 40,000 miles) and appeared in so many places that *The New Yorker* magazine published a cartoon of her exploring a mine shaft as a miner blurted, "Good gosh, here comes Mrs. Roosevelt."

Although she hadn't at that point visited workers in a coal mine, she soon did. Early one morning when FDR hadn't seen Eleanor, he inquired of her secretary if she knew where his wife was. Knowing that she'd left the White House before sunrise for another inspection tour, Malvina Thompson replied, "She's in prison, Mr. President."

FDR replied, "I'm not surprised, but what's she in for?"

The president often referred to Eleanor as his "will of the wisp wife." In a note to him during one of her sojourns, she wrote, "We really are dependent on each other though we do see little of each other."

It would be decades before the public learned that years before FDR became president Eleanor had discovered that her husband had been romantically involved with another woman, Lucy Mercer. In the belief that he would keep a promise not to see Mercer again, Eleanor chose to remain his wife, only to learn that on the day he died at his retreat in Warm Spring, Georgia (April 14, 1945), Lucy Mercer had been with him.

The only woman in FDR's Cabinet, Labor Secretary Frances Perkins, recalled that he was "enormously proud" of Eleanor. Confident in her reports and highly amused by the criticism aimed at her by political enemies, he joked, "You know my Missus gets around a lot." Noting that Eleanor was often "considerably ahead" of him on issues, such as civil rights and equality for women, Roosevelt biographer Nathan Miller rightly observed, "No First Lady had a greater effect on policy and public opinion. But it was not a one-way relationship. She learned from him, and under his tutelage became one of the nation's ablest politicians."

The Least You Need to Know

- President Roosevelt prevented a collapse of the monetary system by ordering all banks to close for a four-day "holiday."
- Congress passed a flurry of New Deal legislation during an intense period of activity known as "the first 100 days."
- The first woman ever appointed to a president's Cabinet was a social and labor-rights reformer, Frances Perkins.
- Roosevelt began a series of informal reports to the people over the radio that became known as "fireside chats."

Chapter 7

Alphabet Soup

In This Chapter

- ◆ Protecting the gold supply
- ◆ The second New Deal
- ◆ Government work projects
- ◆ Aid to agriculture
- ◆ Inventing the Social Security system

With the foundations of the restructuring of the economy laid by the legislation of the first 100 days, the problem became how to put the new programs into effect. In what became known as the Second New Deal, the Works Progress Administration (WPA) and Civilian Conservation Corps (CCC) gave hundreds of thousands of government jobs to the unemployed. Struggling farmers also received federal assistance. But the innovation that had the most significant and long-lasting impact on American lives was an "old age" insurance program known as Social Security.

As Good as Gold

In the previous chapter you read that one of the actions taken by the government in the first 100 days was abandonment by the United States of "the gold standard." Until then, every dollar issued by the U.S. Treasury was backed by gold. At the time, the value of an ounce of gold was $20. (Twenty-dollar gold coins, known as "gold pieces," are now collectibles, but they'll cost you a lot more than $20.) After the stock market crashed and the Great Depression began, there'd been a rush by people to insure "*liquidity*" by dumping their stocks for cash and turning in the greenbacks for gold.

The rush to liquidity caused a drain on the U.S. government's gold reserves. By going off the gold standard, that problem was alleviated. But in 1934 there was still a lot of gold in the hands of individuals, banks, and other financial institutions. Consequently, on January 30, 1934, Congress passed the Gold Reserve Act. It allowed the government to seize all the gold held by Federal Reserve banks. Eventually, all U.S. gold was stored at Fort Knox, Kentucky (as anyone who's seen the James Bond movie *Goldfinger* knows).

The day after passage of the Gold Reserve Act, Roosevelt issued an executive order raising the value of an ounce of gold to $35, where it stayed for the next four decades, when the price was allowed to fluctuate in the free market. Later in the year, Congress gave the president power through the Treasury to increase the government's silver holdings to a value equal to a third of its gold stores. In effect, the law made the dollar in your wallet (a "silver certificate") as good as gold.

The Second New Deal

The intent of much of the legislation of "the first 100 days" was to restructure the nation's economy and to help people get back on their feet through state and local relief programs. The agency set up to do that was the Federal Emergency Relief Administration (FERA), headed by Harry Hopkins. The vehicle for accomplishing this goal was called the Civilian Works Administration (CWA).

When it became clear that recovery was not happening fast enough, Roosevelt decided to provide direct federal government help. In what became known as "the second New Deal," he asked Congress to endorse four goals: security of livelihood through better use of national resources; slum clearance and better housing; old age, illness, and dependency assistance from the federal government; and a national employment program.

Because the CWA wasn't getting the job done fast enough, it was replaced by the Works Progress Administration (WPA), authorized by the Emergency Relief Appropriation Act (April 8, 1935). Eventually "Progress" was replaced in the agency's name with a word that more exactly defined its goal. It became the Work Projects Administration. Harry Hopkins explained that the purpose of the WPA was to offer jobs that would serve the public good while conserving the skills, self-esteem, and pride of the needy people who took them.

You Say "Work," I Say "Boondoggle"

People who were opposed to the WPA saw it as a great leap into Socialism. They saw WPA men as "loafers" who did nothing but stand around and lean on shovels. Many of the WPA projects were called *boondoggles*.

A Lot of Lovely Things

One reply to the scoffers came from an unknown WPA worker who wrote this little poem:

Talk of the Time

In the old definition of the word, a **boondoggle** is an ornamental leather strap. In the modern meaning it's something that's usually done by a government that's pointless and wasteful of money.

> We've made a lot of lovely things.
> Just "leaning on a shovel";
> Parks with flowers and sparkling springs,
> Just "leaning on a shovel."
> The winding roads and the highways straight,
> The wonderful buildings that house the great,
> We built them all at our "lazy" gait,
> Just "leaning on a shovel."

Not All Pick and Shovel Work

When the WPA began, the goal was to provide 3.5 million jobs. The number of people who would depend directly and indirectly upon its federal, state, and local projects actually ranged between 20 and 25 million. They were not all handed picks, shovels, and other tools and sent out to build, improve, or fix.

If you want to see what the people who went to work for the WPA did in the late 1930s, look for the results in school buildings, highways, bridges, airports, post offices, and other kinds of public works. The WPA built or improved:

- 651,087 miles of highways, roads, and streets
- 124,031 bridges
- 125,100 public buildings
- 8,192 parks
- 853 airports or landing fields

You can also find their accomplishments in murals, sculptures, and other works of art in U.S. government and state and local buildings, public libraries, and parks.

Federal Arts Project (FAP)

Chances are excellent that if you go into a courthouse or post office that was built in the 1930s, you'll find it decorated with paintings and sculptures that were created by WPA artists. At its peak of activity in 1936, the FAP employed 5,300 visual artists and related professionals. They produced more than 2,500 murals. Other painters turned out 108,000 works. Its sculptors made more than 18,000 pieces. A photographic division took many thousands of pictures of contemporary life and of WPA people in action. It even had divisions for making posters, architectural models, and articles of stained glass. Hundreds of artists joined the Art Teaching Division to conduct classes in schools, settlement houses, and community centers for an estimated 8 million children and adults in 22 states.

Famous Faces

WPA artists included Jackson Pollock, Mark Rothko, Jacob Laurence, and Philip Guston.

Federal Music Project (FMP)

Directed by a former conductor of the Cleveland Symphony, the FMP gave work to about 16,000 musicians. Its orchestras, chamber groups, choral and opera units, military bands, and dance bands gave some 5,000 performances for more than three million people a week. They also taught music to an estimated 132,000 school kids in 27 states. Others compiled an index of 1,500 composers that listed 5,500 works. FMP people also went into rural areas, many in the South and the mountains of West Virginia, to record and preserve folk music.

Famous Faces

Many talented people who worked for the FTP went on to become famous. They included actors Burt Lancaster, Orson Welles, Joseph Cotten, Will Geer (Grandpa on *The Waltons*), John Houseman, and E. G. Marshall, as well as directors Sidney Lumet and Nicholas Ray.

Federal Theater Project (FTP)

Headed by Hannie Flanagan, an old Iowa friend of Harry Hopkins, the FTP employed 12,700 theater workers in 31 states and New York City. In its four-year history, it produced more than 1,200 plays, and put on more than 1,000 performances a week for an estimated total audience of nearly a million. The FTP also reached about 10 million radio listeners through its coast-to-coast broadcasts of *Federal Theater of the Air.*

An FTP service bureau provided research, consultation, and play-reading services. And the *Federal Theater Magazine* kept everyone in the FTP informed about its activities. You will read in Part 4, "Crackpots and Monsters," that the FTP drew a lot of criticism for employing people whose true objective was alleged to be the use of the FTP to promote the cause of communism of the Soviet Union variety.

Federal Writers' Project (FWP)

Without the work of men and women who participated in the FWP, writing the book you have in your hand would have been a whole lot harder. The Federal Writers' Project produced the *WPA Guide* series of books on every state, plus Washington, D.C., and the territories of Alaska, Puerto Rico, and Guam. Many of the books have been recently reprinted in paperback. Going through these guidebooks to the 48 states and their towns and cities, you'll feel as if you have gotten into a time machine and been taken back to the 1930s. In addition to the guidebooks, FWP writers produced 800 titles in a broad variety of topics that amounted to 3.5 million copies.

It Helped You Grow Up

If you were 18 to 25 years old, unemployed, and broke, but you weren't an artist, a writer, sculptor, actor, or somebody with creative talent, you could enlist in the Civilian Conservation Corps (CCC). Authorized by Congress in the 1933 Civilian Conservation Corps Reforestation Relief Act, the CCC's objective was to put 250,000 young men to work in planting trees, preventing soil erosion, flood control, and other projects. Supervision of the work camps was given to the U.S. Army, along with the Interior, Agriculture, and Labor departments. Pay was $30 a month, part of which had to be sent home if you had dependents.

By the end of 1941 more than two million youths had worked on CCC projects. The CCC's many accomplishments included ...

Famous Faces

FWP writers who later achieved prominence included John Cheever, Saul Bellow, Richard Wright, Studs Terkel, Ralph Ellison, and Margaret Walker.

- More than three billion trees planted.
- 3,470 fire towers built.
- 97,000 miles of fire roads built.
- 84.4 million acres of farmland opened to irrigation.
- 20 million acres brought under erosion control.
- One million sheep rescued in a Utah blizzard.
- More than four million man-hours spent fighting forest fires.
- 1.24 million man-hours spent fighting floods.

Another aspect of federal assistance to youth was in education. Although not part of the CCC, the National Youth Administration was created by executive order in June 1935. Its purpose was to pay for the education and training of young people who otherwise would have gone without it.

Many of the young men who joined the CCC had never been away from their homes. Most hadn't been out of their state. An unintended and unexpected result of these young men uprooting themselves to join "Roosevelt's Tree Army" is that a lot of them didn't return to their homes. Many settled in communities where they'd worked in camps. Almost all came away from the experience more confident in themselves and feeling more optimistic about the country's future. Looking back on the experience, a CCC veteran who became a judge said, "It helped you grow up."

Facts and Figures

Between 1930 and 1936 production of cigarettes rose from 123 billion to 158 billion a year.

The establishment of CCC camps in every state brought with it the largest shift of young men from their homes to government camps since World War I. Only the drafting of men into the army at the start of World War II would surpass it.

Can a Blue Eagle Fly?

You'll recall that one of the actions taken by Congress that was listed in Chapter 6's discussion of the first 100 days of the New Deal was passage of the National Industrial Recovery Act. The idea behind it was that industries and labor should get together and work out "codes" in the areas of minimum wages and maximum work hours and rules of fair competition—all subject to approval by the federal government.

The agency set up to carry out these objectives was the National Recovery Administration (NRA). At its head was a former Army officer, General Hugh S. Johnson. The NRA emblem was a blue eagle. Firms that took part in NRA displayed it in plant and office windows, on flags, and on the labels on their products. With the Blue Eagle appeared the slogan "We do our part." (You can see the Blue Eagle symbol in the credits at the end of many movies of the mid-1930s.)

By midsummer 1933 more than 500 industries had signed codes that covered 22 million workers. Thousands of enthusiastic people had marched in NRA parades. Even New York City burlesque theaters and their strippers adopted a code. It limited the number of times a day the girls would undress.

But by 1935 the NRA had become such a bureaucratic mess that a lot of frustrated businessmen said that the initials NRA stood for "national run around." The main complaint of labor unions was that the NRA was under control of "big business," with the result that wages were set too low. On the other hand, the labor unions found that all this talk about wage fairness and shorter working hours had helped the union cause by increasing membership. (More on the labor movement in Part 4.)

Timeline

When FDR signed the NRA into law in June 1933, he said, "History probably will record the National Recovery Act as the most important and far-reaching legislation ever enacted by the American Congress."

Nine Old Men

As of May 27, 1935, what FDR, businessmen, and the leaders of labor unions thought about the NRA didn't matter. On that Monday, nine men known as the United States Supreme Court blew the NRA out of the water. The justices ruled that it was not in keeping with the separation of powers required by the U.S. Constitution. The Court found that the Congress had illegally delegated excessive power to the executive branch. It also said the federal government had no right to get involved in the affairs of businesses that did not cross state lines.

Facts and Figures

In *United States* v. *Schechter Poultry Corp.*, the chicken firm claimed the NRA had no authority to charge it with violating an NRA code by selling diseased poultry. The unofficial name given to the federal lawsuit was the "sick chicken case."

A furious FDR denounced the decision by "nine old men" and said that their ruling set the Constitution back to "horse-and-buggy days." He was so angry that in 1937 he tried to get the number of justices on the Court increased from 9 to 12. But the attempt to "pack the Court" failed in Congress.

Nothing to Do with Automobiles

In the list of agencies created by Congress in the New Deal's first hundred days was the AAA. It had nothing to do with the American Automobile Association. This Triple-A was the Agricultural Adjustment Administration headed by Henry Wallace (the man from Iowa who'd developed a hybrid corn). It had met a great deal of resistance in persuading farmers to take land out of production and in slaughtering livestock, so as to boost prices. But in many ways the policy had worked. For example, a wheat farmer in 1933 earned 33 cents a bushel. In 1935, he could sell a bushel for 69 cents.

Timeline

Some typical food prices from the mid-1930s:

- A dozen eggs: 29 cents
- A pound of coffee: 35 cents
- Box of Ritz crackers: 17 cents
- Bottle of tomato juice: 15 cents
- Two-pound can of corned beef hash: 23 cents
- Four packages of Jell-O: 15 cents

Talk of the Time

Under the **Townsend Plan,** every unemployed person over age 60 would get $200 a month from the government. The money would come from a 2 percent tax on business transactions.

The downside of the financial improvement for farmers was that a large number of them had gone so deeply into debt that they were defaulting on mortgages. To alleviate the problem, the president had asked for and gotten the Federal Farm Bankruptcy Act of 1934. Unfortunately, it also failed to pass constitutional muster in the eyes of the U.S. Supreme Court. FDR's response to this setback was the Farm Mortgage Moratorium Act (1935). It blocked all land seizures for three years and let farmers get permission from a court to keep their land by paying a fair and reasonable rent as determined by the court.

What the Doctor Saw

One morning in Long Beach, California, in 1933, as a physician by the name of Francis Edward Townsend was shaving, he looked out a window and saw three old women scrounging through garbage cans for scraps of food. Shocked, outraged, and feeling overwhelmed with compassion, the good doctor came up with an idea that he called the Old Age Revolving Pension. In the era of alphabet soup agencies, it became known as OARP. Sociologists and politics called it "the *Townsend Plan*." It soon had millions of Americans enthusiastically behind it.

No Good Deed Goes Unpunished

Dr. Townsend promoted his OARP by selling a booklet for 25 cents. Dubious observers saw it as a nefarious Townsend scheme to get rich. Congress investigated. Townsend refused to cooperate and was cited for contempt. He was convicted and sentenced to 30 days in jail, but President Roosevelt eventually pardoned him. Angrily blaming his troubles on a "Communist conspiracy," he faded into obscurity.

A Task for Frances Perkins

You've read that FDR's choice for the job of Secretary of Labor was Frances Perkins, the first woman ever appointed to the Cabinet. As the country was rallying behind the Townsend Plan, Roosevelt and some members of Congress were also thinking about a way to provide assistance to the elderly population. To keep Congress from taking action, FDR appointed Perkins to head a committee to come up with a federal old-age insurance plan that would include everyone. "From the cradle to the grave," he said, "they ought to be in a social insurance system."

The Social Security Act

During congressional hearings on the proposal that the Perkins committee came up with, the plan was attacked by opponents who saw it as a scheme to establish Socialism in the United States. Business interests saw it as the end of initiative, thrift, and the American way of life. But the idea that was the basis of the Townsend Plan was so popular that re-election-minded members of Congress brushed aside these objections.

Roosevelt signed the Social Security Act in August 1935. After it was challenged on grounds that it was unconstitutional, the U.S. Supreme Court ruled in 1937 that it wasn't.

Here's what the law did:

1. Established federal and state unemployment compensation systems.
2. Imposed a federal tax on payrolls of employers of 8 or more workers of 1 percent in 1936, 2 percent in 1937, and 3 percent thereafter.
3. Started a tax for "old-age and survivors' insurance" paid by all employers and employees that would rise from 1 percent to 3 percent by 1949. Out of the fund that it created, the federal government would pay retired people over the age of 65 a pension ranging from $10 a month to a maximum of $85, calculated on the number of years in which a worker contributed.
4. Gave grants to states to assist in relief payments to the blind, disabled, and homeless.

The Wealth Tax

Just as the Social Security Act established the FICA system of payroll taxes that are deducted from your wages today (and which generally amount to more than you pay in income taxes), a second tax that was imposed at the same time as Social Security is still part of the federal tax system today. It was called the Revenue Act of 1935, but known as the "wealth tax." It established an "inheritance tax," also known as the "death tax." It meant that the government was entitled to a large bite of the estates of rich people who died.

The law also slapped a surtax on individuals with incomes over $50,000 and a tax on millionaires that escalated to a top rate of 75 percent. FDR justified these levies in his tax message of June 19, 1935, in these words: "Our revenue laws have operated in many ways to the unfair advantage of the few, and they have done little to prevent an unjust concentration of wealth and economic power."

The concept is known as "redistribution of wealth." It has been the main bone of contention in our national political debate ever since, and it is the main difference in governmental philosophy between Democrats (for it) and Republicans (against it).

A Nation in Shock

On August 15, 1935, in Fairbanks, Alaska, Will Rogers climbed into a small airplane that belonged to one of the world's best aviators. With a cocky manner and a black patch over an eye that he'd lost in an oil field accident as a boy, Wiley Post was the first person to fly solo around the world. On this trip he and Rogers were continuing a happy-go-lucky aerial tour of Alaska as a prelude to an odyssey to Siberia and then on to Moscow.

Timeline

In July 1933 Wiley Post flew around the globe alone in his plane, the *Winnie Mae*, in 7 days (July 15 through July 22), 18 hours, 49 minutes, covering a distance of 15,596 miles.

Taking off from Fairbanks, Post headed the plane toward Point Barrow, some 500 miles north. When they ran into thick fog, Post was unsure of his bearings. He landed briefly to ask Eskimos for directions. Ten minutes after take-off, the single engine failed. The plane plunged 50 feet and slammed head-on into a river bank.

Not since the death of Harding had Americans been as shocked as they were when the news flashed from Point Barrow that they could no longer have their funny bones tickled by a Will Rogers jab at the high and the mighty. When word of his death reached Congress, the House and Senate adjourned in tribute, but not before voting to authorize the Smithsonian to buy the plane in which Post had set his around-the-world record.

Famous Faces

Here are some of humorist Will Rogers's most memorable quotes:

- "If you think you're a person of some influence, try orderin' somebody else's dog around."
- "The quickest way to double your money is to fold it over and put it back in your pocket."
- "Never miss a good chance to shut up."

Heading Home from Havana

With the end of the Spanish-American War in the summer of 1898, the island of Cuba became a United States Territory. During the Prohibition years, the island had been at the center of the illicit trade in Caribbean rum (hence the term "rum runner"). Its colorful and lively capital, Havana, was a year-round resort for Americans who could afford to book passage on numerous cruise ships and oceanliners that made Havana a port of call. One of the tourist attractions was an old historic fort, Morro Castle, overlooking the harbor in which, in 1898, the American battleship *Maine* had blown up, triggering the war in which Teddy Roosevelt led a cavalry unit known as the Rough Riders to fame and glory in a charge up San Juan Hill.

On the night of September 5, 1934, a liner flying the flag of the Ward Line bore the name of the fort. For the next three days and nights, 318 passengers on the *Morro Castle*, served by a crew of 231 men and women, partook of all the luxuries of the graceful liner. On the night of September 8, they'd joined in a traditional "last night out" party, then gone to bed expecting to awake at their destination, New York City. As the ship leaded for the Ambrose Channel, three miles off Barnegat, New Jersey, a fire broke out.

As radio alarms were sent out, crews of other nearby ships looked through rain and across choppy water at the horrible sight of the *Morro Castle* ablaze. Onboard the burning liner, the passengers were in full panic. Half-clothed and terrified, they rushed to the ship's lifeboats. Many leapt into the cold Atlantic.

At four o'clock, Coast Guard cutters that had recently patrolled the area looking for rum runners were making their way in thick fog and rain in a desperate race to the rescue. One crew member, Warren L. Moulton, later wrote of that terrible night, "Most of the boats were heavily loaded, but a few were not, and these were either hauling people out of the water or doing all in their power to draw up to the stern of the *Morro Castle*, where there must have been 200 people crowded, either along the deck rail, in the water, or hanging by ropes from the stern."

When it was all over, 137 people were dead. The *Morro Castle* was a burned-out hulk drifting toward shore. On Sunday morning she wallowed in shallow water less than 40 yards from the Convention Hall of the resort of Asbury Park. Suddenly, the scene of the disaster turned into a tourist attraction for a crowd estimated at between 125,000 and 250,000 of the morbidly curious.

Timeline _____

Bank robbers Bonnie Parker and Clyde Barrow were shot to death in a police ambush in Louisiana on May 23, 1934.

Big Show on the Beach

Most of the people came by car. Others scrambled into a special Pennsylvania Railroad train from New York City, while many more rushed to take in the sight on Jersey Central trains from all over New Jersey. Reporter Stanley Walker noted, "It was the largest crowd in any one day in the history of the resort."

Local businessmen, from hot dog vendors to hotel proprietors, saw chances to cash in. So did the town's officials. With accesses to the beach roped off, the town of Asbury Park charged 25 cents a head for the best views of the derelict ship, which still held about a hundred bodies.

On Monday afternoon the City Council voted to make the corpse of the *Morro Castle* a permanent attraction. That bright idea was soon scuttled when the odors of dead bodies, plus a smelly cargo of animal hides, made it necessary to have the ship towed way. The job took salvage companies six months to get her unstuck from the sand and to complete the work of getting the wreck to New York, where it was scrapped.

A legacy of this tragedy, and the disgraceful show that *Morro Castle* became, can be found in towns and cities all over America. To cope with the thousands of cars that jammed into Asbury Park, the city's police department decided to control the vehicle flow by opening some streets to cars coming in and others to autos going out. It was the first time in U.S. history that a town or city had imposed "one-way" traffic.

The Least You Need to Know

- When the Roosevelt administration recognized at the end of its first year that the U.S. economy was not recovering as fast as had been hoped, new programs proposed in the second year were known as "the second New Deal."

- Opponents of New Deal public works programs called them "boondoggles" and denounced them as a step toward Socialism.

- Following a Supreme Court decision declaring the National Recovery Act unconstitutional, FDR called the Justices "nine old men" and tried, without success, to expand the Court.

- At Roosevelt's request, Congress created the Social Security system.

Chapter 8

Listen to This!

In This Chapter

- ◆ Radio as the great communicator and unifier
- ◆ The shows everyone listened to
- ◆ Religious revival and the "radio priest"
- ◆ Widespread interest in self-improvement books
- ◆ The craze over daring aviators

In choosing "fireside chats" to inform the people of the country what the government was doing, and to gain popular support for programs that sought to manage the economy by centralizing power in Washington, President Roosevelt made use of the most popular and effective medium of mass communication in U.S. history to that time. The 1930s were "the Golden Age of Radio" in which Americans were not only entertained and informed but also unified as never before.

As people sought meaning and a ray of hope while the Depression dragged on, there was an upsurge in church membership. A "radio priest" attracted a huge following, got rich, and turned his mind to politics. There was a national fascination with famous fliers.

Friends and Fellow Americans

While Franklin Delano Roosevelt is remembered in history as the president who first had to struggle with the Great Depression and then run a world war, he must also be credited with having been our first media-savvy chief executive. Everything about his image was tailored for political purposes: his tone of voice, the way he cocked his head, a dazzling smile, the jaunty angle at which he held a cigarette in a long holder, and pince-nez glasses which reminded people that he was related to nose-glasses-wearing and venerated Teddy Roosevelt. In his fireside chats, he never failed to start with the inviting and folksy greeting "My friends," or "My fellow Americans."

The FDR public persona also entailed a deception. He and those around him, including worshipful reporters and photographers who covered the White House, went to great lengths to obscure the fact that the president of the United States was paralyzed from the waist down. In hundreds of thousands of FDR pictures snapped during his 12 years in office, two showed him in a wheelchair, and they weren't published. When a new cameraman was seen by another as he framed a shot that included the chair, the novice was politely but forcefully told by the veteran photographer that what he'd done was a no-no.

While a cameraman could snap a shot of FDR in a car, as in this 1936 picture, the unwritten rule was that FDR could not be shown being lifted in and out and never in his wheelchair.

It was not until our time of "political correctness" and the rise of an "equality movement" by disabled Americans that a statue was erected at the new Roosevelt Memorial on the Capitol Mall which seated FDR in the wheelchair. A few critics of the statue claim that it falsifies history because FDR persistently avoided being known as a crippled man. Note: In the pre-political correctness era, there was great stigma to the adjective "crippled."

Facts and Figures

The armless wheelchair that FDR used was made of wood. If he had to move a long way, an aide carried him. When he stood to deliver a speech or to be photographed with a visiting dignitary, he held on to an arm of an assistant. In photos of him standing, he was often steadied by one of his sons.

Best Show in Town

FDR was also skillful in handling the press. He was the first president to have regular press conferences at which questions weren't submitted in advance in writing. Held twice a week, the meetings with the newsmen took place in his office. One reporter noted after a 20-minute session that FDR's facial expressions went from amazement, curiosity, mock alarm, genuine interest, concern, and pleasure. Another newsman said in admiration that a Roosevelt press conference was the best show in town. Americans who were not in attendance observed clips of FDR in action in newsreels.

Timeline

Newspaper headline writers who had to worry about the number of letters in a line of type took to referring to Roosevelt by the initials FDR. Later, they were delighted that Eisenhower's life-long nickname was Ike. And, as everyone knows, John F. Kennedy became JFK. Before FDR, a president's name was always printed in full, preceded by "Mr." or "President."

America's Best-Known Voice

Through radio and newsreels, Roosevelt's voice became the best-known in America. It had at the same time a cultured tone (some called it "patrician") and an intimate quality that gave a radio listener the feeling that he was speaking only to that person. He frequently said "you and I," "we," and "together." He came across as a man with the quiet confidence and strength of a friend who would never talk down to anyone.

Facts and Figures

Of the 30 fireside chats made over the 12 years of FDR's presidency, 4 were in 1933, 2 in 1934, 1 in 1935 and 1936, 3 in 1937, and 1 in 1938 and 1939. (Subjects of Great Depression chats are listed in Appendix B, "Roosevelt's Fireside Chats in the 1930s.")

Gotta Have My Radio

Just a decade after radio pioneer David Sarnoff had dreamed of a "musical box" in every home in America, his concept was almost a reality. Since the time the first "sets" went on sale in 1928, Americans were so crazy about radio that when Roosevelt went "on the air" with a fireside chat, his voice could be "tuned in" by 85 percent of the population.

Facts and Figures

The cheapest radios sold for around $8, but if you wanted a really nice one, you would have paid around $50. A console was the size of a bedroom bureau and became the central piece of furniture in the living room. Some of these were priced in the hundreds. They were the work of some of the best industrial designers. A Stromberg-Carlson eight-tube console cost about $500, as did RCA's Radiola.

Smaller radios that were put on a table (called "table models") came in many styles. One the most popular was the "cathedral" radio because it was shaped like an arched church window. A "portable" radio made by such manufacturers as Emerson, Cyart, DeWald, and Fada ran on batteries. They weighed five pounds, were as big as a small suitcase, and had a large handle. Portables could also use electricity.

Timeline

Although FM (frequency modulation) was invented in 1933, it did not come into its own until after World War II. TV began in the late 1930s, but its development was also delayed by the war. The transistor, which made pocket-sized radios available, was not invented until the 1960s.

Now a Word from Our Sponsor

While the first makers of radios saw them as a way of presenting music so that people would buy records and phonographs, the men and women whose job was to sell all kinds of goods by advertising soon saw radio as a unique opportunity to pitch products right in the homes of consumers. And so was born the program's "sponsor" and the advertisement, known as the "commercial."

This break for a sales pitch led almost immediately to "singing commercials" and a product identifier called "the jingle." These brief musical ditties were heard so often and were so catchy that people went around whistling or singing them, thus extending the reach of the commercial.

A Radio Show for Everybody

To reach specific audiences, radio stations and networks created shows designed for women (the soap opera to keep the "housewife" company mornings and afternoons); kids' programs (after-school and before-supper adventure shows); and musical, variety, and dramas for the entire family (from 7 to 11 P.M.).

By presenting dramas, radio became known as "the theater of the imagination" because it required the listener's mind to come up with a picture to match what the ear was taking in. The "sound effects" man used coconut shells to simulate horses' hooves, a shaken sheet of thin metal for the rumble of thunder, kernels of rice on tin for rain, crinkling cellophane for a crackling fire, and recordings of real sounds that could not be faked. (If a gun had to be fired, a real one was used to shoot blanks.) The most famous (and blood-curdling) of these sound effects for a mystery show was a squeaking door. It was achieved with a nail scraped on a piece of glass.

As silly as it may seem today, radio shows even presented tap dancers. And one of the most popular shows of all starred Edgar Bergen, a ventriloquist, with his dummy Charlie McCarthy. As one of the characters in Woody Allen's 1990s movie *Radio Days* asked, "How do you know if his lips are moving?" Actually, the listener didn't care, because Charlie came across so real in the theater of the imagination that no one thought of him as a dummy.

Shows That Couldn't Be Missed

If you had been a radio listener in the 1930s, you would have made it a point not to miss:

◆ *Amos 'n' Andy*, featuring two black characters in Harlem who were played by white men, Freeman Gosden and Charles Correl.

◆ *Fibber McGee and Molly*, a situation comedy (although the term was not invented until the TV era). The highlight of every show was McGee opening "the hall closet." A sound effects man created a hilarious stream of crashing sounds as junk from the closet tumbled out.

◆ *Mr. First Nighter*, a drama show that recreated the excitement of going to a "little theater just off Broadway."

◆ *The Lone Ranger*, for kids, but the whole family listened as the orchestra played "The William Tell Overture" and the announcer invited them to "return to those thrilling days of yesteryear." The Lone Ranger's famous cry to his horse was "Hi Yo, Silver, away!"

◆ *The Shadow*, a mystery, with "Lamont Cranston," a detective who could make himself invisible. You knew he was invisible when his voice sounded as if he were speaking over a bad phone line.

◆ *Gangbusters*, a crime show that started with a police car siren and a blast of machine gun fire.

◆ *Baby Snooks*, starring Broadway star Fanny Brice as a naughty child (Brooks was played by Barbra Streisand in the 1960's stage show and movie *Funny Girl*).

◆ *The Jack Benny Show*, a Sunday night comedy half-hour that made a successful transition to TV. It featured the many voices of Mel Blanc, who also provided the voices of Bugs Bunny, Porky Pig, and numerous other characters in movie cartoons. Sound effects men created tightwad Benny's dilapidated Maxwell automobile and a multi-lock underground safe being opened.

◆ *One Man's Family*, a soap opera.

♦ *The Voice of Firestone*, a musical program with the Firestone rubber company symphony orchestra, opera stars, and classical and semi-classical compositions.

♦ *Lux Radio Theater*, dramatizations of hit movies with the stars from the films. The host was famed director Cecil B. DeMille.

♦ *The Kate Smith Show*, America's most popular (and fattest) singer whose rendition of "God Bless America" made the Irving Berlin song a second national anthem (it's still the best version of the song ever recorded).

♦ *The Chase and Sanborn Hour*, sponsored by the coffee company of that name, starring Edgar Bergen and Charlie McCarthy.

Radio's Most Famous Lines

Charlie McCarthy: "So help me, I'll mow him down."

Molly McGee: "No, McGee, not the hall closet!"

Cecil B. DeMille at the end of each *Lux Theater Show*: "Good night ... from ... HOLLY-WOOD!"

Jack Benny: "Well!"

The Shadow: "The Shadow knows!"

Kate Smith: "Good night folks."

Rudy Vallee: "Heigh-ho everybody." (He was the most popular male singer of the time.)

The famous feud that had been going on for 18 years looks only script deep in this picture of Jack Benny (left) and Fred Allen. It was taken as the two comics got together for the first reading of the show they did together for Benny's television program April 19, 1953. The feud would continue in the show, their first on TV together.

(AP Photo)

Ah, There's Good News Tonight

Americans got news over the radio in early evening in 15-minute broadcasts by Lowell Thomas, H. V. Kaltenborn, Elmer Davis, Drew Pearson, Boak Carter, Edwin C. Hill, and Gabriel Heatter. The latter was famous for leading into some items with "Ah, there's good news tonight." News programs also included commentary in which national and international affairs were "interpreted."

Radio also provided "on the scene" reports broadcast direct from locations of newsworthy events, as well as sports, including boxing, the World Series, and the Kentucky Derby. For people interested in gossip, there were broadcasts by Walter Winchell (mostly Broadway items) and Louella Parsons and Hedda Hopper (Hollywood).

The Radio Priest

With the exception of President Roosevelt and Charlie McCarthy, no voice on the radio in the 1930s was better known than that of Father Charles E. Coughlin. A Roman Catholic priest in Michigan, he was pastor of the Shrine of the Little Flower. He first went on the radio on a Detroit station, WJR, then coast to coast on a program called *The Radio League of the Little Flower*. An earlier supporter of FDR, "the radio priest," as Roosevelt called him, backed the New Deal so heartily that he termed it "Christ's Deal." He eventually broke ranks with the New Deal's policies and became a thorn in FDR's side.

Coughlin also became rich. Decades before television evangelists such as Jim and Tammy Bakker and others raked in thousands of dollars in contributions, Coughlin had radio listeners sending nickels and dimes to his "National Union for Social Justice." The organization became Coughlin's personal political machine. His targets were "money changers," Communists, the League of Nations, labor unions, banks, the AAA, the Supreme Court, and FDR. The NUSJ and another group, the People's Lobby, had members numbered in the millions. By 1936, he was being heard on 35 radio stations.

On June 19, 1936, he announced the formation of a new political party, the Union Party, and that he would be its presidential candidate. In the retrospect of seventy years, Father Coughlin is seen for what he was—a demagogue, a political quack with devious goals, a shifty manipulator of the truth, and a man greedy for power. But in 1936, with 30 million radios tuned in to his weekly broadcasts, he was a formidable and scary figure. (Read more about the other demagogues of the 1930s in Part 4, "Crackpots and Monsters.")

That Old-Time Religion

When Robert and Helen Merrell Lynd returned to Muncie, Indiana, in 1935, to continue their study of "Middletown," they noted that the Depression brought a resurgence of "religious fundamentalism" in the working class. But in the "uptown" churches of the town's better-off class, they found "little similar revival of interest" in religion.

One woman interviewed by the Lynds summed up the feeling of many in the better-off class about attending churches in this way: "We don't go. I believe the church is a good thing for the community, and the beliefs it stands for are probably a good thing, but I've just pretty well lost any belief in church and God and immortality I ever had. If you do the very best you can, that's all anybody can do anyway."

Famous Faces

In addition to being the most conspicuous thinker in American Protestantism of his time, and well into the 1950s, Reinhold Niebuhr was active in politics as a founder of the Liberal Party of New York and the later Americans for Democratic Action. His biographer correctly called him the "prophet to politicians."

Offering Another Way

Two years before the stock market crash of 1929, a theologian by the name of Rheinhold Niebuhr published a book that asked in its title *Does Civilization Need Religion?* It was followed in the 1930s by a series of books that were concerned with social ethics and the role of religion in politics. The crux of his message, known as the "new religion" and "Neo-orthodoxy," was an attempt to restate Christian teaching in a form that was relevant to the great issues of contemporary life.

The Living Spirit of Religion

The Lynds' analysis concluded that organized religion appeared to be "an emotionally stabilizing agent," but that the people looked elsewhere for the defining of values. Among these resources were the mass media (a term that came into use much later) of radio and the movies. (For the influence of movies, see Part 5, "Better Tomorrows.")

Although the Lynds didn't see much of a change in the religious nature of Middletown, statistics for the nation during the first eight years of the Great Depression show a brisk upturn in the number of people claiming church membership. Between 1929 and 1937, the number of Roman Catholics increased by a little over a million. Methodist, Baptist, and Lutheran churches also saw an increase. And in 1931 a new church appeared on the scene in the form of the *Jehovah's Witnesses*.

One final note on religion in the Great Depression: The novelist Pearl Buck saw evidence of an America with a spiritual core. She wrote, "I am amazed at all the religion I see everywhere." But it was not the religion that attracted believers into churches. She spoke of "those men and women who cannot endure the suffering of others, who feel it as their own suffering, and who give out of their own longing to see a better world." The plain truth is that on a Sunday in 1938 more people turned on their radios to laugh away their woes with Charlie McCarthy and Jack Benny than went to church that day to pray for God's help.

Talk of the Time

Organized under the leadership of Judge J. F. Rutherford, **Jehovah's Witnesses** are Christian fundamentalists best known to most Americans for their practice of distributing their publication "The Watchtower." To do so freely, they won several cases in the U.S. Supreme Court in the 1930s that reaffirmed the constitutional right to disseminate religious literature without a license and to solicit money for religious ends without being subject to taxes.

The Gospel of Help Thyself

Americans have always taken to heart the "pursuit of happiness" promised in the Declaration of Independence, and never more so than in the late 1930s. This desire for self-fulfillment took the form of books that rocketed to the top of best-seller lists. The most popular was Dale Carnegie's *How to Win Friends and Influence People*. Published in 1937, it's still in print. Other guides to a better life included Lin Yutang's *The Importance of Living* (1938) and Dorothea Brande's *Live Alone and Like It* (1936).

Timeline

Here are some of the other books popular in the mid- to late 1930s:

- ◆ *While Rome Burns* (1934), by radio personality Alexander Woollcott
- ◆ *Way of the Transgressor* (1936), by Negley Ferson
- ◆ *Inside Europe* (1936) and *Inside Asia* (1939), by John Gunther
- ◆ *The Yearling* (1938), by Marjorie Keenan Rawlings
- ◆ *The Best of Damon Runyon* (1938), by Damon Runyon
- ◆ *Gone with the Wind* (1936), by Margaret Mitchell (see Part 5)
- ◆ Detective novels by Ellery Queen, Erle Stanley Gardner, and Rex Stout (the Nero Wolfe mysteries)

Eyes and Hearts in the Skies

As you've read, America's beloved cowboy-humorist Will Rogers was killed in the crash of a small plane in Alaska. The pilot, Wiley Post, was one of many aviators whose daredevil exploits in the skies had captivated hearts and fired imaginations since the 1927 transatlantic solo flight of Charles Lindbergh.

One of these was Douglas Corrigan. The 31-year-old pilot took off from New York in 1933 with the goal of being the first to make a solo flight coast to coast. Instead, he wound up in Ireland. He explained that his compass had failed. Americans immediately fell in love with "Wrong Way Corrigan," but only the naïve believed that his "mistake" wasn't a planned publicity stunt.

Another hero of the skies was Howard Hughes. In 1939 to help promote the opening of New York World's Fair (see Part 5), he set an aviation record by flying around the world in 3 days and 19 hours.

The Big Balloon That Burst

You've read that the Empire State Building was topped by a tower that was intended to be a mooring mast for dirigibles. The goal was never realized because strong wind currents made such a thing impossible. But that did not mean an end to the dirigibles. A huge, hydrogen-filled airship from Nazi Germany that plied the skies of the Atlantic on a regular schedule was the *Hindenburg*. (Germans called dirigibles zeppelins.) Its base in the United States was at Lakehurst, New Jersey. But as it was coming in for a landing on May 6, 1937, something went wrong. It erupted into a ball of flame, killing 36 passengers and crew. That's what put an end to "lighter than air" travel.

Facts and Figures

One way on the *Dixie Clipper* from its base in Post Washington, Long Island, to Southampton, England, cost $375. A round trip ticket was $675.

Whether the *Hindenburg* blew up because an accidental spark ignited its hydrogen tanks or it was sabotaged to embarrass the Nazis is still a matter of debate.

Cheerfully Clipping Along

In the opinion of the author of this book, the most romantic way of air travel introduced in the 1930s was a "flying boat" called the "Clipper." Flown by Pan American Airways and Great Britain's Imperial Airways, these "boats" took off and landed on water in regular service across the Atlantic and Pacific. With flying boat service approved by the Civil Aeronautics Authority on May 19, 1939, and approved by FDR the following day, the first of the Boeing 314s, named *Yankee Clipper*, flew from New York via the Azores and Lisbon to Marseilles in 29 hours. Each of the graceful planes had seats and sleeping accommodations for 22 passengers.

America's Darling of the Skies

On July 2, 1937, on an airfield at Lae, New Guinea, a group of men waited nervously beside a twin-engine Lockheed Electra as a woman in a flying suit walked confidently toward the plane. Her name was Amelia Earhart. With a striking resemblance to Charles Lindbergh, she was his equal in daring as a pilot. She'd been the first woman to fly solo across the Atlantic. She'd set several speed records. President Hoover had said of her skill, modesty, and good humor, "All these things combine to place her in spirit with the great pioneering women to whom every generation of Americans looked up, with admiration for their firmness of will, their strength of character, and their cheerful spirit of comradeship in the work of the world."

Earhart and her navigator, Fred Noonan, took off from Lae, heading toward the west coast of the United States on the last leg of a historic around-the-world flight. They never made it. Somewhere between New Guinea and Howland Island, about halfway to Hawaii, their plane vanished. Because it and its famous pilot were never found, a sad and intriguing legacy of the 1930s is the nagging question "What happened to Amelia Earhart?"

The generally accepted theory is that she and Noonan got lost, the plane ran out of fuel, and they crashed into the Pacific. Another explanation put forward 30 years later was that she'd taken on the role of spy by changing her route at the request of FDR so that she would fly over islands that were occupied by Japanese, and that her plane was shot down.

 Timeline

The Motor Carrier Act of 1935 empowered the Interstate Commerce Commission (ICC) to regulate rates for buses and trucks engaged in commerce that crossed state lines.

Fat Man at the Dinner Table

In the year the stock market crashed, four young brothers from the lower east side of New York broke into the movies with the screen version of *The Cocoanuts*, a smash Broadway comedy written by George S. Kaufman. The zany movie proved so successful that Paramount Pictures immediately signed the brothers to make *Duck Soup*. From that point on, everyone in the country knew that the one with the painted-on mustache and low-slung way of walking was named Groucho, Chico played the piano, Harpo never spoke, and Zeppo was the solid and serious Marx.

The Marx Brothers' Depression-era movies included:

The Cocoanuts, 1929

Animal Crackers, 1930

Monkey Business, 1931

Horse Feathers, 1932

Duck Soup, 1933

A Night at the Opera, 1935

A Day at the Races, 1937

Room Service, 1938

At the Circus, 1939

Go West, 1940

The Big Store, 1941

Yet if it hadn't been for a glowing review of the stage production of *The Cocoanuts* by Broadway's most influential theater critic, the Marx Brothers might not have enjoyed such a skyrocketing success. One of the most famous, charismatic, controversial, and acid-tongued personalities during the Great Depression, fat, owlish-looking Alexander Woollcott set literary and theatrical standards as a writer for *The New Yorker* and drama critic for *The New York Times*. In the 1920s he'd founded a circle of famous writers known as the Algonquin Round Table, then ruled over it with sarcasm and wit. On his CBS network radio show, *The Town Crier*, heard on Sunday nights in the late 1930s and early 1940s, he amused and lectured a spellbound nation.

A friend of the Roosevelts, he recommended mystery novels to FDR and called First Lady Eleanor Roosevelt's White House "the finest boarding house for actors that I've ever stayed in." One of the most powerful critics in the nation, he boosted not only the careers of the Marx Brothers, but also Helen Hayes, "the fist lady of the theater" Katharine Cornell, the husband-and-wife acting team of Alfred Lunt and Lynn Fontanne, and dancers Fred and Adele Astaire. He urged W. C. Fields to turn from a juggling act to comedy and Will Rogers from a *Ziegfeld Follies* comedian twirling a lasso into a writer. He knew all the celebrities of his time, including Winston Churchill. Orbiting his sun were motion picture stars, scientists, royalty, journalists, and leading figures of the criminal world.

He admitted that, as a critic, he blatantly catered to popular tastes and said of himself. "I am the greatest writer in America with absolutely nothing to say." Millions of Americans would not miss his newspaper columns, magazine articles, and *The Town Crier*. In 1938, his outlandish behavior provided inspiration for the title character, Sheridan Whiteside, in George S. Kaufmann and Moss Hart's hit Broadway comedy, and later movie, *The Man*

Who Came to Dinner. Continually revived by regional theater groups, it was recently re-staged on Broadway, then presented on Public Television, starring Nathan Lane as Whiteside.

When Woollcott died in 1943, *The New Yorker* magazine noted, "Alexander Woollcott's unique contribution was his peculiar ability to infect one and all with the notion that they were at some sort of play. He always seemed to be at a play himself, whether he was in the bathtub, at the White House, or on a battleship."

Columnist Walter Lippmann wrote, "Woollcott had a sharp taste. He had a piercing eye for sham. He had an acid tongue. But he had gusto, he really liked what he praised, and he cared much more for the men and women he liked than he worried about those he did not like."

If you want a riotously entertaining "time-capsule" look at what life was like in the 1930s, you'll find it in *The Man Who Came to Dinner.*

The Least You Need to Know

- The main form of entertainment for Americans was the radio.
- A Roman Catholic priest, Charles E. Coughlin, used radio to build a national organization that opposed Communists, the League of Nations, labor unions, banks, the Supreme Court, and FDR.
- Many Americans sought inspiration by reading self-help books by such authors as Dale Carnegie and Dorothea Brande.
- Hopes for commercial travel by dirigibles were dashed with the explosion of Germany's *Hindenburg* at Lakehurst, New Jersey, on May 6, 1937.

Part  3

This Land Is Your Land

This section deals with the 1936 election, a business recession that threatened to stall recovery, and a disastrous drought in the West that turned America's "breadbasket" into the "Dust Bowl."

As a result of the drought, industrialization of agriculture, and people being kicked off farms because of debts, there was a wave of migration to California that novelist John Steinbeck used as the theme of a best-selling book, *The Grapes of Wrath*. The Dust Bowl also produced a "hard times," wandering troubadour named Woody Guthrie.

Chapter 9

Soup and Dust Bowls

In This Chapter

◆ The 1936 presidential election
◆ FDR's failure to change the Supreme Court
◆ Philosophy of the planned economy
◆ The Dust Bowl

As President Franklin D. Roosevelt ran for re-election in 1936, millions of people were still dependent on government relief. His opponent was Gov. Alfred M. (Alf) Landon of Kansas. Landon condemned the New Deal for its policy of a "planned economy." FDR saw one issue in this campaign. "It's myself," he said. "People must be either for me or against me."

Re-elected in a landslide, FDR embraced the concept of a planned economy. But nothing he proposed came in time to cure the worst drought in U.S. history. Millions of parched acres of the Great Plains became a "dust bowl."

Rendezvous with Destiny

Governor Alfred M. Landon of Kansas had one thing in common with President Franklin D. Roosevelt. Both had been elected in 1932. Their differences provided the issues for the 1936 presidential election campaign.

A successful independent oil producer before entering politics, Landon was a friendly, likeable family man whom some Republicans praised as "the Kansas Coolidge." He ran on a GOP platform that accused FDR of usurping the powers of Congress and of displacing the free enterprise system with rule by the federal government.

What Landon did not have on his side was a pleasant voice. His was raspy and harsh. FDR's was warm, friendly, and familiar. As one observer put it, a Landon speech did not throw out sparks, while Roosevelt on the radio could be thrilling. Landon's oratorical theme was fear. Claiming a "campaign to save America," he warned voters to be on their guard against "fanatics, theorists, and impractical experimenters." He drew a frightening picture of New Dealers creeping up silently in the night "seeking to impose upon us, before we realize it, a new and alien kind of government."

Roosevelt's acceptance speech at the Democratic convention gave future editors of books of quotations one of the most famous, and far-seeing, utterances in U.S. political history. FDR declared, "To some generations much is given. Of other generations much is expected. This generation of Americans has a rendezvous with destiny."

Cherokee chief Jerry Blythe gives President Franklin D. Roosevelt a bonnet of brown turkey feathers during the president's visit to the Cherokee Indian Reservation in North Carolina in this September 10, 1936, photo.

(AP Photo)

Saying that he was running against old enemies of business and financial monopoly, speculation, reckless banking, class antagonism, and sectionalism, he told a rally in Madison Square Garden in New York, "I would like to have it said of my first administration that in it the forces of selfishness and lust for power met their match. I should like to have it said of my second administration that in it these forces have met their master."

As Maine Goes, So Goes Vermont

When all the votes were in, Roosevelt carried every state but Maine and Vermont. His coat-tails gave Democrats an overwhelming majority in Congress. In the House, it would be 328 to 107. In the Senate, 77 to 19.

Facts and Figures

In the 1936 election, Roosevelt garnered 27,751,612 popular votes to Landon's 16,681,913. Roosevelt captured 523 electoral college votes, while Landon received just 8.

Gloomy Day in Washington

As a result of the 20th Amendment's shortening of the time from the election to the date of the president's swearing-in, FDR was the first president inaugurated on January 20. In 1937 it was a rainy day as he admitted in his inauguration address that after four years of the New Deal "a substantial part" of the nation's population was denied "the very lowest standards of living." Millions of families were "trying to live on incomes so meager that the pall of family disaster hangs over them every day."

"I see," he said, "one third of a nation ill-housed, ill-clad, ill-nourished."

"Hands Off the Supreme Court!"

As noted earlier, key parts of Roosevelt's New Deal were found to be unconstitutional by the Supreme Court. To say FDR was angry about this is an understatement. He was so furious that after his re-election, he came up with a plan to increase the membership of the court. He proposed that the number of judges be raised from 9 to a maximum of 15. Shocked opponents accused him of trying to "pack" the court with men who would go along with the New Deal. The outcry against the plan was summed up by a newspaper headline that warned, "Hands Off the Supreme Court."

To defend his idea, FDR went on the radio with a fireside chat (March 9, 1937). He declared that the Supreme Court had "cast doubts on the

Famous Faces

The justices who joined the U.S. Supreme Court during FDR's administration were:

- Hugo Black, 1937
- Stanley Reed, 1938
- Felix Frankfurter, 1939
- William O. Douglas, 1939
- Frank Murphy, 1940
- Robert H. Jackson, 1941
- James F. Byrnes, 1941

ability of elected Congress to protect us against catastrophe by meeting squarely our modern social and economic conditions." Although the court-packing plan did not succeed in Congress or in winning popular approval, over the next four years enough members of the Supreme Court left the bench that FDR was able to name seven new members. The result was a dramatic switch to a more liberal judicial philosophy.

The Planned Economy

The crux of the New Deal's design for getting the country out of the Depression was government intervention in the economy through massive spending to boost employment, increase purchasing power, stimulate investment, and raise production. In order to do this, the government would have to spend more money than it took in. The term for this is "deficit spending."

In following this policy, the New Deal had actually embraced the ideas of a British economic theorist that would not be published until 1936 in a book with the weighty title *The General Theory of Employment, Interest, and Money.* The author was John Maynard Keynes. His ideas became so important that his name is now an adjective and a noun. If you adhere to "Keynesian" economics, you are a "Keynesian." That is, you're someone who believes in a big government that assumes an active part in managing the economy.

Who Was This Guy Keynes?

The son of a distinguished economist, Keynes went to Eton and then King's College, Cambridge. A deep thinker in the area of economics, he'd published several controversial works in which he advocated abandoning the gold standard and deficits and recommended the use of public works to cut unemployment.

An important member of the Roosevelt administration who embraced Keynesian theory was Marriner Eccles, a member of the Federal Reserve Board. A friend of Keynes was Secretary of Labor Frances Perkins. After meeting Keynes in 1934, FDR had told Perkins that Keynes had given him "a whole rigmarole of figures." Not all impressed with the economist, FDR said to Perkins, "He must be a mathematician rather than a political economist."

Keynes had gone away disappointed. He told Perkins he'd expected Roosevelt to have been "more literate, economically speaking." How much FDR knew about Keynes's theories is debatable, but the consensus of students of New Deal policies is that he'd adopted Keynesian theories. While they may or may not have been the New Deal blueprint for ending the Depression, Keynes's book is now regarded as a classic, and Keynes is esteemed by many experts as the most important figure in the history of economics.

Sticky Prices, Sticky Wages

One of the maxims of economics is that prices and wages change in terms of the scarcity of goods and labor in relation to the amount of money that's on hand to buy them. But often in trying to strike the proper balance, prices and wages get stuck. When it happens, people buy less, production is cut, and jobs are lost.

This cycle was a major cause of the Depression. Remember the term "maldistribution of wealth"? The objective of the New Deal was to cure it by pumping money into the economy through direct relief payments, tax policy, government jobs, and the projects known as "public works." Although neither Roosevelt nor Keynes had impressed one another in 1934, the economist wrote a letter to FDR in 1938 in which he advised the president that the key to breaking the back of the Depression was large-scale public works.

Stampeded Like Cattle

While Roosevelt's policies had gotten a ringing endorsement by voters, his and the people's confidence got a rude shock when the stock market took another nose dive in 1937 that left everyone wondering if the country would ever recover. Opinions among the president's advisors were split on what to do. The Secretary of the Treasury, Henry Morgenthau, felt that the thing to do was wait "to see what happens this spring." FDR agreed. But during a vacation at his retreat in Warm Springs, Georgia, FDR's advisor Harry Hopkins and others with a Keynesian outlook persuaded FDR to launch a massive spending program.

When Morgenthau heard about this, he griped, "They stampeded him like cattle."

To Prime the Pump

Taking to the airwaves again for a fireside chat on April 14, 1938, Roosevelt explained to the country that he was asking the Congress in a special message for a doubling of the rolls of the WPA (from 1.5 to 3 million). The RFC would "prime the pump" of production with loans to industries. And the Federal Reserve would make more money available.

When the legislation he requested (Emergency Relief Appropriation Act) became law on June 21, Roosevelt exclaimed in a speech at Bowling Green, Kentucky, "We are on our way again." When he spoke (nine years after the Wall Street crash and five years since the New Deal was launched), as many as nine million Americans still did not have jobs.

If at First You Don't Succeed

Just as troubling as industrial unemployment was the realization that the 1933 Agricultural Adjustment Act (AAA), aimed at reducing farm surpluses as a means of supporting crop prices, had flopped. Following the tried-and-true American belief that if at first you don't succeed, you must try again, the law was revived in amended form as the Agricultural Adjustment Act of 1938.

This second shot at stabilizing prices dropped a federal tax that farmers had found objectionable. Instead, Agriculture Secretary Wallace was empowered to impose production quotas. It also set up a "parity" program in which the government would buy surpluses in order to regulate market prices. With so much farm surplus on hand by May 1939, another government program was created to make the excess available to the needy in the form of federal food stamps.

Down on the Farm

Another problem "down on the farm" was the result of increasing mechanization. With the introduction of the tractor and other types of labor-saving machinery, American agriculture had changed from family-owned farms to a modern "agri-business" in which the farmer was a tenant employed by a large industrial enterprise, or in many instances working on land that had been taken over by a bank, insurance firm, or loan company which held the mortgage. In 1880 only 25 percent of U.S. farms had been run by tenants. But in the mid-1930s 42 percent were "tenant farms."

Tenant farming put many farmers in the same position as those who worked in factories. They held their jobs only as long as their bosses needed them. Ironically, as a result of the federal policy of encouraging farm owners to cut back on production as a means of keeping up prices, many of the tenants found themselves either out of work or employed part-time as day workers. Forced to go on the relief rolls, many men who once had raised food were now applying for the new food stamps.

Timeline

The steam-powered farm tractor was invented in 1886, followed in 1892 by the gas-powered version. The diesel-powered tractor joined the line-up in 1930, with the Caterpillar version debuting the next year.

Facts and Figures

In 1934 nearly 30 percent of Americans lived on farms.

River Keep Away from My Door

An annual problem for farmlands adjacent to rivers was flooding. It was a rare year when at least one of the major waterways did not overflow and inundate crops. Despite this annual soaking, the federal government had done little in the way of flood control. But in 1936 Congress passed legislation authorizing construction of some 200 river control works. Unfortunately, the action was not in time to prevent a disastrous flood on the Ohio River in January 1937. Before the water subsided, 900 people died and half a million families lost their homes.

In that year of major floods in the East and Midwest, only the Tennessee River was kept under control, thanks to one of FDR's earliest successes. On May 18, 1933, as part of the first 100 days' tide of legislation, Congress created the Tennessee Valley Authority (TVA). An independent public corporation, it was given the right to build dams and power plants along the course of the river in Tennessee, North Carolina, Kentucky, Virginia, Georgia, and Alabama.

The author of the TVA legislation, Senator George Norris, said, "It is emblematic of the dawning of that day when every rippling stream that flows down the mountainside and winds its way through the meadows to the sea shall be harnessed and made to work for the welfare and comfort of man."

Electricity generated by the dams would be supplied to homes, farms, and industries for the first time. Roosevelt saw the TVA leading "to national planning for a complete watershed involving many states and the future lives and welfare of millions" that "touches and gives life to all forms of human concern." One of the lasting achievements of the New Deal, the TVA made possible in its first 10 years the building of nine main dams and numerous smaller ones. During World War II, it supplied the power facilities for manufacturing munitions and for the atomic bomb plant at Oak Ridge, Tennessee.

The Saddest Land I've Ever Seen

While the government could take action to control rivers, there was another phenomenon of nature that no action by the government could have prevented. And once it began, there was nothing anybody could do about it. Land that was once called America's "breadbasket" was being ravaged by the worst and longest drought in the nation's history.

It started in 1930 with a heat wave. A Weather Bureau official called it "the worst in the climatological history" of the United States. First to feel the effects was the East. By 1934 the drought had spread West to the Great Plains, from North Dakota to Texas. It's the settled opinion of agricultural historians that the dry spell was made worse by the hand of man. You'll recall that in the years right after World War I, there had been a burst of speculation, not just in the stock market, but in buying land.

Timeline ————

Congress set the minimum wage at 40 cents an hour and the maximum work week at 40 hours for industries engaged in interstate commerce.

Unfortunately, the desire to own farm property was not matched by wise use of the land. As millions of acres were plowed, little or no effort was made toward conservation. The result was erosion of the topsoil. The 1934 *Yearbook of Agriculture* reported that 100 million acres were "rapidly losing topsoil." Much of the loss was attributed to plowing, but millions of acres of grassland had been ravaged in overgrazing by livestock.

Too Little, Too Late

In June of 1934, Roosevelt signed the Taylor Grazing Act. It gave the government power to establish grazing districts for cattle and sheep on federal land. Its use would be monitored by a new agency, the Grazing Service, within the Department of Interior. It was a case of locking the barn door after the horse had gone.

In 1935, Congress passed the Soil Conservation Act. It created a permanent unit of the Agriculture Department for the control and prevention of soil erosion. When it became apparent that this unit had failed in its purpose, crop losses from drought, flooding, and other natural causes (most of which could have been prevented by conservation measures) ranged between 50 and 75 percent of the average annual yield.

Between 1933 and 1934 the Federal Emergency Relief Administration spent $85 million in an effort to rehabilitate ruined farmland. It was also an exercise in futility.

The Dry Spell Blues

As the drought gripped the nation's heartland, a blues musician named Son House wrote in "Dry Spells Blues" that the drought was "drivin' people from door to door" as farmers abandoned homes to seek relief in the cities. Countless others just moved away. In 1934 the state of Oklahoma had a net population loss of more than 400,000. Kansas lost 227,000. The Plains States experienced a shift elsewhere of 2.5 million residents. (More on this mass migration in Chapter 10, "Keep It Movin', Buddy!")

Timeline ————

On November 11, 1933, the first dust storm struck Beadle County, South Dakota. The cloud of dust darkened skies over Chicago and eventually reached as far east as Albany, New York. Between May 9 and May 11, 1934, an estimated 350 million tons of soil disappeared from the West and caused Boston, New York, and Washington, D.C., to turn on streetlights.

Agricultural machinery is buried under a mound of dust in a Guymon, Oklahoma, farm on March 14, 1936.

(AP Photo)

Voices from the Dust Bowl

In June 1936, a roving newspaperman from Garden City, Kansas, by the name of Ernie Pyle wrote, "If you would like to have your heart broken, just come out here. This is the dust-storm country. It is the saddest land I have ever seen."

A victim of dust storms wrote, "We dream of the faint gurgling sound of dry soil sucking in the moisture, but we wake to another day of wind and dust and hopes deferred." Another desperate sufferer scribbled in a daily log, "This is ultimate darkness. So must come the end of the world."

Farm wife Caroline Henderson wrote "Letters from the Dust Bowl" for *The Atlantic Monthly* in May 1936 in which she described "the sunlight turning smoky, shadows gone, distance vanishing, the sky blown out."

In "The Life and Death of 470 Acres" for *The Saturday Evening Post* of August 13, 1938, R. D. Lusk wrote: "By mid-morning a gale was blowing, cold and black. By noon it was blacker than the night. When the wind died and the sun shone forth again, it was on a different world. There were no fields, only sand drifting into mounds and eddies that swirled in what was now an autumn breeze. In the farm yard, fences, machinery, and trees were gone, buried. The roofs of sheds stuck out through drifts deeper than a man is tall."

As the wind blew, Lusk noted, it kicked up a wall of dirt "that eyes could not penetrate, but it [the dirt] could penetrate the eyes and ears and nose."

Dust storms became a health hazard. Doctors recorded a rise in the number of bronchitis cases, asthma, tuberculosis, and a new malady that they called "dust pneumonia."

Rippling dunes of dust, piled up against fences and an abandoned farm home, barn, and windmill, illustrate the desolation in part of the Dust Bowl in Oklahoma on March 27, 1937.

(AP Photo)

Dust Bowl Balladeer

In 1938 a 26-year-old wanderer with a harmonica, a knack for linking words and music, and a sympathy for the plight of people who'd been dispossessed by the Depression composed a song that he titled "Dust Pneumonia Blues." That year he also wrote "Dust Can't Kill Me," "Dust Bowl Refugee," and "Dusty Old Dust," better known to you as the folk-music classic "So Long, It's Been Good to Know You."

Born on July 14, 1912, in Okemah, Oklahoma, this troubadour of troubles was named for the man who became president that year. But Woodrow Wilson Guthrie would gain fame as "Woody" and earn the title "father of American folk music." A school dropout who became an itinerant entertainer in his teen years, he'd married in 1933 at age 21, then struck out again on his own. He was described as wiry, with a shock of hair and a guitar slung over his back. He tramped all over the country singing songs of protest. Hitting the road through Texas, Oklahoma, and Arkansas, he encountered displaced people. Tales they told of their hard times and his own experiences, took the form of Guthrie songs whose titles alone tell the story of the years of the Great Depression.

Woody Guthrie would say of his songs and himself, "I am out to sing songs that will prove to you that this is your world and that if it has hit you pretty hard and knocked you for a dozen loops, no matter what color, what size you are, how you are built, I am out to sing the songs that make you take pride in yourself and in your work. And the songs I sing are made up for the most part by all sorts of folks just about like you."

The best example of that Guthrie philosophy is found in his most famous Depression song, "This Land Is Your Land." But what you probably don't know is that Guthrie wrote the song as a protest against Irving Berlin's "God Bless America." The original "This Land Is Your Land" contained bitter references to Guthrie seeing hungry people outside a federal relief office and wondering "if God blessed America for me."

Woody Guthrie will appear again in the following chapter, linked with John Steinbeck, who wrote the Great Depression's most famous book, *The Grapes of Wrath*.

Facts and Figures

Popular Woody Guthrie Depression songs included:

- "All In and Down and Out"
- "If You Ain't Got the Do Re Me"
- "Death of the Blue Eagle"
- "Dust Bowl Blues"
- "I Ain't Got No Home"

Not Since the Pyramids of Egypt

In describing the challenge of the New Deal's building projects, the man in charge of the Public Works Administration (PWA), Harold Ickes, declared, "We set for ourselves at the outset the perhaps unattainable ideal of administering the greatest fund for construction in the history of the world."

Not since ancient Egyptians built the pyramids had a government launched such a vast enterprise. Among the achievements were the 100-mile causeway between Key West and mainland Florida, New York City's Triborough Bridge, 70 percent of all new schools between 1933 and 1939, municipal buildings, sewage plants, airports, hospitals, and the Bonneville, Grand Coulee, and Boulder dams.

Taming the Colorado

While the waters of the Colorado River had given America one of the world's most spectacular natural wonders in the Grand Canyon, the river that over millions of years had gouged and worn away rocks to cut its course to the Lower California Gulf had a disturbing record of wreaking havoc by flooding. Calls for taming the river with a flood control dam had been raised for decades. But the federal government had turned a deaf ear until construction got the green light from the Depression-embattled Hoover administration.

When Roosevelt came into office, construction of the project, to be named Boulder Dam, was well under way near a speck of a town in the Nevada desert called Las Vegas. The purposes of the dam were to provide the much-needed flood prevention, silt control, an irrigation system, electricity, and water supply for faraway Los Angeles, California. To carry a billion gallons of water over desert and mountains, a 239-mile viaduct with pumping stations was built. The irrigation network would water a million acres downstream of the dam at a cost of $60 million more than the amount spent on building the dam. Only the building of the Panama Canal exceeded the project in the list of great building efforts in the modern world.

The Mighty Boulder

Two-thirds the height of the Empire State Building, the dam was 600 feet wide at the base. Behind it the water of the Colorado River would eventually create Lake Mead. Some 115 miles long and eight miles wide, it would hold enough water to cover all of New York State to a depth of one foot. It was estimated that it would take 10 years to fill. One observer writing about first seeing the dam described "a vast wall of new gray-white concrete, curved in a beautiful bow with its arch upstream for strength." Just beyond were four concrete intake towers containing generating plants, two on each side of the dam.

The biggest single piece of masonry ever attempted—six million tons of concrete—if poured into a square block, it would rise higher than the Empire State Building. If 500 miles of water pipes hadn't been put in as it was being built, and instead the concrete left to cool by itself, it was estimated that the setting process would take a century.

Built with a combination of private construction firms and money from the federal government, the project entailed building a 330-mile branch railway, miles of first-class highways, and 222 miles of power lines. To provide a highway that would lead to Los Angeles, the top of the dam had a roadway that provided a view of the chasm on one side and the lake on the other.

The building of this immense project required six-million man-hours of risky labor by as many as 5,000 workers per day. They labored in three shifts a day. Paid $35 a week, they ate box lunches or sit-down meals in a huge restaurant. With temperatures over 120 degrees, they slept in air-conditioned dormitories.

On days off, many of the men sought respite in the little town nearby.

Does This Sound Familiar?

In *The New Republic* of December 11, 1935, reporter Bruce Bliven took a look at the town just to the north of Boulder Dam and wrote, "So far as anyone can discern from casual observation, the only occupations of Las Vegas, Nevada, are drinking, gambling, and prostitution. They must do something else there, but if so, it is not discernable to the innocent tourist's eye. Probably the dam, with up to 5,000 men, mostly single, has helped, though old inhabitants tell me that Las Vegas has always been one of the most wide-open towns in a wide-open state."

Founded in the nineteenth century by the Mormons, 1930s Las Vegas was not yet the mecca of casinos that exists today. That didn't come about until 1946, when Hollywood-based gangster Benjamin "Bugsy" Siegel used mob money to open the Flamingo. But on the day that Bliven ventured up from the dam, he was startled to find that on a walk down the main street at 11 A.M. almost every block had one or more gambling houses, doors open to every passerby, crowded with men and women, old and young, playing Keno, roulette, and poker, shooting craps, or betting on horse races. Las Vegas's "painted ladies" wore raspberry-colored sailor pants, coral-tinted blouses, and high-heeled slippers.

Shocked by what he saw, Bliven compared the dam site with Las Vegas and found Las Vegas "a pretty awful spectacle" that carried over the habits of the old West "into an era of long-distance buses, radio sets, and ubiquitous Ford V-8s."

Today, visitors to Las Vegas can take a break from gambling in the casinos for a trip to the dam site or spend a day boating on Lake Mead. But the colossal dam is no longer called "Boulder." In a tribute to the president whose administration started work on it, the very same president whose name was applied to so many of the shantytowns built by victims of the Great Depression, it is now called "Hoover Dam."

The Least You Need to Know

- Although re-elected in a landslide in 1936, Roosevelt was unable to gain approval for his plan to "pack" the Supreme Court by increasing the number of justices from 9 to 15.

- The federal government launched vast projects to build dams in order to prevent annual flooding of rivers.

- A prolonged drought, poor land management, and wind storms resulted in displacement of farmers in parched areas that became known as "the Dust Bowl."

- Itinerant song-writer Woody Guthrie became the balladeer of the Great Depression with such songs as "This Land Is Your Land" and "Dust Bowl Blues."

Chapter 10

Keep It Movin', Buddy!

In This Chapter

◆ A fireside chat on the Great Plains drought

◆ The United States is a nation of migrants

◆ Novelist Upton Sinclair offers a radial recovery plan

◆ A flood of refugees swamps California

◆ John Steinbeck publishes *The Grapes of Wrath*

As drought and dust storms drove farmers from their lands in the Great Plains, Roosevelt predicted in a fireside chat that the drought would not depopulate the affected area. He was proven wrong by a wave of migrants that flooded into California.

Writer Upton Sinclair proposed a state takeover of industry and agriculture in California. Displaced Oklahomans who moved to the state became known as "Okies." Their plight was depicted for the rest of the country in a best-selling novel by John Steinbeck.

A Journey of Husbandry

When Franklin D. Roosevelt was running for re-election in 1936, he traveled through nine states that were in the heart of the Dust Bowl. In a fireside chat on the night before Labor Day, he reported what he'd seen on the tour that he called "a journey of *husbandry*."

FDR told listeners that he'd talked with families who'd lost their wheat crop, lost the water in their well, lost their garden, and had reached the end of the summer without one dollar of cash resources, facing a winter without food for themselves and seed for the next planting season.

Talk of the Time

Husbandry is the management of domestic resources, such as farming.

Speaking to a nation of radios on September 6, 1936, he pledged, "I shall never forget the fields of wheat so blasted by heat that they cannot be harvested. I shall never forget field after field of corn stunted, earless, and stripped of leaves, for what the sun left the grasshoppers took. I saw brown pastures which would not keep a cow on fifty acres."

What he had not seen, he told his listeners optimistically, was "permanent disaster" in the drought regions. "No cracked earth, no blistering sun, no burning wind. No grasshoppers," he said, "are a permanent match for the indomitable American farmers and stockmen and their wives and children who have carried on through these desperate days, and inspire us with their self-reliance, their tenacity, and their courage."

The chat was FDR in full flight. He sounded undaunted, full of confidence, and brimming with what Americans called "grit." Much has been made of the morale-boosting power of Winston Churchill's oratory in Britain during World War II. But in the seven years before Churchill became Prime Minister in 1940 and spoke about Britain's "finest hour," Franklin D. Roosevelt was a master of the art of the uplifting speech.

But he was wrong on one point. He said he did not see in all of the suffering that he'd witnessed on his tour of the Dust Bowl the "depopulating" of those areas. The truth was that even as he spoke, thousands of devastated, demoralized farmers in Oklahoma, Arkansas, and other Dust Bowl states were already on the move.

An Arkansas farmer and his sons are shown in 1936 in the Dust Bowl.

(AP Photo/Arthur Rothstein/FSA)

A Nation of Migrants

Soon after the stock market crash of 1929, the Missouri Pacific Railroad took "official cognizance" of 13,745 migrants who'd used the railway to get from one place to another without bothering to buy a ticket. In 1931, the number of these "hoboes" riding the rails stood at 186,028. Two years later, it was estimated that over a million people were "transients." The number of these freight-car hoppers grew so much that many railroads just gave up trying to remove them from trains and train yards.

It Was a System

Reporting on the rising tide of migrants in 1932 in an article titled "No One Has Starved," *Fortune* magazine found the "social curiosity" of destitute families "in search of a solvent relative or a generous friend." The article continued, "Dull mornings last winter, the sheriff of Miami, Florida, used to fill a truck with homeless men and run them up to the county line. Where the sheriff of Fort Lauderdale used to meet them and load them into a second truck and run them up to his county line. Where the sheriff of Saint Lucie's would meet them and load them into a third truck and run them up to his county line. It was a system."

States and communities faced with having to shelter and feed the wave of wanderers simply did not have the resources. Signs went up at state borders and town and city lines telling migrants in one form or another, "Keep it movin', buddy, there's no work for you here."

Eyewitness Account

An unemployed youth who observed this movement of jobless men was 20-year-old Eric Sevareid. He would eventually become a famed war correspondent for CBS and enjoy a long career as a newsman and commentator in radio and on television. A native of Minnesota, he'd set out to hitchhike across the country in search of work. Part of the way he hopped onto freight trains.

Writing of the experience in his 1946 memoir, *Not So Wild a Dream*, he told of waking up one morning next to the Union Pacific tracks at Spark, Nevada. Finding an "empty" in a long freight train, he entered "a new social dimension" that he called "the great underground world, peopled by tens of thousands of American men, women, and children, white, black, brown, and yellow." They ate from blackened tin cans, found warmth at night in boxcars, and stole one day and begged with cap in hand the next.

"They had worked—once," Sevareid noted, "but jobs did not last, pay was low, they had to move on and on for new jobs, until finally it became easier just to move on."

If This Isn't Depopulation, What Is?

While FDR told Americans in his 1936 fireside chat that he did not foresee the depopulation of Dust Bowl regions, those states were, in fact, losing people at an astonishing rate. Between 1930 and 1940 the losses in numbers and percent of population were:

- Kansas: 79,791; 4 percent
- Nebraska: 62,179; 4 percent
- North Dakota: 38,910; 3 percent
- Oklahoma: 440,000; 18.4 percent
- South Dakota: 49,586; 7 percent

No one knows exactly how many uprooted Americans there were. The estimate is 3.5 million, with 2.5 million of them leaving their homes after 1935.

Highways to Heaven

"Drive out on any of the main highways of our state," said U.S. Senator William Borah of Idaho during the height of the Dust Bowl crisis, "and you will see cars, sometimes almost caravans, fleeing from the devastation of the drought."

Where were they going? "They roll westward like a parade," wrote Richard Neuberger in *Our Promised Land* (1936). "In a single hour from a grassy meadow near an Idaho road I counted 34 automobiles with the license plates of states between Chicago and the mountains."

Thousands of people who hadn't gone to the poor house in a car, as Will Rogers had joked, were now broke and in Ford cars and Model T trucks, Dodges, Chevies, La Salles, and every other make. With, roofs, running boards, and back and rear bumpers loaded with as many possessions as they could hold, they limped along highways that had been built in the good years.

U.S. Route 30 cut through mountains of Colorado and Idaho. The two-lane wonder of American know-how and the can-do spirit that stretched from the Mississippi to California was U.S. Route 66. Not since the trains of Conestoga wagons headed west across the plains after the Civil War had so many Americans moved at one time in search of a fresh start. And not since 1848, when Johann Augustus Sutter struck gold on a branch of the American River in Eldorado County, California, had so many people set their eyes and hearts on starting life over in the place known thereafter as "the Golden State."

California, Here I Come

As noted earlier, California experienced a spurt in popularity among the land speculators of the boom years of the 1920s. As a result, the state's population had risen by more than a million. The *WPA Guide to California* recorded that by 1930 the population had grown to 5.6 million, a jump of 65 percent in 10 years. But by 1934 the balloon had deflated. Like every state in the Union, California found itself in the throes of the Great Depression.

Jobless, their savings exhausted, their businesses bankrupt, and their farms foreclosed, Californians had rallied in 1933 to the banner of a most unlikely leader of a movement who came up with a plan that he called EPIC ("End Poverty in California"). His name was Upton Sinclair, and he was not a politician but a *muckraking* novelist.

Famous Faces

A writer and reformer, Upton Sinclair wrote critical studies of American life, including *The Jungle* (1906), *The Metropolis* (1908), *King Coal* (1917), *Oil!* (1927), and *Boston* (1929).

Talk of the Time

A **muckraker** is a writer or journalist who exposes real (and sometimes imagined) corruption by public officials and businessmen. The term was coined by Theodore Roosevelt in a 1906 speech that compared such journalists to the character with a muck rake in John Bunyan's *The Pilgrim's Progress*.

Talk of the Time

The biggest and richest studio in Hollywood, with the largest array of stars, **Metro-Goldwyn-Mayer,** or MGM, also owned the most movie houses (Loew's theaters). Its newsreel was called "Metrotone."

Production for Use

The Sinclair plan included a graduated income tax that would be used by the state to rent or buy idle factories and put them back to use, but in the hands of the unemployed. EPIC's motto was "Production for Use." The state would also buy up agricultural products that could be traded for goods produced in factories. It was a kind of state "co-operative" system intended to supplant the capitalist system.

Sinclair's ideas on how to end poverty in California were set out in a self-published tract titled *I, Governor of California, and How I Ended Poverty: A True Story of the Future*. It appeared in 1933, along with Sinclair's announcement that he was running for governor as a Democrat. (He'd been a registered Socialist.) To the dismay of "regular" Democrats, Sinclair got the nomination.

Calling Sinclair a Socialist in Democratic clothing, Republicans and many Democrats lined up against him. Among the opponents was Louis B. Mayer. The boss of the powerful movie studio *Metro-Goldwyn-Mayer* (see Part 5, "Better Tomorrows") and his head of production, Irving Thalberg, produced a series of fraudulent newsreels showing California being invaded by railroad-riding bums and other shiftless types. Sinclair lost the election.

Ham, Eggs, and a Bunch of Baloney

In the seven decades since the Great Depression, California has earned a reputation as the state where people have a knack for starting movements that at the time seem out of the mainstream, but eventually find acceptance everywhere. You'll recall that it was Dr. Francis Townsend of Long Beach, California, who thought up an old-age insurance plan before the Roosevelt administration devised Social Security.

While many Californians were embracing Upton Sinclair's EPIC, others joined a short-lived Utopian Society that thought the way out of the Depression was to educate its members in social and economic affairs. This notion that you can think your way into a utopia may have been the basis for the Wizard of Oz in the 1939 movie presenting the brainless Straw Man with a diploma making him a Doctor of Thinkology. (More on *The Wizard of Oz* in Part 5.)

In 1938 another project for economic recovery was called "Thirty Dollars Every Thursday." It promised to pay the elderly of the state $30 a week, to be financed by a 2-cent state sales tax. The plan was also called "Ham-and-Eggs." At a time when the most the federal government promised in Social Security was $20 a month, people soon saw "Thirty Dollars Every Thursday" for what it was: a bunch of baloney.

Arrival of the Okies

Although Sinclair's EPIC program never happened, the prediction of MGM's fake newsreels that California would find a flood of immigrants pouring into the state came true. Highways 30 and 66 and all the roads that led to California brought thousands of refugees from the Dust Bowl. They came from several states, but because so many of them hailed from Oklahoma, the general term to describe them was "Okies." The second-largest group, from Arkansas, got the name "Arkies."

The situation was described in the 1934 *WPA Guide to California* this way: "Over the spirits of the starving immigrants the desolation they had seen lay heavily—until they remembered they were going to California. That horizon was a bright one, for they were sure that in a State which supplies nearly half the Nation's fresh fruit and a third of its truck crops there would be a place for them among the pickers. What few of them had learned was that earlier immigrants—Japanese, Mexicans, Filipinos—had swarmed so thickly over the fertile acres that wages never rose above the standard accepted by coolie and peon labor."

Facts and Figures

In 1936, nearly 100,000 people arrived in California. In 1938, they were coming in at a rate of 10,000 a month.

But poor pay, if they could get it, was not the only hardship. The hopeful migrants discovered, as the *WPA Guide to California* noted, "that they would have to make their homes in districts like the one where in 1934 the National Labor Relations Board found 'filth, squalor, an entire absence of sanitation, and a crowding of human beings into totally inadequate tents or rude structures built of boards, weeds, and anything that was found at hand to give a pitiful semblance of a home at its worst.'"

Okies, Arkies, and others who were "California Dreamin'" long before The Beach Boys were born also found themselves caught in a nightmare of labor-union struggles, strikes, and violence.

Proposition One

The California of our time is known as a state in which voters routinely find themselves asked to approve (or not) a variety of "propositions" that appear on their ballots. Recent issues laid before the electorate have included limiting property taxes and ending "affirmative action" in state universities and colleges. In 1938 "Proposition One" was aimed at curbing labor unions by banning picketing and strikes for the purpose of getting workers, especially those on farms, to join unions.

Known as the "inland march" because unions targeted workers in the agricultural areas of central California, the movement was met with violent opposition in the form of anti-union vigilante raids on migrant-worker camps. They'd started in 1933 and 1934 in the Imperial Valley lettuce fields. Spreading elsewhere, the violence reached a peak in April 1938 when about 300 mine workers, along with their wives and children, were driven from their homes in Grass Valley and Nevada City, site of the second-largest gold mine in the country. Only with the intervention of police were the miners returned to their homes and the mines re-opened.

Talk of the Time

Originally called The Patrons of Husbandry, the **National Grange** was organized in 1874. Its goals were to promote farming, oppose monopolies, establish agricultural colleges, and urge laws to regulate produce shipping rates.

Led by the AFL and CIO (see Chapter 15, "Brown Shirts, Black Shirts, No Shirts"), maritime workers, tunnel miners, carpenters, railwaymen, newspapermen, clergy, and some movie stars organized a campaign to defeat Proposition One that proved successful. Had the proposition been approved, it would have resulted, in the words of the official publication of the California State *Grange*, in "taking away the constitutional rights of labor."

The City of Angels

Not all Okies and other migrants went to California's farmlands. More than 100,000 headed for Los Angeles. Known nationally as the city with the nation's best relief program, the City of Angels found its aid programs stretched to the breaking point. As the influx continued, the city's chief of police, James F. Davis, sent 125 policemen to the borders of Arizona and Oregon to turn away penniless migrants, with force if necessary. This effort was answered with a lawsuit against the city by the American Civil Liberties Union. It also prompted Woody Guthrie to write:

> Oh, if you ain't got the do-re-mi, folks,
> If you ain't got the do-re-mi,
> Why you better go back to beautiful Texas,
> Oklahoma, Kansas, Georgia, Tennessee.
> California is a garden of Eden,
> A paradise to live in or see,
> But believe it or not, you won't find it so hot,
> If you ain't got the do-re-mi.

Life in the Little Oklahomas

Migrants who looked for work in California's agricultural areas settled into camps that became known as "Little Oklahomas" and "Shacktowns." No better than the Hoovervilles, and usually a lot worse, they were filthy, overcrowded, fly-infested in summer, and battered by freezing rain and wind in winter. Health inspectors found them ridden with diphtheria, typhus, and other diseases.

One shocked relief worker who'd visited a Shacktown at Sacramento reported, "The outside appearance of most dwellings is repellent. Decay has rotted scrap construction material and the overflow piles of sodden junk help prepare the visitor for a sordid look within the household. Even in mid-day the interior is dark, but the noxious odors are strong of dampness, rot, stale atmosphere. Some shacks contain nothing but a bedroll."

An unidentified 80-year-old woman from Oklahoma, who is grandmother to 22 children, is photographed at a refuge camp set up for Dust Bowl migrants near Bakersfield, California, in 1937.

(AP Photo)

The Feds Step In

In late spring 1935, the federal government launched a program in California to improve conditions in the camps. It began in the towns of Marysville and Arvin with tents and cabins for as many as 230 families. The camps provided communal cooking sheds, bath and toilet facilities, nurseries, and laundry rooms. Managers of these camps were told to be in charge "at all times" and to "protect the camp population from abuses by contractors [who hired laborers], peddlers, and others." They were also told to "avoid paternalism and regimentation."

The program proved so successful that it was expanded and placed under the authority of the federal Resettlement Administration, then shifted in 1937 to the newly created Farm Security Administration. By 1941 there would be 13 such camps with 45,000 tenants residing in sturdy, clean, safe, and healthy houses.

Timeline

The Food, Drug and Cosmetic Act of 1938 required for the first time that product labels list ingredients.

Big Wind Back East

If you'd been living on the East Coast of the United States in September of 1938, you would have felt sympathy for the people of the Great Plains and the trouble that the drought had brought to them. But as you were thanking your lucky stars that you weren't in their shoes, you also would have gotten a taste of the tricks that Mother Nature can play. The difference between you and the Okies was that they suffered from a lack of water, while what you suddenly had to face was too much of it in the form of a hurricane.

Timeline

The worst hurricane in U.S. history hit Galveston, Texas, in 1900, killing 10,000 people.

Because there was no early warning system such as we have now, the hurricane struck areas that weren't prepared. Long Island, New York, got it the hardest on September 21. By the time it (hurricanes back then didn't have names) blew out to sea, the toll in deaths in seven states and the Canadian province of Quebec was 700. It was far and away worse than any storm experienced on the East Coast to that time.

A Voice for the Okies

In August 1936 the *San Francisco News* asked a California author by the name of John Steinbeck to write about the migrants. The writer had just published a novel about the labor strife in the agricultural areas titled *In Dubious Battle*. His weeklong series for the newspaper, "The Harvest Gypsies," was run in October. Born on February 27, 1902, in Carmel, California, Steinbeck attended Stanford University but did not earn a degree. Moving to New York City in 1925, he worked as a reporter and bricklayer, then went back to California in 1927. Two years later, he published his first novel, *Cup of Gold*.

But two books in quick succession made him famous, *Tortilla Flat* (1935) and *Of Mice and Men* (1937).

When he took on the *San Francisco News* assignment, he'd just finished writing the novel that would thrust the plight of the Okies under the noses of their countrymen, earn Steinbeck the 1940 Pulitzer Prize for Literature, and be made into a classic movie directed by John Ford and starring Henry Fonda. Titled *The Grapes of Wrath*, it told the story of the Joad family of Oklahoma. Evicted from their Dust Bowl farm, they packed all they had into a Hudson automobile and joined the Okies' trek on Route 66 to California. They were, Steinbeck wrote, "a people in flight, refugees from dust and shrinking land, from the thunder of tractors and shrinking ownership."

Meeting another Okie who had preceded them, Tom Joad and his brother Noah and their "Pa" are told, "Okie use'ta mean you was from Oklahoma. Now it means you're a dirty son of a bitch. Okie means you're scum."

When Eleanor Roosevelt read the book, she wrote in her syndicated newspaper column that it was "an unforgettable experience that both repels and attracts you." The horrors presented, she said, "made you dread sometimes to begin the next chapter, and yet you cannot lay the book down or even skip a page."

Facts and Figures

By the end of 1939, 430,000 copies of *The Grapes of Wrath* had been sold. One of the largest sellers of the 1930s, the book has never been out of print.

When Woody Guthrie saw the movie version of the novel, he wrote in his column in the leftist publication *People's World* that it was the "best cussed pitcher" he'd ever seen. He noted that the story was "about us pullin' out of Oklahoma and Arkansas, and a driftin' around over the state of California, busted, disgusted, down and out, and a lookin' for work."

The message, he said, was that "you got to get together and have some meetins, and stick together, and raise old billy hell till you get your job, and get back your farm, and your house and your chickens and your groceries and your clothes, and your money back."

Worried that "the people back in Oklahoma haven't got two bucks to buy the book, or even thirty cents to see the movie," he wrote a song named after the book's central character, Tom Joad. Together, Steinbeck's novel and Guthrie's songs gave generations yet to be born a vivid portrait of one aspect of the struggles of the Great Depression.

The Belly vs. the Book

Looking back to the Depression years, John Steinbeck wrote, "When people are broke, the first things they give up are books." What he meant was that in the 1930s they gave up buying books at the pace with which they'd done so in the previous decade. Book sales dropped from about $42 million in 1929 to about half that amount in 1933. In a choice between buying food for a family or a book, the belly will always win over nourishment of the mind.

But people didn't quit reading. They found books in the public libraries (lending of books rose nearly 40 percent), and in a new way of borrowing called a "private circulating library." One could rent a book from a bookstore for three cents a day.

Faced with the decline in book buyers, publishers reacted in two ways. They brought out fewer books and cut back on royalties paid to authors. Of the hard times he knew while living in Pacific Grove, California, before finding success as an author, Steinbeck recalled, "Being without a job, I went on writing—books, essays, short stories. Regularly they went out and just as regularly came back, because publishers were hit hardest of all."

Except for the most famous authors whose name on a book cover was a guarantee for a best-seller, the typical author of a book that sold modestly in the 1930s, but was a loss or a break-even for the publisher, could earn about $2,500 a year. Unable to carry such writers, publishers adopted a survival policy of "fewer books but better ones."

A Wealth of Writers

Despite the hard times that plagued the literary world, the 1930s produced a wealth of new writers. In addition to Fitzgerald, Dos Passos, Lewis, and Hemingway, out of the Great Depression came a generation of authors whose books withstood the test of time and preserved for today's readers a picture of America in the 1930s.

Making their literary marks were William Faulkner, Thomas Wolfe, James T. Farrell, Erskine Caldwell, William Saroyan, Katherine Anne Porter, John Marquand, Richard Wright, Marjorie Kinnan Rawlings, Jerome Weidman, and John O'Hara.

Extra! Extra! Read All About It!

Also hit hard were magazines and newspapers, but not for any lack of readers. A newspaper boy standing on a city street corner and yelling, "Extra! Extra! Read all about it!" still parted passersby from three cents, and the daily *Bugle* was still being left on doorsteps. The papers' problem was a decline in advertising. In the first four years of the Depression, the amount of magazine ad space dropped more than 30 percent. Newspapers reduced the number of editions by half, resulting in the closing or mergers of some newspapers and a decline in the number of weekly papers by the end of the decade of more than 2,000. Fewer than 125 cities had more than one newspaper.

Fewer papers meant fewer jobs for reporters and editors. Drastic economies imposed by the Great Depression had thrown so many of these "ink-stained wretches" out on the street, notes historian Frederick Lewis Allen, that what had once been hopefully spoken of as the "profession of journalism" had become one of the most crowded and ill-paid of all white-collar occupations.

To help fill a paper's pages, owners turned to greater usage of material from news syndicates. Among the most popular features were columnists Walter Winchell and O. O. McIntyre (covering New York and Broadway); Louella Parsons, Hedda Hopper, and Jimmy Fiddler (Hollywood), Dorothy Dix (affairs of the heart), and in the fields of political analysis and commentary: Walter Lippmann, David Lawrence, Dorothy Thompson, Westbrook Pegler, Drew Pearson, Frank Kent, and Robert S. Allen.

Sunday Morning Giggles

A staple of American lives on Sunday mornings was the part of the Sunday newspaper known as "the funnies." Daily and weekly since the 1880s, the "comic strip" could be counted on by everyone in the family to provide not only laughs, but, beginning in the 1930s, also a taste of adventure from a hatchet-jawed police detective named Dick Tracy, the swashbuckling of *Terry and the Pirates*, stories of two-fisted *Steve Canyon*, historical action with *Prince Valiant*, the future in the form of *Flash Gordon*, and thrills in the jungle with *Tarzan*.

Timeline

On June 22, 1938, in a heavyweight championship boxing match at New York's Madison Square Garden, Joe Louis KO'd Germany's Max Schmeling.

Slices of very different kinds of domestic life in the funnies were available in strips offering *Blondie* and her sandwich-making hubbie, Dagwood Bumstead; and the hillbilly humor of a place called "Dogpatch" in *L'il Abner*. The funnies also gave sports fans a choice in a strip about boxer *Joe Palooka*.

Something to Kill Time With

Among the many effects of the Great Depression on average Americans who found themselves out of work and surviving on "relief" was having a lot of time on their hands. To "kill" it, millions of people got caught up in "crazes." Some took part in "marathon dances" in hopes of staying on their feet long enough to win a little prize money. Colleges were the scenes of nutty stunts such as goldfish-swallowing. And huge numbers of people took up bowling and golfing (on courses built by the government).

In a broke nation that still somehow managed to hold on to its automobiles, people went for "rides" and ventured on longer excursions to "camp" or park a "trailer" (a new idea) in a woodsy area. By the middle of the 1930s some 30 million Americans were zipping around the country to pay a visit to relatives or just "take in the sights."

The Least You Need to Know

- ◆ A major challenge to the New Deal was keeping farmers at work and supporting the price of their crops.
- ◆ Author-turned-politician Upton Sinclair proposed a plan for economic recovery that he called "Production for Use," but it wasn't good enough to elect him governor of California.
- ◆ The migration of millions of desperate people resulted in a "depopulation" of some regions of the country and a huge influx of settlers in California, known as "Okies."
- ◆ John Steinbeck wrote a classic novel, *The Grapes of Wrath*, about the plight of a family of "Okies."

Chapter 11

Black, White, and Blues

In This Chapter

- ◆ The federal government conducts a census of the unemployed
- ◆ Efforts to provide assistance to Negroes
- ◆ The Scottsboro Boys and lynchings
- ◆ Segregated America embraces black music and entertainers

As the Great Depression took hold and worsened the already poor economic and social conditions of blacks, many joined a migration from the rural South to cities of the North. While efforts were made to assist them through federal aid programs, a large segment of the population turned to their own leaders, such as W.E.B. DuBois, Father Divine, and A. Phillip Randolph, as well as the Urban League, National Negro Congress, and National Association for the Advancement of Colored People. Despite racial segregation and second-class citizenship for "the Negro," whites accepted blacks as entertainers and musicians who popularized jazz and "the blues."

Facts We Do Not Now Possess

It's hard to believe in our day in which the federal government issues a monthly count of the unemployed that in November 1937 it did not have a precise tally of Americans who were out of work. As a result of this, FDR

Facts and Figures

In the mail, people got a double postcard. The part they sent back contained 14 questions about their age, job history, wages, and other facts of their lives. There was also a message from FDR calling upon "the unemployed and everyone else in this land to help make this census complete, honest, and accurate."

went on the air with another fireside chat, this one to announce an "unemployment census." Explaining that in order to have "a better long-range program of re-employment" the government needed "facts which we do not now possess." He said that "every abode in the United States" would be receiving "an Unemployment Report Card."

"There is neither logic nor necessity," Roosevelt said in the fireside chat, "for one third of our population to have less of the needs of modern life that make for decent living. Our national purchasing power is the soil from which comes all our prosperity. The steady flow of wages to millions of workers is essential if the products of our industry and of our farmers are to be consumed."

We know now that as FDR spoke, there were roughly 11.3 million, or nearly 22 percent, of the working population still without jobs. When he went on the air about the unemployment census, the help promised to the jobless and elderly through Social Security was only a trickle. At the end of 1937, 32.9 million were signed up. This aid amounted to a small part in recovery programs and would remain so for the rest of the 1930s.

Year	Recipients	Total Paid
1937	53,236	$1,278,000
1938	213,670	$10,478,000
1939	174,839	$13,896,000
1940	222,000	$35,000,000

The Other Migration

You've read that the Midwest drought, Dust Bowl conditions, and farm foreclosures drove scores of thousands of white tenants off their land to create a huge westward migration. As the Okies took to the highways, there was a second massive shift of agricultural workers from the South to the cities of the North. This flow was caused by the overall effects of Depression and by mechanization. The victims were black men and women who'd been employed as field hands on plantations. Some had been sharecroppers.

As thousands of blacks had flocked to northern cities looking for work during World War I, those who found themselves jobless in a segregated South headed there throughout the 1930s. Of all the northern cities, New York was known as the place with easy and generous relief programs, thanks mainly to the liberal policies of its mayor, Fiorello H. La Guardia (see Chapter 12, "A Little Flower Blooms"). As a result, between 1930 and 1940, more than 145,000 blacks settled in the city's five boroughs. Most of them went to Harlem, raising its population to half a million.

FDR's "Black Cabinet"

Students of American presidential elections agree that in 1936 there was a massive shift of black voters from the Republican Party (the "party of Lincoln") to the Democratic. They went for FDR because of New Deal programs, not because they saw Roosevelt as particularly sensitive to their race. FDR biographer Nathan Miller noted that the only blacks Roosevelt knew were servants and that "he easily accommodated himself to the segregationist ways of the south." He was "a gradualist on the race issue" who believed that the New Deal was the answer to problems of blacks, just as it was seen as a panacea for whites.

While Roosevelt appointed more than 40 black men and women to administrative positions, it was his wife, Eleanor, who became the champion of blacks. She was aided in this by a group of advisors who formed the Federal Council on Negro Affairs. Unofficially, they were known as Roosevelt's "Black Cabinet."

The "Mother Superior"

A leader of the Black Cabinet was Mary McLeod Bethune. A black friend of Mrs. Roosevelt, she was appointed in 1936 to head a new Division of Black Affairs within the previously created National Youth Administration. The position made her the highest-ranking black in FDR's administration. The others of her race who were in the government took to calling her "Mother Superior."

A famous story about her involved her arriving at the White House one day and being challenged by a black gardener. "Hey, there, Auntie," he exclaimed, "where do you think you're going?" A very large woman, Bethune gave him a withering look, seized on being addressed as "Auntie," and retorted, "I didn't recognize you. Which of my sister's children are you?" The gardener beat a hasty retreat.

During her tenure as head of the Division of Black Affairs, the agency was able to employ 300,000 black men and women, which was about 12 percent of the blacks who'd sought assistance. In 1937 she told a meeting of the Kentucky Negro Educational Association, "Above all, the NYS has dispelled the thick and oppressive clouds of despair under which Negro youth has long struggled until they now see through the rift the blue sky of hope and promise."

The Scottsboro Boys

No group of young black men embodied the prejudice of whites in the 1930s more than nine wanderers known as the Scottsboro Boys. On March 24, 1931, they were accused by two white girls of raping them on a freight train en route to Alabama from Chattanooga, Tennessee. Dragged from the train at Scottsboro, Alabama, the youths (aged 13 to 20) were jailed, indicted, and put on trial. All but one were convicted and sentenced to death.

While the verdict was on appeal on the claim that the boys hadn't gotten a fair trial, one of the girls retracted the charge of rape. But the boys remained in jail. Their plight became a movement to free them. It failed to do so. When the last of them was exonerated and freed decades later, it was the end of one of the most shameful cases of racial injustice in the history of the United States.

At the End of the Rope

As outrageous as the Scottsboro Boys episode was, they were lucky that they hadn't met the fate of other black men in the South who found themselves lynched. In 1930 a commission on interracial cooperation had authorized a study of lynchings in the South. Its 1933 report, *The Tragedy of Lynching*, warned "until America can discover and apply means to end these relapses to the law of the jungle, we have no assurance that ordered society will not at any moment be overthrown by the blind passion of an ever-present mob."

Another study of lynchings, published in 1944, found that in the hangings that occurred in 1929, one third of the victims had been falsely accused. Among atrocities committed by "tens of thousands of lynchers and onlookers" before their victims were strung up, were cutting off fingers and toes, pulling teeth and nails, disemboweling, and being dragged behind cars. Often the body of such a victim was set afire or used for pistol and rifle practice. How effective was the 1933 report in stopping the practice? The year after it came out, 28 black men were lynched.

Facts and Figures

Since keeping of statistics began in 1892, there'd been 3,745 lynchings, almost all of them in the South. Classified by race: blacks, 2,954; whites, 791. Most in one year: 255, in 1892. Reasons for lynchings were murder, 1,406; rape of white women (or attempted), 878; "insult to whites," 67.

"Supper Time"

The problem of lynchings of black men in the South found a most unlikely airing in one of the Broadway musicals of 1933. With songs by Irving Berlin, and the script by Moss Hart, *As Thousands Cheer* introduced one of Berlin's all-time hits, "Easter Parade." But it was in a star turn by the black singer Ethel Waters that the white audience was confronted with the tragedy of lynching.

The song was "Supper Time." It was a widow's lament for a husband who'd been lynched. Having fled from the South and settled in New York, she also sang of her loneliness in "Harlem on My Mind." The show was a triumph, running a year and making a profit, which was, as Broadway historian Gerald Bordman noted, "a rarity during Depression days."

"An American Folk Opera"

Two years after *As Thousands Cheer*, theatergoers met an entire cast of Negro performers in *An American Folk Opera*, with music by George Gershwin. The show was *Porgy and Bess*. A collaboration with black writer DeBose Hayward was carried on through the mail, with Hayward at his home in South Carolina and Gershwin in New York. Based on Hayward's novel *Porgy*, it was set in a black area of Charleston called *Catfish Row*.

The show gave America songs by Gershwin that became classics: "Summertime," "A Woman Is a Sometime Thing," "Bess, You Is My Woman Now," "It Ain't Necessarily So," and a pair of numbers that caught the essence of blacks living in the South in the years of the Great Depression: "I Got Plenty of Nothin'" and "There's a Boat Dat's Leavin' Soon for New York."

Other Gershwin hits include:

> "The Man I Love"
>
> "A Foggy Day"
>
> "Oh, Lady Be Good"
>
> "'S Wonderful"
>
> "Fascinating Rhythm"
>
> "Embraceable You"
>
> "I've Got a Crush on You"
>
> "They Can't Take That Away from Me"
>
> "Nice Work If You Can Get It"
>
> "Love Is Here to Stay"
>
> "Let's Call the Whole Thing Off"
>
> "Someone to Watch Over Me"

> **Famous Faces**
>
> Born Jacob Gershvin in Brooklyn on September 26, 1898, George Gershwin and his lyricist-brother Ira wrote 500 songs, many of them among the most popular tunes of the 1920s and 1930s. A musical genius who wrote for movies starring Fred Astaire and Ginger Rogers, George also composed a symphonic jazz piece titled "Rhapsody in Blue" (1927) and "American in Paris" (1928). Two years after "Porgy and Bess," he died in Hollywood, California, on July 11, 1937.

Green Pastures in Heaven and on Earth

In the year that the stock market crashed, Broadway theatergoers had gotten a first taste of an all-black show in a play titled *The Green Pastures*, written by a white man, Marc Connolly. He was one of the 1920's famed group of literary wits who lunched every day at a large round table in the Algonquin Hotel and publicized themselves in their newspaper and magazines articles. A fable of Heaven in which everyone is black, *The Green Pastures* portrayed God ("De Lawd") as the kind of earthly black preacher who was familiar to American blacks both in the South and the North, if not to the white audiences who made the comedy a hit.

While whites generally did not flock to churches seeking comfort during the Great Depression, as was noted earlier, the 1930s saw an increase of interest in religion among blacks. Some of this was attributable to the fact that their churches were often the only places where blacks could get food, clothing, and other aid. The ministers of these churches, many of which were storefronts, found themselves not only operators of soup kitchens but also leaders in a fight against white racism. One of their tactics was to lead boycotts of white businesses in black areas that didn't employ whites. A "Don't Buy Where You Don't Work" movement sprang up in all the major cities.

Father Divine

One of these emerging black leaders was a charismatic figure who was born George Baker Jr. in Rockville, Maryland, in 1897. By the mid-1930s, he was the "Reverend Major Jealous Divine," head of the "Peace Mission" movement. While feeding the hungry who came to his mission, he preached an end to racism, peace on earth, and food for all. Fervent followers, both black and white, exclaimed, "God is here on earth and Father Divine is his name."

If you had gone into his Peace Mission's "banquet hall" in Harlem, you were likely to have heard him exhorting everyone with, "Sisters and Brothers, I want you to eat and eat and eat, and dine and dine and dine. And when you have eaten and eaten and eaten, and dined and dined and dined, I want you to get up and give your places to others that they might eat and eat and eat, and dine and dine and dine. Peace! It's truly wonderful."

The Happy News Preacher

Almost as well known as Father Divine was Elder Lightfoot Solomon Michaux. A minister of the Church of God in Washington, D.C., he offered a daily morning radio program to preach "the happy news" of the gospel of Jesus Christ. When wealthy health-enthusiast and magazine publisher Bernard McFadden gave him money for a lunchroom, Michaux named it the "Happy News Café." Hundreds of hungry people ate there every day. He also acquired a large, rent-free building that housed 40 homeless families.

The Transformation of Elijah Poole

No black leader to appear in the 1930s would have a more lasting influence than Elijah Poole. Converted to Islam in Detroit, he took the name Elijah Muhammad and founded the Nation of Islam, also known as the Black Muslims. With patience and zeal over a period of 30 years, he gathered a following that would not become widely known outside the black population of America until the 1960s when everyone who had access to a TV set got to know another convert to Islam. The former Malcolm Little, he chose the name Malcolm X because he considered "Little" to be a "slave name."

Two Warring Ideals in One Dark Body

While religious men such as Father Divine and the Rev. Michaud saw the possibility that blacks could find the rewards of Heaven in America, another voice proclaimed that the answer would be in a "self-separation" of blacks from whites in which blacks would develop a separate "group economy." Born on February 23, 1868, in Great Barrington, Massachusetts, a town of 5,000 people and less than 50 blacks, W.E.B. (William Edward Burghart) DuBois, was a graduate of Fisk and Harvard and had studied at the University of Berlin. A Marxist and the author of several books on blacks and racism in America, he had played a major role in the formation in 1909 of the NAACP.

Summing up the frustration of being black in a white country, he'd said in 1897, "One never feels his two-ness—an American, a Negro, two souls, two thoughts, two unreconciled strivings, two warring ideals in one dark body." Originally a believer that social science and education would bridge America's racial divide, he came to the conclusion that only protest and agitation would force white America to put an end to lynchings, black disenfranchisement, and the segregation imposed by Jim Crow laws. But his ideas on Pan-Africanism and black cultural nationalism, and criticism of the NAACP for ignoring the problems of the black masses, led to his resignation from the NAACP in 1934.

Since Booker T. Washington (1856–1915) and until the emergence of Dr. Martin Luther King Jr. in the 1950s, no black leader had more influence on his people. He eventually left the United States to take citizenship in Ghana. Ironically, he died there on the eve of Dr. King's August 27, 1963, civil rights march on Washington.

A Few Words from Senator Bilbo

With so much outrage and attention centered on lynching, a bill to make it a federal crime was introduced in Congress in January 1934. Co-sponsored in the Senate by Edward P. Costigan and Robert Wagner, it provoked furious opposition from southern Senators, and especially from Theodore Bilbo of Mississippi. Taking to the Senate floor one day, Bilbo observed that race consciousness was "developing in all parts of the world." He declared, "The Germans [in their insistence on Aryan purity] appreciate the importance of race values."

Therefore, he said, "It is beginning to be recognized by the thoughtful minds of our age that the conservation of racial values is the only hope for future civilization." Because of filibustering by southern Senators, the anti-lynching bill lost. When a second try at passage failed, it was withdrawn.

Negroes and the New Deal

Recognizing that the sudden loss of jobs after the stock market crash of 1929 would be felt especially hard by Negro workers, one of the early black civil rights organizations, the National Urban League, launched a "jobs for Negroes" drive. But it was not until FDR's New Deal created the NRA and its public works projects that blacks were promised substantial relief.

Timeline _____

The National Urban League was founded in 1910 as the Committee on Urban Conditions Among Negroes. The name was changed in 1920. The National Association for the Advancement of Colored People (NAACP) was founded in 1910. Its goals were prevention of violence against blacks, providing a legal defense system for blacks, and overturning "separate but equal" segregation laws. Its magazine, *Crisis*, was edited for many years by W.E.B. DuBois.

Blacks who were disappointed with the results of the NRA soon complained that the initials NRA really meant "Negro Run Around," and "Negroes Rarely Allowed." While blacks were griping that they'd been left out of the New Deal, many whites believed that FDR's administration showed too much sympathy for Negroes, primarily because of the influence of Mrs. Roosevelt.

The following is an anonymous imaginary conversation between FDR and Eleanor. Just as she was hated by white bigots because of her friendships with blacks, FDR was hated for having Jews in his administration. FDR says to Eleanor:

> You kiss the niggers,
> I'll kiss the Jews,
> We'll stay in the White House
> As long as we choose.

The Negroes Everybody Liked

In 1934 Mrs. Roosevelt declared in a speech to a conference on black education, "The day of working together has come, and we must learn to work together, all of us, regardless of race or creed or color."

She was asking a lot. As she spoke, there was almost no contact between whites and blacks, except when blacks worked for whites. While segregation was official in the South, in most places in the North it was an unwritten law. When the majority of whites spoke of the Negro, he was a "nigger," "Sambo," and "coon," and among the polite, "colored" and "darky." Popular novelist Fannie Hurst called this interracial contact an "osmosis" in which whites knew blacks as maids, cooks, janitors, elevator operators, "red cap" railroad porters, shoeshine boys, entertainers, and the world heavyweight boxing champ.

The Brown Bomber

Born Joseph Louis Barrow in Chambers County, Alabama, on May 13, 1914, he began boxing in Detroit in 1930 while working at the Ford auto plant in River Rouge. After winning the National AAU light-heavyweight title in 1934, he turned pro. He was given the nickname "Brown Bomber of Detroit."

As much as for a powerful punch, he was admired by all Americans in the years of the Depression for his personal style, grace, sportsmanship, and soft-spoken, gentlemanly demeanor. For blacks, he was a figure of heroic and mythic proportions.

 Famous Faces

In 26 bouts from 1937 to 1949 Joe Louis lost only once, to Max Schmeling in 1936. But he got his revenge in a 1938 rematch by knocking out Schmeling in round one.

The Emperor Robeson

As Joe Louis in the world of sports was the pride of blacks, one of the greatest figures of the theater was the son of a runaway slave. A graduate of Rutgers University, where he'd twice been an All-American football player (1917 and 1918), and with a degree in law from Columbia, Paul Robeson had taken up acting. For his work in Eugene O'Neill's *Emperor Jones* (1923) and in *All God's Chillun Got Wings* (1924) he was hailed as one of the world's greatest actors. With a rich bass voice, he also earned a reputation as a superb interpreter of Negro spirituals. But real stardom came because of his performance of "Old Man River" in the movie *Show Boat*.

The best-known black man in America and praised as a "symbol of Negro achievement," he used his status to fight for black rights. Frustrated by the lack of change, he made frequent trips to the Soviet Union. Like many who became enamored of the USSR in the 1930s (see Part 5, "Better Tomorrows"), he would be called to account for his "pro-Red" activities in the 1950s.

Amos 'n' Andy

By far the most famous black people in the United States in the 1930s were on the radio. But they weren't black. The roles of Amos Jones and Andrew H. Brown on the most popular show of the decade were played by Freeman Gosden and Charles Correl. On the program they portrayed fictional residents of Harlem, speaking with "Negro" accents.

Millions of Americans, blacks and whites, tuned in to laugh at the antics of Amos, Andy, "Kingfish" of the "Mystic Nights of the Sea Lodge," a saucy woman named Sapphire, Madame Queen, Ruby (Amos's wife), Miss Genevieve Blue (secretary of the Fresh Air Taxi Co.), Shorty the barber, crooked-lawyer Stonewall, and Arabella (Amos's daughter).

Amos 'n' Andy had a listenership estimated at 40 million, about one third of the population. Many movie theater operators stopped showing films when it was on the air and turned on a radio so audiences could listen to it. In retrospect, the program has been denounced as racist, but the people who tuned it in at the time, including blacks, found it just plain funny.

Satchmo and All That Jazz

When the prosperity bubble burst in 1929, the crash brought an end to "the Jazz Age." Americans who were worried and depressed (in more ways than one) in the early 1930s were more interested in easy-going music. But jazz persisted, though interest in it was mainly among blacks. The best known of the jazz musicians was Louis Armstrong, nicknamed Satchelmouth, which was shortened to Satchmo. With his cornet and gravelly voice, he'd almost single-handedly introduced jazz to white America. He also became the performer by which all jazz musicians measured themselves and were measured by audiences.

Among the jazz musicians and jazz singers in the 1930s were Duke Ellington, Art Tatum, Jelly Roll Morton, Sidney Bechet, Fats Waller, Willie "The Lion" Smith, King Oliver, "Leadbelly" Ledbetter, Billie Holiday, Maxine Sullivan, Hot Lips Page, Coleman Hawkins, "Stuff" Smith, Erroll Garner, and Wingie Manone. A hotbed of jazz in the 1930s was the block of West 52nd Street in New York City between Fifth and Sixth avenues. It consisted of former speakeasies named Famous Door, Onyx Club, Jimmy Ryan's, Tony's, Three Deuces, Reilly's Tavern, and Hickory House.

The story of jazz in the years of the Great Depression is so rich and complex that it's too vast to be contained in this book, so if you're interested in knowing more, you will have to look it up elsewhere. Along with jazz came "the blues." It was defined by recording company executive Ahmet Ertegun as both sad and happy music with "the beauty of the black people expressed in it," because "it's got a soul that came from suffering." By the late 1930s, the jazz of the Roaring Twenties was taking a new form called "swing," played by "big bands." It and they will be discussed in Part 5.

The Singer and the Lincoln Memorial

One of the most celebrated black entertainers in the 1930s was an operatic contralto by the name of Marian Anderson. In March 1939 the Roosevelt administration wanted her to give a concert in the capital. The ideal place for the performance was Washington's largest auditorium, Constitution Hall.

But it belonged to the Daughters of the American Revolution (DAR), and the ladies refused to let it be used by a black person. An outraged member of the DAR, Eleanor Roosevelt, resigned, then arranged for Miss Anderson to perform on the steps of the Lincoln Memorial. A racially integrated crowd of more than 70,000 came to hear her on Easter Sunday.

The Harlem Renaissance

As you've read, mechanization in farming in the South caused a vast migration of blacks into most large northern cities. The greatest influx took place in New York City's uptown neighborhood called Harlem. Because New York is a port city, it also attracted people from the West Indies and Africa. The result by the 1930s was that Harlem was the recognized black "capital" of the nation, and a mixture of other "nonwhite" groups.

"Here in Manhattan is not merely the largest Negro community in the world," noted the black writer and educator Alain Locke, "but the first concentration in history of so many diverse elements of Negro life. In Harlem, Negro life is seizing upon its first chances for group expression and self-determination."

This flowering of intellectual dialogue, literary, and artistic creation, along with jazz, blues, dance, black theater, poetry, and literature, got the name "Harlem Renaissance."

Picking up on W.E.B. DuBois's description of the black American's sense of "two-ness, two souls, two thoughts, two unreconciled stirrings," the themes of the work of black writers and artists were alienation and marginality. No Harlem Renaissance writer was as effective at expressing black feelings than a young poet who had been born in Joplin, Missouri, but grew up in Ohio.

Harlem's Poet

When Langston Hughes arrived in New York to study engineering at Columbia University, the neighboring Harlem in which he found a home was an elegant and exciting place with wide boulevards and fine townhouses. Quickly enthralled by the intellectuality and cultural vibrancy, he abandoned all thoughts of an engineering career, dropped out of school, and began writing poetry.

Unable to make a living, he joined the crew of a ship sailing for Africa, then wandered through Italy, Holland, Spain, and France. Back in New York in 1926, he published his first book of poems, *The Weary Blues*, about Harlem life. "I knew only the people I had grown up with," he recalled, "and they weren't people whose shoes were always shined, who had been to Harvard, or who had heard Bach."

By the time of the Scottsboro Boys, he was one of the leading, if not *the* leading, black literary voice. His contribution to the controversy and the cause of "the boys" was *Scottsboro Limited: Four Poems and a Play in Verse*, 1932.

Langston Hughes's Significant Works

Opera and Drama:

The Negro Mother and Other Dramatic Recitations, 1931

Mule Bone (with Zora Neale Hurston), 1932

Mulatto, 1935

Little Ham, 1936

When the Jack Hollers, 1936

Don't You Want to Be Free?, 1937

Soul Gone Home, 1937

Emperor of Haiti, 1938

Front Porch, 1939

Langston Hughes's Significant Works

Nonfiction:

The Ways of White Folks, 1934

Proletarian Literature in the United States, 1935

A New Song, 1938

Poetry:

Scottsboro Limited: Four Poems and a Play in Verse, 1932

Ultimately, the Harlem Renaissance fell victim to the Depression, and with an unemployment rate that was far worse than among the white population, there came a widening of the economic, social, and political gap between the races. Hughes noted, "The Depression brought everybody down a peg or two. And the Negro had but few pegs to fall."

Big Trouble Uptown

On March 19, 1935, a 16-year-old Puerto Rican boy helped himself to a penknife in Kress five-and-dime store on West 125th Street in the heart of Harlem. Two store guards grabbed him for shoplifting. A cop was called. The boy was taken to the rear of the store, questioned, then let go through the back door. A woman who observed the boy being led into the back room cried, "They're taking him to the basement to beat him up."

A rumor quickly spread that a white cop had killed a black man. A crowd that had gathered went wild, invading the store and looting it. As more police arrived, a riot broke out. Fanning the flames were members of a militant black group, the Young Liberators, and the Young Communist League.

By nightfall the disorder was widespread. Before order was restored and the story was refuted, three people were dead, 125 men arrested, and more than 100 people injured. More than 250 stores and shops that were "white-owned" had been looted.

When order was at last restored, the Harlem of the "renaissance" that Langston Hughes and other black intellectuals had expected to continue to flower was viewed by whites as a dangerous place. And so began a decline in Harlem's fortunes that would continue for the remainder of the century.

The Least You Need to Know

♦ In November 1937 the unemployment rate was 22 percent, with more than 11 million Americans unable to find jobs.

◆ Technological innovations such as the tractor and mechanical cotton picker displaced black farm workers in the South, creating a huge migration of blacks to northern cities.

◆ The Scottsboro Boys case, lynchings of blacks in the South, and general white prejudice were used by some black leaders, such as W.E.B. DuBois, to urge black separatism.

◆ Black voters shifted allegiance from the Republican Party to the Democrats.

12

A Little Flower Blooms

In This Chapter

- ◆ An ape climbs the world's tallest empty building
- ◆ The Depression leaves New York City facing bankruptcy
- ◆ Mayor Fiorello La Guardia makes good use of the New Deal
- ◆ The nation's first public housing projects
- ◆ The rise of tenant activism

When a giant ape climbed to the top of New York City's newest skyscraper in the 1933 movie *King Kong*, the nearly empty Empire State Building was a symbol of the desperate shape of the U.S. economy. Being the city with the largest population, New York had the biggest problems in coping with the Great Depression.

Disgusted with the corrupt government of Mayor James J. Walker, and with the city facing bankruptcy, voters rebelled and elected a reformer. A congressman who'd backed all of FDR's programs in the first 100 days, Fiorello H. La Guardia, as mayor, and with FDR in the White House, made the city a New Deal proving ground.

Big Gorilla and Little Flower

In 1933, the fourth year of the Depression, people all across the country watched with fascination as two amusing figures took the city of New York by storm. One was the product of the imagination of Hollywood moviemakers in the form of a huge gorilla named Kong. The other was a diminutive politician with a squeaky voice and funny first name. He was Fiorello La Guardia. In English, his given name meant "little flower."

Timeline

King Kong premiered at both Radio City Music Hall and the Roxy Theater on March 3, 1933, the day before FDR became president. *New York Times* critic Mordaunt Hall liked it. He wrote that it was "a fantastic film" that was "worked out in a decidedly compelling fashion."

The dramatic ending of the movie, *King Kong*, in the view of film critic Leonard Maltin in his 1990s guide to movies, became a bit of "cinematic folklore." In the unlikely event you've not seen the film, its last scenes have Kong (smitten with love for Fay Wray), holding on to the spire of the Empire State Building as he swats at a swarm of attacking planes with machine guns blazing away. After Kong plummets 102 stories to his death, the moviemaker (Carl Denham), who had brought Kong from Africa, declares that the planes didn't finished the big ape. "It was beauty," he says, "that killed the beast."

White Elephant on 34th Street

When Hollywood chose to set *King Kong's* ending at the Empire State Building, the skyscraper was the tallest and most famous manmade structure in the world. Because of the effects of the Depression, it was almost vacant. Rising 1,250 feet above 34th Street at the corner of Fifth Avenue in the center of Manhattan, it was a beautiful but forlorn symbol (people called it the Empty State Building) of a bankrupt city in a nation gone broke.

As construction started on the Empire State Building, it had been a godsend to men in the construction trade. If it hadn't been for the project, thousands of them wouldn't have had jobs. But rather than taking their time in erecting it, they built it in record fashion. Demolition of the old Waldorf-Astoria Hotel had begun on October 1, 1929. The ribbon-cutting by Al Smith to formally open the Empire State took place on May 1, 1933. On average, they built four and a half floors per week.

The money that kept the Empire State open didn't come from rent paid by a handful of tenants. It was forked over by tourists who flocked to its eighty-sixth floor observation deck. The building did not start making money as a piece of real estate until the 1950s.

Another White Elephant on Sixth Avenue

Five months before the Empire State was completed, one of the theaters that premiered *King Kong* had opened for business at the corner of Sixth Avenue and 50th Street. It was named "Radio City Music Hall" because it was across the street from NBC's studios, known as Radio City. But the immense showplace (6,200 seats, the largest theater in the world) wasn't built to show movies.

It was to have been a vaudeville house. Unfortunately, that type of variety show was dying out, due in large measure to movies and radio. Consequently, Radio City Music Hall's owners were forced to put on their live shows, always featuring a line of dancing girls known as "the Rockettes," between movies.

(Read more about the Radio City Music Hall as an example of the 1930s "Art Deco" style architecture in Part 5, "Better Tomorrows.")

Timeline

With a Radio City Music Hall ticket, a person got at least two hours of entertainment consisting of the stage show and always a "first run" movie. There were four shows presented per day, starting at 11:30 A.M. Depending where one sat, tickets ranged from 40 cents to $1.65.

Fiorello Gets a New Job

The day that *King Kong* started scaring movie audiences was the last day in Congress for Representative Fiorello H. La Guardia of New York City's 20th District. Because he was a Republican, he'd been defeated in November 1932 in the Democratic landslide that sent FDR to the White House. But he wasn't out of a job for long. In November of 1933 he was elected mayor.

In the final months of his congressional term, he'd been an ardent supporter of all that Roosevelt asked for in the first 100 days. As mayor of New York, he would use those programs to turn the city into a New Deal proving ground. In doing so, he'd earn a reputation as the most dynamic, colorful, effective, and beloved mayor in the city's history.

Born in New York City in 1882, La Guardia grew up in Prescott, Arizona, where his Italian-immigrant father was bandmaster of the U.S. Army's 14th Infantry Regiment. First elected to Congress in 1914, Fiorello took a leave of absence to serve as an army aviator during World War I. After the war he left Congress to become president of the city's board of aldermen, then went

Timeline

Fiorello La Guardia served three terms as mayor of New York, spanning January 1, 1934, to December 31, 1945. If he'd chosen to run again, he certainly would have been re-elected. He died of pancreatic cancer two years after leaving City Hall.

back to Congress from a different district (the 20th). In 1929, he made a bid for mayor, but lost to James J. Walker.

When Walker was forced to resign (by Governor Franklin Roosevelt) because of corruption in his administration, La Guardia won the office in 1933 by promising scandal-weary New Yorkers an honest government. But as he took office, he found that as a result of mismanagement by Walker and effects of the Depression, the city was on the brink of bankruptcy.

The Worm That Walks Like a Man

Eleven months after the stock market crashed, one of New York's most celebrated journalists, Gene Fowler (he would write a best-selling biography of Mayor Walker titled *Beau James*), conducted an unofficial census of jobless men who were selling apples on the city's streets. He counted 6,000, "crouching like half-remembered sins sitting upon the conscience of the town."

When newspaperman Heywood Broun observed one of many Salvation Army bread lines in 1932, he described it as "the worm that walks like a man." One out of four employable New Yorkers had neither a job nor a hope of finding one.

General view of the bread line at Times Square and 43rd Street in New York City on December 8, 1930, to receive sandwiches and coffee from a truck to help feed the unemployed and needy.

(AP Photo)

At that time it was estimated that 85,000 meals a day were being handed out by 82 bread lines. Two in Times Square were established by newspaper magnate William Randolph Hearst. After observing one of them, Louis Adamic wrote, "The wretched men, many without overcoats or decent shoes, usually began to line up soon after six o'clock—in good weather or bad, rain or snow."

Reluctant Gypsies

According to police department records, one night in the spring of 1931, a six-story Municipal Lodging House on East 25th Street provided cots for 3,300 homeless people (300 of them women). The city's parks blossomed with countless makeshift shacks.

Called "reluctant gypsies" by one observer, the dispossessed were found "squatting" wherever there was a vacant lot. Social worker Anna Arnold Hedgman described a Harlem scene where people lived in cellars and basements. "Packed in damp, rat-ridden dungeons," she wrote, they existed in squalor "with only slits for a window and a tin can in the corner was the only toilet."

In 1934 as La Guardia took office at City Hall, another writer, Emily Hahn, estimated that there were 75,000 homeless women but that many more were too proud or ashamed to apply for charity, or join the bread lines. Hahn quoted one 55-year-old woman as saying, "I thought perhaps God would be good to me and let me die."

Comedian Groucho Marx said he knew things were bad when "pigeons started feeding the people in Central Park."

Forging an Alliance

It wasn't that the city government was indifferent. It was also broke. The Walker administration had tried to cope, but to do so, it had borrowed far beyond its means to repay.

When La Guardia took over, he wanted to put relief on a pay-as-you-go basis. He planned to foot the bill by raising taxes, but even this fell short. If the city was to handle the rising tide of need, he realized, help had to come from the federal government.

Having wholeheartedly backed the New Deal while in Congress, he found a grateful ally in President Roosevelt. He made so many trips to Washington to plead with FDR for aid to the city that Roosevelt joked, "I listen to Fiorello, and then I give him everything he wants."

Facts and Figures

From 1934 to 1939 New York benefited from more than $1 billion in federal assistance through the PWA and other agencies. In the peak year of 1936, 1.5 million New Yorkers (20 percent of the population) got some form of public assistance.

President Franklin D. Roosevelt (wearing hat) smiles at New York mayor Fiorello La Guardia (at right, holding hat) before the opening of the Triborough Bridge in New York City on July 11, 1930. Others are unidentified.

(AP Photo)

When FDR celebrated his first birthday as president, La Guardia sent him a telegram that was congratulatory, flattering, and a reminder that Fiorello was his number-one ally:

> YOU CAN COUNT ON NEW YORK CITY DOING ITS PART BY FOLLOWING YOUR SPLENDID LEADERSHIP IN THE GREAT BATTLE NOW BEING WAGED AGAINST DEPRESSION, POVERTY AND UNHAPPINESS

Patience and Fortitude

While FDR had occasional fireside chats, Mayor La Guardia went on the radio every Sunday afternoon to report on what the city was doing. A combination of facts, civic lectures, tips on ways to save money, and morale-boosting pep talks, the broadcasts always ended with La Guardia telling New Yorkers to have "patience and fortitude."

A long line of men wait along Broadway for their ration of a sandwich and a cup of coffee in Times Square, New York City, on February 13, 1932, during the Great Depression.

(AP Photo)

The Dreamer and the Builder

To organize and carry out the numerous civic projects that were made possible by federal funding, La Guardia appointed as the city's parks commissioner a no-nonsense urban planner by the name of Robert Moses. Together they built highways and both improved and expanded parks. In one burst of activity in 1936 so many new public swimming pools were built by Moses to be officially opened by La Guardia that *Fortune* called it "the swimming pool year."

Although Moses and the mayor frequently fought with each other over projects like a pair of Brooklyn junkyard dogs, they laid the foundations for New York to become the place it is today. The mayor was a romantic who imagined a utopia of lovely scenery, friendly surroundings, trees, sun, fresh air, civility, art, happy people, laughing and healthy children at play, crime-free neighborhoods, and beautiful music wafting everywhere. Moses was a man who knew how to get things done.

Boondoggling Exhibit A

You read earlier that a lot of people thought that much of the work done by the WPA and other New Deal agencies was nothing more than "boondoggling." That's the way many critics of FDR and La Guardia described their announcement that New York City would use federal funds for a housing project. It was to be erected on Manhattan's Lower East side on blocks that once held tenements. The land was bought and donated to the city by the millionaire Vincent Astor.

This first try at "public housing" was given the logical name "First Houses." Eight new or renovated buildings provided 122 modern, centrally heated, fireproof apartments at an average rent of $6 a room. Each unit had a common laundry room. There were recreation areas indoors and several playgrounds.

When First Houses opened in December 1936, with Mrs. Roosevelt on hand, La Guardia proudly, gleefully, and gloatingly took a jab at the doubters. Waving an arm in the direction of the new homes, he said, "This is boondoggling exhibit A."

Similar projects were built all over the city. They remain in use today, including the La Guardia Houses in Greenwich Village. Having shown that public money could be used to provide low-rent housing, the federal government would eventually subsidize many similar projects in all the major cities.

Unless You Demand It

Speaking at the opening of First Houses, WPA head Harry Hopkins said, "Private capital has never spent a dime to build a house for the poor person."

This was not true. Until First Houses opened, all the residences in the city had been built with private capital, whether it was the money that went into the mansions of Fifth Avenue that were known as "millionaires' row," or the tenements of the Lower East Side and Harlem. What Hopkins was getting at was that private capital had never gone into housing that didn't promise a profit.

A result of this was that when the floor dropped from under the nation's feet, there was no rush to build new housing in a nation in which few people were in a position to buy or rent.

The Plight of the Renter

Someone who couldn't afford the rent or the mortgage payments found an eviction notice tacked to or slipped under the door or was met by a sheriff with the paper in hand. With no place of his or her own, he or she moved in with others. If it happened that no one there could come up with the rent, they were all given the heave-ho.

This situation led to the organization of tenant groups to fight evictions, often at the instigation of Communists, and literally, with fists, clubs, and whatever else was at hand to drive off the person who'd come to serve a notice of eviction.

In 1937 Mayor La Guardia's housing commissioner, Langdon Post, told a meeting of one such group, calling itself the City-Wide Tenants Council, "You will never get anything unless you demand it." He added, "Nothing was ever gotten in this country except when the people forced it."

Revolt of the Tenants

Tenants in New York and in other cities with housing problems united to demand not only new housing but also rent controls. In the presidential election year of 1932 in which La Guardia lost his congressional seat in the FDR landslide, a rent-strike movement, led largely by Communists, arose on the Lower East Side, in Harlem, and in the Bronx and Brooklyn. When La Guardia became mayor, he understood that if nothing were done on a grand scale to provide low-rent housing, he would have to deal with a rebellion in the poorest parts of the city.

Fortunately, First Houses and other forms of housing relief kept the lid on. But tenants' organizations born during the Depression have remained active to this very day in the form of rent control and "rent stabilization." An annual staple of TV news programs in New York City is a rowdy meeting of a city rent board, which says how much landlords of certain apartment houses can charge.

The housing crisis of the 1930s is viewed by sociologists and urban experts as a watershed in the history of tenant activism. Seeking government action to control rents, these groups were a significant factor in the realization of public housing, better conditions in existing housing, urban renewal, and recognition of tenants' rights.

Mr. Rockefeller's Center

One man who didn't have to worry about paying his rent or being booted out of his house was John D. Rockefeller. You have read that at the suggestion of a public relations expert, he made a practice of handing out dimes. One of the world's richest men, he certainly could afford it. He also had plenty of money to pour into a building project that over a 10-year period would employ 75,000 construction workers.

After buying up all the buildings between Fifth and Sixth avenues and West 48th and 51st streets, he launched New York City's most important

Facts and Figures

To build the Rockefeller Center, more than 200 buildings had to be demolished. Workers hauled away 250,000 tons of debris, poured 88,000 tons of cement, and laid 39 million bricks. The mortgage from Metropolitan Life Insurance Co. was $44,300,000.

architectural project: Rockefeller Center. Consisting of 12 buildings on 12 acres (the land was leased from its owner, Columbia University), it was the largest building effort ever undertaken by private enterprise.

The elegant centerpiece of Rockefeller Center was the 70-story RCA Building, which became the home of NBC's Radio City. When the building opened, visitors could take a guided tour of the NBC studios. It cost 55 cents. Those who took it watched radio shows being broadcast, learned how radio worked, and were given a demonstration by a "sound effects man" of how sounds such as rain, fire, and the stuff falling from Fibber McGee's closet were created. Tourists also were given a glimpse at a future form of entertainment called television.

The man running NBC was David Sarnoff. Remember his prediction that radio could be a "music box" in everyone's home? As the RCA Building opened for business, he had another prognostication. He told anyone who'd listen to him that in five years television would be "as much a part of our life as radio." He was wrong in his timetable, primarily because World War II delayed development of television.

Another forecast about TV, this one on the subject of using TV to sell things, also proved wrong. *The New York Telegram* warned that if the medium was used "to distribute miniature billboards into the home, its growth will be stifled at the outset."

Movie and stage star Lionel Barrymore predicted that television would "scrap theaters throughout the country." He was also wrong.

Timeline

During the 1931 Christmas season, construction workers at the Rockefeller Center put up and decorated a small Christmas tree. The tradition has lasted right up to today, although today's trees stand several stories high and are the focus of a "tree lighting" ceremony that's carried coast to coast on television.

Timeline

Actor Alan Alda was born in New York City, January 1, 1936.

That there might be a role for television in bringing news events into American homes was demonstrated on a hot, cloudy Thursday morning, July 26, 1938. A breath-holding real-life drama unfolded at the Gotham Hotel, just five blocks uptown from NBC's studios.

The Man on the Ledge

Four floors down from the 20-story hotel's roof, a young man stood on an 18-inch-wide ledge about 200 feet above the busy sidewalk with the apparent intention of jumping. Although no one below him knew it, John William Warde had attempted to commit suicide before.

Minutes after he was noticed around noon, hundreds of spectators looked up and waited. Police arrived. Reporters heard about the man on the ledge and raced to the scene. So did newsreel cameramen. Eventually, a big truck with "NBC Television" on its sides appeared. A bulky camera was set up on its roof.

Radio was represented by Dave Driscoll of the Special Features Section of the Mutual Broadcasting System. Through his words, a nationwide audience was kept informed of every move made by the nervous and indecisive man on the ledge.

When a resourceful photographer asked the minister of the Fifth Avenue Presbyterian Church if he could climb the steeple to get a better vantage point for his camera, the clergyman refused him permission, reportedly in decidedly un-Christian language.

Also observing was Joel Sayer. A reporter for the *New York Herald Tribune*, he'd published a 1932 best-selling satirical novel about gangsters, gin, jazz, and college football. Sayer's account of the man on the ledge noted the inevitable phenomenon of such public dramas in New York City. "Hawkers circulated among the crowds on the streets," he wrote, "and peddled cheap opera glasses so that John's fellow citizens might see him better. Passengers craned and goggled at John from the buses that crawled along Fifth Avenue."

As though the crucial game of a World Series were being played, people all over Greater New York gathered about parked taxicabs equipped with radios. At ringside, so to speak, on the northeast corner of Fifth Avenue and 55th Street, a cluster of John's co-mortals discussed his dilemma.

One onlooker with binoculars exclaimed to his wife, "My God, Louise, the way he's got his head turned now, he's a dead ringer for Tyrone Power." Another said to no one in particular, "Five bucks'll getcha ten he don't jump."

It would have been a losing wager. Despite the valiant efforts all through the afternoon of the police to talk, or trick, John in from the ledge, he went off it feet first. He slammed against another ledge on the eighth floor, then cartwheeled down to the hotel's marquee, where he bounced to the ground, partly on the sidewalk and partly in the gutter. A priest sprang forward to administer last rites, but John was, of course, dead. He was buried in Brooklyn, but the time for the service was moved up four hours to avoid curious throngs.

Newspapers published photos of John's leap while editorial pages offered the opinion that New Yorkers had disgraced themselves by forming a morbid mob that had waited with bloodthirsty glee to see him jump.

The manager of a Fifth Avenue department store complained that John's lengthy period of indecisiveness had cost the store at least $100,000 in lost sales. By the end of the week, newsreels showing John's leap boosted movie ticket sales in New York City by a million dollars. The latter fact moved John Sayer to write, "Perhaps it can be argued that in the end John William Warde more than paid his debt to metropolitan society."

Fashion City

There's no doubting that millions of people across the United States who heard about the story of the man on the ledge shook their heads and muttered, "It could only happen in New York." Many of such folks were also likely to say, "New York's probably a nice place to visit, but I wouldn't want to live there." But no matter how someone in the United States felt about the country's biggest city, there was no way of avoiding its influence upon every aspect of life.

And this was not just because it was the home of the stock market, or the radio shows came from there, or on account of the domination of baseball by the Yankees, or that it was the country's greatest seaport. It was the center for arts and culture, of course, and while it was true that movies were made in Hollywood, the money men who controlled the big studios were based in New York.

But the part of New York City that touched American lives, day in and day out, wasn't any of these. It was the garment business. When you got dressed in the morning, donned your Saturday night duds to go out to the movies, and spruced up in your going-to-church finery, the clothing in your closet and bureau drawers was sure to be New York–made, if not entirely, then in part.

In the 1930s, "fashion" was dictated by New York designers, the "cutting rooms" in lofts on the West Side, and department stores with the names Saks Fifth Avenue, Macy's, Peck and Peck, B. Altman, Bergdorf Goodman, Best & Co., Bloomingdale's, and Lord & Taylor.

Introducing the "American Look"

It was at Lord & Taylor's posh store on Fifth Avenue that styles broke with the tradition of following the dictates of the fashion salons of Paris. The introduction of the "American look" took place there when designer Elizabeth Hawes presented the first all-American fashion show.

Other designers followed by offering U.S. "originals" with their names on their dresses. One of the leaders was known simply as "Schiaparelli." In the words of fashion historian Cecil Beaton, she "injected a healthy note into the 1930s." Inventing her own particular form with colors that were aggressive and even upsetting, she began a "revolution" by using nylon and other new materials.

Suddenly, romance and youth were in vogue. Even Sears and Roebuck, famed for its mail-order catalog, tempted women everywhere with ads that pictured "you, winsome and desirable in clouds of rayon net, your tiny waist sashed with whispering rayon taffeta." The lady of the house who was thousands of miles from New York could be "pretty as a picture" in a formal of celanese rayon, agleam with rayon satin stripes, with proud puffed sleeves, and softly shirred bodice, slashed in a V.

Beauty from Head to Toe

Throughout the 1930s, women's dresses and skirts rose from 10 inches off the floor to just below the knee. Fingernails were painted. Women flocked to hairdressers for a "permanent wave" or a shoulder-length "page boy" cut. The downside of this rage for stylish hairdos for millinery makers was nearly disastrous as women abandoned wearing hats. Stockings became sheerer and sheerer, and falling prices for silk made them affordable. At the beginning of the Great Depression, a pair of silk stockings cost $1.50. By 1938 they were 91 cents.

If lower prices didn't attract buyers fast enough, manufacturers enlisted "endorsements" from glamorous movie stars. When Ginger Rogers appeared in ads, sales skyrocketed. Women who didn't have Ginger's trim waistline bought corsets at such a rate that makers raked in $67 million from ladies who wanted to emulate her flat tummy, even if they had no chance of spinning across a dance floor in the arms of Fred Astaire.

Timeline

In 1938, New York City's population was 7,505,068. A city cab charged 20 cents for the first $1/4$ mile and 5 cents for each additional $1/4$ mile. And dinner at the Stork Club was $2.50 (not including drinks).

The Great Garbo

Although screen actress Greta Garbo did not lend her famous face to ads, the Swedish star's films had an enormous influence upon fashion. Women who saw her pictures wanted copies of what she'd worn on the screen. They also copied her makeup. "Before Garbo," wrote Cecil Beaton, "women's faces were pink and white. But her very simple and sparing use of cosmetics altered the face of the fashionable woman."

"Of all the stars who have ever fired the imagination of film audiences," wrote motion picture historian Ephraim Katz, "none has quite projected a magnetism and a mystique equal to Garbo's. Mysterious, unattainable, and ever-changing, she appealed to both male and female audiences."

Although she appeared in dozens of films, silent and talkies, she never got an Academy Award. With a reputation for aloofness and a reticence to speak, and the words "I want to be left alone," she starred in the films *Grand Hotel* (1930), *Queen Christina* (1933), *Anna Karenina* (1935), and *Camille* (1937). In *Ninotchka* (1939) she played a Soviet official on a visit to Paris who resisted both romantic advances from co-star Melvin Douglas and the temptations of capitalism. Ads for the film exclaimed, "Garbo laughs."

After shocking the nation and world by announcing her retirement in 1941, she virtually disappeared from public view. So well did she stay out of the limelight that when she died in 1984, many of her fans believed she'd passed away long before. As Ephraim Katz noted, Garbo's films of the 1930s are "a legacy of nostalgia for a very special time in the history of American cinema."

The Least You Need to Know

- New York's Mayor Fiorello La Guardia made the city a kind of testing ground for programs of the New Deal.
- In 1932 there were 82 bread lines in New York City serving 85,000 meals a day to homeless men, women, and children.
- The first federally financed public housing project opened in New York City in December 1936.
- New York's Rockefeller Center was built.

Part 4

Crackpots and Monsters

This section examines how some Americans dealt with the Great Depression by turning to radical political and social movements. One of these advocated by Louisiana's Democratic U.S. Senator Huey P. Long promised to "share the wealth" and make "every man a king." Following his assassination for a personal reason, Long was succeeded by a white-supremacist named Gerald L. K. Smith. Other people joined fascist organizations. Some Americans who believed that the wave of the future was communism joined in the fighting in the Spanish Civil War as members of the Abraham Lincoln Brigade.

Among the gangsters who were hunted by the FBI was John Dillinger. In the "crime of the century" the infant son of famed aviation hero Charles Lindbergh was kidnapped and murdered.

Chapter 13

Every Man a King

In This Chapter

- ◆ The New Deal is challenged by Louisiana Senator Huey Long's "Share the Wealth" program
- ◆ When Long is assassinated, the movement is taken over by a fiery orator and demagogue named Gerald L. K. Smith
- ◆ The Union Party, based on racial and religious prejudices, is formed
- ◆ Growth of the power of labor unions results in numerous violent strikes

As the effects of the Great Depression spread, many frightened and confused Americans were looking for a savior. Many arose who claimed to be that economic, social, and political messiah. They attracted millions of disciples. But the one who drew the most attention was a Louisiana politician, first as governor and then in the U.S. Senate. Huey "Kingfish" Long proclaimed "every man a king." While leading a movement called "Share the Wealth," he posed a threat to the New Deal, until he was assassinated.

Long's successor, Gerald L. K. Smith, joined in founding a third party in 1936. The Depression also sparked a massive membership growth in labor unions. Numerous strikes took place. Some of them turned violent.

The Unmistakable Edict

To give you a taste of how close the United States was getting to having a second American Revolution in the 1930s, here's what a leader of one of the decade's movements, Gerald L. K. Smith, said in a speech in Cleveland, Ohio, on August 17, 1936, about such organizations:

> These great phenomenal assemblies represent the unmistakable edict that is being issued to the corrupt, seething politicians of America that the baby-having, stump-grumping, sod-busting, go-to-meeting, God-fearing American people are about to take over the United States Government.

The people he was describing were not the same as the "silent majority" that Richard Nixon appealed to in the 1970s to express themselves in the ballot box. The great phenomenal assemblies of the 1930s that Smith referred to were so dismayed, disgusted, and downright angry that they were prepared to follow almost any of the crackpots who came down the pike with a catchy slogan and an easy cure for what ailed the country. (Most of the these groups are discussed in detail in Chapter 15, "Brown Shirts, Black Shirts, No Shirts.")

For now, all you need to know is that the cure they offered people had nothing to do with American democracy, but everything to do with fear, resentments, class warfare, the "have-nots" taking from the "haves," regional rivalries, and racial and religious bigotry. The leader of the biggest of these groups was a radical political rogue from Louisiana. Known as the "Kingfish," Huey Long became President Franklin D. Roosevelt's wide-awake nightmare.

"My Enemies Believe I'm Faking"

If you were not wealthy when the stock market crashed, there may have been worse places to live in America than the state of Louisiana. If so, there weren't many. At the bottom of the American economic ladder even before the Depression, the state was mainly agricultural with a sizeable black population.

Noting that "very few full-blooded Negroes are to be found in the state," the *WPA Guide to Louisiana* cited "all manner of physical variations" that defined blacks of mixed parentage by "percentage of Negro blood."

Facts and Figures

The total state population of Louisiana in 1930 census was 2.1 million, of which 776,326 were blacks.

Facts and Figures _____

Louisiana's blacks were classified according to their percentage of Negro blood.

◆ **Mulatto:** 50 percent Negro, 50 percent white

◆ **Quadroon:** 25 percent Negro, 75 percent white

◆ **Octaroon:** 12.5 percent Negro, 78.5 percent Quadroon

◆ **Griffe:** 75 percent Negro, 25 percent Mulatto

◆ **Sacatro:** 87.5 percent Negro, 12.5 percent Griffe

The Languages of Huey Long Country

A designation most associated with Louisiana is "Creole." It was originally a term for a descendant of early French and Spanish settlers. It was adopted by many blacks in the hope of bettering themselves socially and financially. Whites called them "Negro Creoles."

The name "Cajun" came from "Acadian" and was applied to French-speaking city-dwellers (most of them in New Orleans) and to French-speaking country folk. In the 1930s the term "gumbo," which most people today know as a kind of stew made of fish and anything else one cares to toss in the pot, was a French-based household language of blacks living mainly in southern parishes (counties) in such towns as Lafayette and St. Martinville.

Long Country's Black Parishes

Blacks were found almost everywhere, but in 17 parishes they were in the majority. In five of these areas they outnumbered whites two to one. In two parishes, it was three to one. Some villages were wholly black. There were some places where blacks were not to be found. One of these towns posted signs that warned blacks that they'd better not be caught in town after the sun went down.

The Kingfish

For a young, wily, would-be politician named Huey Pierce Long in the years after World War I, there was hay to be made from the state's poverty. Born in 1893 in a log cabin (yes, a log cabin), he studied law at Tulane University, plunged into politics, and served for 10 years on the state's railroad commission (later the Public Service Commission).

After an unsuccessful run for governor in 1924, he won the office in 1928. He kept getting re-elected. In 1930 he was elected to the U.S. Senate but didn't assume his seat until

1932. By the spring of 1935, in the words of Louisiana newspaper publisher Hodding Carter, "Huey Long owned Louisiana."

Long said he succeeded because "My enemies think I'm faking." He achieved all this clout by appealing to poor farmers and laborers in factories with a message of "us against them," meaning us and the rich and powerful. But he also delivered on his promises by paving roads, building public schools (including Louisiana State University), and carrying through on other highly visible improvements. His slogan was "Every Man a King."

When he was elected to the Senate, he delayed taking his seat until he had a puppet installed as governor, then he continued running Louisiana's affairs from Washington.

Facts and Figures

Huey Long took his nickname from the "Kingfish" character on the popular radio show, *Amos 'n' Andy.*

Senator Huey "Kingfish" Long shown here at the Democratic National Convention in Chicago, Illinois, on June 28, 1932, at the speaker's platform defending his group of delegates.

(AP Photo)

Share the Wealth

As early as 1918, Long recognized an easy target. At age 24, he wrote in a letter to the *New Orleans Item* that with about 65 percent of the entire wealth of the country owned by only 2 percent of the people, "there is not the opportunity for the Christian uplift and education and cannot be until there is more economic reform."

The way to fix this, he believed, was to "share the wealth." In 1933 he started a national newspaper, *The American Progress*, to push his ideas. He wrote, "We must fight to avoid the country being opened up on a basis of mere economic slavery for the masses, with the ruling classes greater in power and standing than ever." He also came up with a slogan for the program that he proposed to correct the maldistribution of wealth that had been a cause of the Depression.

Long called it "Share the Wealth." Its foundation was limitation of the size of fortunes to whatever degree was necessary to give $5,000 to each "deserving family" in America. In doing this, he promised, the rich would still have "all the luxuries they can possibly use."

Long's "Share the Wealth" program promised that every family would be guaranteed:

An annual income of $2,000 to $3,000 a year

A 30-hour work week

An annual one-month vacation

Old age pensions

Free college for "deserving" students

Government purchase of farm surpluses

Suddenly, "Share the Wealth" clubs appeared all over a country in which millions of people were looking for a strong man to lead them out of the Depression. In April 1935 his Senate office received about 60,000 letters of support. In one 24-day period 30,000 letters arrived. More than 27,000 clubs formed. They took the name "Share Our Wealth" and had at least 4.6 million members.

As the "Share the Wealth" idea spread, Huey Long set his sights on achieving a goal he'd set for himself as a boy—being elected president of the United States. In 1935 it wasn't such a crazy dream. When the Democratic National Committee took a secret poll of Democrats, it showed that between three and four million of them would think about voting for Long in 1936. The survey also found Long's strength throughout farm states, on the West Coast, and even in New York.

Senator Huey Long is shown here addressing the students of Louisiana State University in New Orleans on November 12, 1934.

(AP Photo)

Panic in the White House

Concerned that Huey Long represented a real threat, Roosevelt began a secret war against him. It included ordering the Justice department and the Federal Bureau of Investigation (FBI) to look into the possibility of sending the army to take over Louisiana and "restore republican government."

For evidence of Long's disregard for rights guaranteed in the Bill of Rights, FDR's men could point to a ruling by the United States Supreme Court in February 1936. A Long law in Louisiana that sought to control the press by putting a tax on newspapers was struck down as a violation of the guarantee of a free press. Long had called the levy a "two cents a lie" tax. He also tried (and failed in the courts) to cripple Hodding Carter's paper by denying it a contract to print an official government record.

Gods and Monsters

Roosevelt wrote to a friend in 1935 that Americans were "jumpy and ready to run after strange gods."

To 1930s film buffs, FDR's comment about strange gods might be taken as evidence that Roosevelt had been to the movies to see the sequel to 1931's *Frankenstein*. The sensational horror picture was followed in 1935 by *The Bride of Frankenstein*. In a scene in which Dr. Frankenstein renews his experiments in giving life to a corpse, the mad Professor

Pretorius, with a head of wild, frizzy hair and a very long nose, exclaimed, "Gods and monsters!"

Both of these movies reflected the aspect of life in the Depression that would prove so appealing to demagogues. It's the poor and hard-working simple people of the village in the valley below Dr. Frankenstein's castle who become victims of the indifference of the wealthy class.

All the King's Men

So confident was Huey Long that the presidency was in reach that he took a page from the life of Upton Sinclair. (Remember him? He wrote a book in which he spoke as if he were already the governor of California.) In 1935 Huey Long started dictating a tome that he titled *My First Days in the White House*.

On the night of September 8, 1935, the Kingfish was back in his home state to check up on what *his* governor and legislature were doing. Surrounded by bodyguards, he hurried toward the governor's office when a slender, bespectacled man in a white suit stepped from behind a pillar. He drew a small pistol and fired one shot. But his lone bullet that hit Long was followed by a volley from the bodyguards as they gunned down the assassin.

When all the shooting was over, Long's body was riddled with 61 other bullets. He died 30 hours later. This burst of gunfire led to speculation that Long and his killer (Dr. Carl Austin Weiss) had both been set up by enemies of Long who'd enlisted the bodyguards to execute the deadly scheme. The truth behind Huey Long's death thus finds itself a matter of continuing debate, similar to the assassinations of John F. Kennedy and Martin Luther King Jr.

A figure patterned on Huey Long became the central character of a Pulitzer Prize–winning novel, *All the King's Men*, by Robert Penn Warren. Published in 1946, it was made into a movie of the same title in 1949. As "Willie Stark," Broderick Crawford provided a chillingly realistic portrayal of a not-much fictionalized Kingfish.

Famous Faces

Kentucky-born (1905), educated at Yale, University of California, and at Oxford as a Rhodes Scholar, Robert Penn Warren taught at Louisiana State University. He wrote nine other novels about the South and its people. In the 1950s and 1960s he wrote extensively on the Civil Rights movement. In 1986, three years before his death, he was named the first poet laureate of the United States.

Heir to the Movement

One of the most ardent of Long's early followers was the radical minister of the First Christian Church of Shreveport. His name was Gerald L. K. Smith. When the gifted and eloquent orator used his pulpit to preach the gospel of the Kingfish, instead of that of Jesus Christ, the elders of the congregation dismissed him.

Long saw to it that the preacher's spell of unemployment would be brief. He hired Smith to proselytize for "Share the Wealth." Smith was so devoted to Long that he wore Long's used clothing. Once, according to Smith himself, he slept on the floor next to Long's bed just so he could "be close to Huey."

After hearing a Smith speech, journalist H. L. Mencken said he was the "greatest orator of them all." He was "not greatest by an inch or foot or a mile," Mencken continued, "but the greatest by at least two light years."

Smith had described Long as "this young man who came out of the woods of north Louisiana, who leads us like a Moses out of the land of bondage into the land of milk and honey where every man is a king but no man wears a crown."

A Smith Speech Sampler

"Share the Wealth" crowds were brought to their feet in ecstasy with lines such as this: "Let's pull down these huge piles of gold until there shall be a real job, not a little old sow-belly, black-eyed pea job, but a real spending-money, beefsteak and gravy, Chevrolet, Ford in the new garage, new suit, Thomas Jefferson, Jesus Christ, red, white and blue job for every man!"

Turning revolutionary rhetoric into prayer, he would exclaim, "Lift us out of this wretchedness, O Lord, out of this poverty. Lift us who stand in slavery tonight."

Advocating a nationalist movement to "seize the government of the United States," Smith declared, "The democratic method is a lot of baloney. It doesn't mean a thing."

The Minister, the Doctor, and the Radio Priest

When the Kingfish went to his eternal rest with his body riddled by gunshots, Smith wrapped himself in the mantel of "Share the Wealth" leadership. He also formed an alliance with two other leaders of movements, Father Coughlin (remember the "Radio Priest"?) and Dr. Francis Townsend, whose Townsend Plan was a precursor to the New Deal's Social Security.

In 1936 this triumvirate formed the Union Party. It chose as its candidate for president an obscure congressman named William Lemke. From North Dakota, he was known by detractors as "Liberty Bill." The nickname didn't mean that they saw Lemke as a freedom-loving patriot. They meant that his head, like the Liberty Bell, had a crack in it.

Although the "Share the Wealth" movement faded away, Gerald L. K. Smith remained on the public stage. In 1944 he predicted "the flame will spread, and extreme nationalists will come to power."

Described by historian Joseph C. Goulden as "a noisy old bigot associated with most of the nut cases of the 1930s and 1940s," Smith backed the racist Dixiecrats, who broke with the Democratic Party on the issue of racial segregation. At the Democratic convention in 1948, he warned the desegregationists, "There are not enough troops in the army to force the southern people to admit Negroes into our theaters, our swimming pools, our homes."

Founder of the Christian Nationalist Crusade in St. Louis in 1942 to "preserve America as a Christian nation," Smith started a magazine, *The Cross and the Flag*, in which he ranted against "Jews, desegregation, mongrelization" of America by immigration and Communism. He died in 1976.

Timeline

In 1936, the Union Party got 2 percent of the popular vote, but no electoral votes. Four days after the election, the party disbanded.

Famous Faces

Future general and Secretary of State Colin Powell was born on April 5, 1937, in the Bronx, New York.

The Man with the Eyebrows

Meet John Llewellyn Lewis. With a face like a bulldog's and eyebrows for which the adjective "bushy" was an understatement, he was president of the United Mine Workers. Born in Lucas, Iowa, on February 12, 1880, the son a Welsh-born coal miner, Lewis went to work in the mines at age 16. Active in the miner's union that he would eventually lead between 1920 and 1960, he became a protégé of Samuel Gompers, the founder of the American Federation of Labor (AFL).

In the 1930s, when coal was the backbone of industry and the way Americans kept warm in the winter, the UMW was not to be given short shrift. But in the fall of 1935, that's just what Lewis thought his union members were getting from the country's biggest labor organization. Founded in the 1880s, the AFL was an amalgam of "skilled" workers in "craft unions." Its president in 1935 was William Green.

Believing that the AFL should include all kinds of workers, Lewis and other like-minded men formed their own labor conglomeration and called it the Congress of Industrial

Organizations (CIO). To bolster its strength, Lewis set out to bring all the unskilled workers into it, starting with the rubber industry. In a country still crazy over cars, tire-making was a vital part of the U.S. economy.

When the United Rubber Workers went on strike against the Goodyear Tire and Rubber Company in March 1936, it wasn't the AFL that rallied to their cause, but the CIO. Disgruntled rubber workers immediately joined the CIO. Next to sign up were iron and tin workers. The results of this were a division in the forces of organized labor that lasted for decades and the emergence of John L. Lewis as the head of a union organization in a nation in which most of the labor force fell into the "unskilled" category.

Lewis Spots an Opportunity

While the CIO was bringing important unions under its banner, a prime target was the vast automobile industry. There was a union, the United Auto Workers (UAW), led by three brothers, Walter, Roy, and Victor Reuther. But out of a million autoworkers, they'd managed to sign up only about 25,000.

Talk of the Time

In a **sit-down strike,** workers quit working, but in addition to setting up picket lines outside the factory, members remain in the factories, but not doing their jobs, of course.

Consequently, when the UAW called for a *sit-down strike* at the Fisher Body Division of the General Motors Corporation (GM) at factories in Cleveland, Ohio, and Flint, Michigan, Lewis threw the weight of the CIO behind it.

GM's reaction to the sit-down strikes was to seek an injunction from a court. When that failed, the company brought in police. In the resulting confrontation, the cops who attempted to evict the strikers met violent resistance. They were driven back in what was called "the Battle of the Running Bulls."

As the stalemate continued, Secretary of Labor Frances Perkins tried to negotiate an ending, but the UAW said it would settle only when GM recognized the union. GM said it would do nothing as long as the plants were occupied.

Before the strike, GM had been turning out about 15,000 cars per week. The people of the country that went to the poor house in an automobile in 1929 were buying General Motors cars in 1936 at a rate of 1.7 million a year. But with its main parts plants shut down by strikers, production of GM cars dropped to only 151. In the face of this disastrous situation, GM entered into talks with the union, granting the recognition the UAW had demanded.

With GM defeated, the UAW, backed by the CIO, next took on the Chrysler company, which quickly folded. Then came Ford. But the man who had put America on wheels proved a tougher opponent. Henry Ford would not recognize the UAW until 1941, and he did so then only because of the likelihood that the United States would be drawn into the Second World War.

The Memorial Day Massacre

In the spring of 1937 the Steel Workers' Organizing Committee, backed by the CIO, was recognized by United States Steel. But the smaller, independent companies, including Republic Steel, known as "Little Steel," refused to give the union what it had gained at U.S. Steel.

When union demonstrators appeared at Republic's plant in South Chicago on May 30 (Memorial Day), they were fired on by police. When the shooting ended, four men were dead and 84 wounded. As in the case of Ford, "Little Steel" would not sign CIO contracts until 1941.

Between a Rock and a Hard Place

The outbreak of strikes that marked the last half of the 1930s left Franklin D. Roosevelt between a rock and a hard place. He was caught between a need to get industries going at their maximum capacity in order to put people back to work and the demands of people who were working for better wages and conditions. At one point during strikes involving the steel industry, he became so frustrated with the companies and CIO unions that he wished "a plague on both your houses."

John L. Lewis raised his raspy voice and shot back at FDR, "It ill behooves one who has supped at labor's table to curse with equal fervor and fine impartiality both labor and its adversaries when they become locked in deadly embrace."

But it was the institution with which FDR had once been at odds over the New Deal that had the final word on sit-down strikes. In 1939, the U.S. Supreme Court outlawed them.

Facts and Figures

In October 1937 the CIO had 4,000,000 members in 6,000 locals. The AFL had 2.9 million. Combined, they were 18.5 percent of nonfarm employees.

The Manager of Discontent

In some ways John L. Lewis and FDR were alike. Each was a skilled politician, had a superb sense of timing, and possessed a great skill at manipulation. And both men had an instinct for theatrical gestures and dramatic impact.

In assessing John L. Lewis's role in these tumultuous events, historian Robert S. McElvain judged that the labor upheaval of the 1930s would not have followed the course it did without him. His role was that of a manager of discontent. "The CIO," he wrote, "channeled into constructive action the discontent that was so widespread among working Americans in the thirties."

The most important figure in the American labor movement of the twentieth century, John L. Lewis led the UMW and the CIO through the 1930s, World War II, and Truman and Eisenhower Administrations. He died in 1969.

The Birth of the "Sit-In"

When students who demonstrated for civil rights and against the war in Vietnam in the 1960s suddenly began takeovers of college buildings, they believed that they'd invented a new tactic for voicing protests. They called it the "sit-in." In fact, they were taking a leaf from the men who'd fought for the rights of labor unions in the 1930s in the form of the sit-down strike that appeared first in a significant way in the automobile industry, starting with General Motors.

As a result of the success of the action against GM between September 1, 1936, and June 1, 1937, American workers flexed their muscles in the tire-and-rubber industry, ship-building, steel companies, textiles, shoes, aircraft manufacturing, newspaper publishing, bakeries, and other pillars of modern capitalism.

Assessing the effectiveness of these sit-down actions in a 1938 book, *American Labor,* Herbert Harris wrote, "Whereas in the everyday variety [of striking] employees leave mill or mine or store or factory to picket outside their place of business, in the sit-down they remain inside at or near their usual posts but do no work. They just sit or stretch out on the floor or benches or loll around on their feet. And if the sit-down lasts long enough, it becomes a stay-in."

The advantages were obvious. Police and militia could more easily disperse a picket line in the open than in an "occupied" plant. The sit-down also gave individual workers a new and rare sense of power. The traditional union term for this was "solidarity." But in the sit-down strike, the concept was given a new meaning as workers found themselves living together for days and sometimes weeks inside their places of work.

Sit-down strikers even came up with a song:

> When they tie a can to a union man,
> Sit-down! Sit-down!
> When they give him the sack, they'll take him back,
> Sit-down! Sit-down!

When the speed-up comes, just twiddle your thumbs,
Sit-down! Sit-down!
When the boss won't talk, don't take a walk,
Sit-down! Sit-down!

They Didn't Just Sit

While covering the sit-down at GM's Fisher Body Plant No. 1 at Flint, Michigan, for *The New Republic*, reporter Bruce Bliven wrote:

> The degree of organization among these men was something to think about. An elected strike committee was in general control. Every man had specified duties, to be performed at specified hours. Meals were prepared with goods brought in by friends on the outside and passed through a window, these meals being served in the plant cafeteria at stipulated hours
>
> There was even a barbershop in operation in one of the plant's rest rooms. Liquor was absolutely forbidden. An emergency post office was set up and there was a heavy movement of mail in both directions, all of it censored by a special committee.

Timeline

In August 1938 the *Queen Mary* set an England to New York speed record of 3 days, 20 hours, 42 minutes, at an average rate of 31.69 knots.

For recreation, the men played cards or listened to the radio. In one sit-down there was a daily concert by sit-downers with musical talent who put together a small band.

The Lasting Effects

Primarily as a result of the 44-day sit-down strike against GM, the United Automobile Workers union garnered 370,000 dues-paying members out of an industry workforce of 450,000. This success made the UAW the third largest of CIO unions.

During the sit-down strike, John L. Lewis, president of the CIO, said, "You men are undoubtedly carrying on through one of the most heroic battles that has ever been undertaken by strikers in an industrial dispute. The attention of the entire American public is focused upon you."

He was right. As one observer of the Flint sit-down strike noted, the refusal of the auto workers to be dislodged for many weeks "stirred headline writers to new heights, editorial writers, columnists, and radio commentators to new hysterias, provided bitter debates in the Senate and House, and divided most of the population into two emotionally over-strung camps."

And as noted, the sit-downers also provided a blueprint for the sit-ins and takeovers of the 1960s. They were carried out by sons and daughters of men and women who endured the Great Depression, then went off to war to defend freedom—a generation that at the dawn of the twenty-first century would be hailed in best-selling books, in epic movies, and on TV as "the greatest generation."

The Least You Need to Know

- United States Senator Huey Long of Louisiana formed and led a national movement called "Share the Wealth" that posed a real threat to FDR and the New Deal.
- Following Long's assassination by a man with a personal grudge, the "Share the Wealth" movement was taken over by a bigot named Gerald L. K. Smith.
- Labor leader John L. Lewis formed a nationwide combination of unions called the Congress of Industrial Organizations (CIO).
- In a strike against General Motors, members of the United Auto Workers union (UAW) invented the "sit-down" strike.

Chapter **14**

Give This a Try

In This Chapter

- ◆ A frenzy erupts over an idea called "Technocracy"
- ◆ Intellectuals who believe that the Great Depression is proof that capitalism is dead, or at least on its last legs, rally to the red flag of Russian Communism
- ◆ Americans form the Abraham Lincoln Brigade to fight against fascists in a civil war in Spain
- ◆ Congress creates a committee headed by Martin Dies of Texas to investigate "un-American activities"
- ◆ Concerned about the likelihood of another world war, FDR asks for increased spending for U.S. military defenses

In the early years of the Great Depression the country went into a frenzy of enthusiasm for an idea called "Technocracy." It held that the only way of guaranteeing economic stability was reliance on technology and a price system–based energy.

Many intellectuals who questioned the capitalist system believed the wave of the future was communism, like the kind that had been imposed on Russia by the Bolshevik Revolution. The Communist Party of the United States experienced a huge increase in membership or found sympathy from "fellow travelers." Some of them enlisted in the Abraham Lincoln Brigade to fight on the "Republican" side against a fascist revolution in Spain. Worried about the "Red" threat, Congress created the House Un-American Activities Committee.

Methodology of the Most Probable

You've probably never heard of Howard Scott. But as Americans found themselves sinking deeper into the Great Depression, his idea for getting the country out of the mess, and making sure it could never happen again, became a household word. Scott called it "Technocracy."

Claiming to have had an important career in engineering, he was a familiar figure in hangouts of intellectuals in New York City's Greenwich Village. With a reputation as an eccentric braggart, he talked with anyone he could corner about "synthetic integration of the physical sciences that pertain to the determination of all functional sequences of social phenomena."

Would You Say That Again, Please?

Translated, he meant that the answer to the Depression was found in technologies, machine power, and the proper use of energy. To prove it, he managed to persuade Columbia University to give him money to conduct a study. Using the funds to hire some unemployed architects, he conducted an "Energy Survey of North America."

He reported that harnessing machine power had the potential to provide unparalleled prosperity. But first, something had to be done about the existing price system. He argued that advances in technology were being thwarted by those in charge of the economy. What was needed was a system controlled by technologists, hence the name Technocracy. Scientists and engineers would do better because they were able through "scientific method" to understand "the methodology of the determination of the most probable." In other words, these smart guys would know what would work and what wouldn't.

What Happened with Technocracy?

When Scott's findings were publicized at a time when most people saw the old system failing and were in a mood to give a try to almost anything, Technocracy became all the rage. Looking back, you'd be right to call it a fad of that time. It was right up there in popularity with two other 1930s crazes—"miniature golf" and a board game named Monopoly.

A book titled *The ABC of Technocracy*, published by Scott at the end of 1932, rocketed onto best-seller lists. Everyone was talking about the Technocracy idea. Scott became a celebrity. But the problem with the book, and with Technocracy, was that it required the abandonment of the present money system. Anyone with a particle of common sense recognized that it would be an undertaking so vast as to be impossible. On closer examination, the people realized Technocracy would also put everyone's lives in the hands of people who weren't elected.

Rather than embrace the ideas of Howard Scott, Americans went to the polls and voted for Franklin D. Roosevelt's promise of a New Deal. It sounded good, even if no one, including FDR, could say just what it entailed.

Timeline

John Ledbetter and Drake Delanoy laid out the first miniature golf course atop a skyscraper in New York in 1926. They called it "Tom Thumb" golf. In 1929 Garnet Carter of Chattanooga, Tennessee, opened hundreds of them in Florida. By 1930 more than 30,000 courses were in use across the country.

Timeline

Monopoly was created in 1930 by unemployed heating-equipment salesman Charles Darrow of Germantown, Pennsylvania, for his family. Monopoly was offered to Parker Brothers. The game-maker at first rejected it, but then reconsidered. The change of heart resulted in the company's biggest success and multimillionaire status for Darrow.

I Have Been to the Future and It Works

You've read that there was a rush by dismayed, scared Americans toward almost anyone who seemed to have a "better idea," from the Townsend Plan, Sinclair Lewis, Father Coughlin, and Technocracy to Huey Long's and Gerald L. K. Smith's "Share the Wealth." Now it's time to talk about the people in the United States who saw communism as the wave of the future and wanted it here.

Five months before the stock market crash of 1929, the ruler of the Soviet Union offered a prediction from Moscow. Speaking in the Kremlin on May 16, Joseph Stalin said, "I think the moment is not far off when a revolutionary crisis will develop in America."

Echoing Stalin, the head of the Communist Party of the United States (CP-USA), William Z. Foster, saw "increasing militancy of the workers." He greeted it as a "revolutionary upsurge" that boded well for the triumph of the communist doctrine all across America.

He had reason to be optimistic. Suddenly, his fringe group in the political spectrum experienced a significant increase in members. A party that in 1929 had less than 10,000 found in 1934 that its ranks had swollen to more than 25,000, with another 6,000 in the Young Communist League, and half a million more who never took the step of joining. They were known as "Fellow Travelers."

> **Famous Faces**
>
> William Z. Foster was born in Taunton, Massachusetts, in 1881. He joined the Socialist Party in 1901 and then the Industrial Workers of the World (IWW, also known as the "Wobblies"). A founder of the CP-USA, he headed it from 1919 to 1932, and again from 1945 to the 1960s. A devoted Stalinist all his life, he died in 1961 in the USSR.

Knocking on the Steam Pipe

The CP-USA consisted of local "clubs" and state "sections." In one apartment building in the borough of the Bronx in New York City, there were so many communists that the CP-USA chairman in the area, Isadore Begun, boasted that if he needed to convene a meeting, all he had to do was "knock on the steam pipe."

Support and advice on organizing came from Moscow through the Communist International (Comintern). A worldwide organization, it was set up to promote communism with funding for recruitment and to foment demonstrations and the occasional riot.

Whatever Were They Thinking?

With the collapse and dismembering of the Soviet Union in the 1990s, communism had finally proved itself to be just what its critics in the 1930s said it would be—an economic, societal, and political disaster for the Russian people and a menace to the world. After 70 years of promising a People's Utopia, the USSR was never able to deliver. Instead of the true democracy of the masses forecast by Karl Marx, the communism of Lenin and Joseph Stalin had, by the 1930s, relentlessly denied its people any kind of liberty.

Why then, you might ask, would so many bright Americans in the 1930s be so eager to embrace it? A young woman who was fresh out of college recalled that being a communist made her better than she was. "It was," she declared, "the great moral adventure of my life."

A historian of the 1930s, Frederic Lewis Allen, wrote in *Since Yesterday* that such "young rebels" saw communism as the "end-station of the road of disillusionment." They saw that the going order was not working. Deciding that half-measures would not suffice, they chose to believe that nothing short of revolution would do. And what did communism advocate? Just that.

When William Foster's dutiful branch of the CP-USA sent out 100,000 postcards (postage paid by the Communist International) ordering a rally on March 6, 1930, at New York's Union Square, 35,000 people showed up (four times the membership of Foster's group). The biggest communist demonstration in the city's history ended just as its organizers planned.

Goaded by agitators, the crowd waged a pitched battle with the police that spread from Union Square to surrounding streets. When it was all over, communists everywhere unleashed a propaganda campaign that blamed the riot on the cops. It was hailed as "a great success" and "the prelude" to the "overthrow of capitalism and establishment of a revolutionary workers and farmers government" in the United States.

Timeline

Although the Bolshevik Revolution took place in 1917, it was not until FDR took office in 1933 that the United States recognized the Soviet Union. FDR came under pressure from American businesses that saw a huge market in Russia. But he granted recognition only after he was promised that the USSR would not interfere in U.S. domestic affairs, which was, as you've seen, a lie. The Soviet Union's first ambassador to Washington was Maxim Litvinov.

To Russia with Love

To the westward migration of the Okies and the flood of blacks from the South to relief-rich northern cities, you may now add a flow of Marxist-smitten Americans to the Soviet Union. They went to see for themselves how well communism worked in the USSR, and then came home to heap it with praise. One exulted upon his return, "I have been to the future and it works."

A great many of these literal fellow travelers were teachers. One of their groups was observed by Elaine Rozenberg, then a child. Because her father, an unemployed musician, had gotten a modest cash settlement for injuries he'd suffered in a car-truck crash, the family sailed to France in the summer of 1935 to visit their relatives. Recalling the adventure, Elaine described most of the people in tourist class on the *Ille d'France* as teachers "who were headed to Russia to learn more about how Communism works."

On the way over, Elaine recalled, the teachers "taught my parents and me the words to the Communist anthem, the 'Internationale.'" They also looked disapprovingly at little Elaine's Shirley Temple curls (see Part 5, "Better Tomorrows"). They "implored" the

Rozenbergs to turn Elaine over to a commune so that she could be raised with "real" values. But when the trip to France was over, Elaine was enrolled in the Kindergarten of PS 226 in Bensonhurst, Brooklyn.

Many of those who voyaged to Russia were writers and artists who came back to push the Soviet Union in their work (more on this in Part 5).

Seeing Red in Black and White

Another phenomenon of the obsession with the Soviet Union was to be found in a flurry of films. Between 1929 and 1939 you could have gone to see these cinematic glorifications: *Living Russia, Soil, Childhood of Maxim Gorky, Gorky's Mother, Alexander Nevsky, Potemkin* (made in 1925 but frequently re-shown), *Anna Karenina, Tchapayef, Storm Over Asia, Fragment of an Empire,* and *Ninotchka,* which was made in Hollywood and starred Greta Garbo.

When *Alexander Nevsky,* directed by renowned Russian filmmaker Sergei Eisenstein, who also made *Potemkin,* was shown at New York's Cameo Theater, *New York Times* critic Frank S. Nugent saw a "rough-hewn monument to national heroism." He also observed the "comrades" in the audience cheering.

"Freest Country in the World"

Americans who'd been to Russia returned to gush about "the freest country in the world." Many of them did so at "We Have Been to the USSR" dinners. They were sponsored by a Moscow bankrolled operation called "Friends of Soviet Russia." Journalist Eugene Lyons, who'd also been there, wrote of these people, "Their breed was legion." They had been drawn to "the Great Experiment by its magnitude and seeming strength."

They could make their "sacrifices," he wrote, while comfortably "overeating at banquets and overdrinking at cocktail parties for the cause."

Author Morris Ernst, who in 1952 would write *Report on American Communism,* joined the Communist Party in the early 1930s. He was 24 at the time and worked for the federal government. "Probably the thing that pushed me into the party," he recalled, "was that I felt terribly guilty at being employed when there were so many unemployed."

To assuage his feelings, Morris enlisted in a volunteer army of sorts that formed in the United States to fight on "the Loyalist side" against fascists in what's known as the Spanish Civil War.

A War, a Book, and a Movie

What most Americans know today about the Spanish Civil War they probably learned from an old movie. Made in 1943 and based on a novel by Ernest Hemingway, *For Whom the Bell Tolls* starred Gary Cooper and Ingrid Bergman. It's an excellent film, but in no way does it provide a complete understanding of what the Spanish Civil War was about.

The war started in 1936 with an attack on the Spanish Republic by an army led by a young officer, Francisco Franco. His force had the backing of Adolph Hitler's Nazi Germany and Italy's fascist boss, Benito Mussolini. Loyalists were supported by the Soviet Union through the Comintern. Its avowed purpose in raising 35,000 fighters from 52 countries was to make the capital, Madrid, "the tomb of fascism."

The result of this confrontation of two ideologies was to turn Spain into a proving ground for the weaponry that would be used in the showdown between them, along with the capitalist nations, in World War II.

Timeline

Best-selling author Ernest Hemingway was a correspondent in Spain for the North American Newspaper Alliance. His reports favored the Loyalists, as did his novel. By the time it was published in 1940, Gary Cooper's side in the war had lost. Other writers who favored the Loyalists included Ralph Bates, Irving Pflaum, Martha Gellhorn, Dashiell Hammett, Lillian Hellman, Herbert Matthews, and Vincent Sheehan.

The Abraham Lincoln Brigade

Americans who joined the war on the Republican side were part of the "Fifteenth International Brigade." The U.S. units took the names "George Washington Battalion," "John Brown Battery," and the "Abraham Lincoln Battalion." The "Brigade" came from a group at home that called itself the "Friends of the Abraham Lincoln Brigade." At least 60 percent of the Lincoln Battalion consisted of members of the Young Communist League, the IWW (Wobblies), and socialists, who formed a "column" named after socialist leader Eugene V. Debs.

The Lincolns, as they called themselves, came from all walks of life. Integrated racially, they were men who'd been unemployed, or who gave up jobs as teachers, miners, lumberjacks, factory workers, and salesmen to join the cause. The motives of some were the same as Morris Ernst's, who, as noted, joined the Brigade out of a feeling of guilt. Others enlisted because they'd experienced what they considered the deprivations and injustices of the Great Depression, as defined by the Communist Party.

One of the volunteers was Alvah C. Bessie. In his 1939 book, *Men in Battle*, he wrote, "And this is the meaning of it all (the people's war); these men behind these fragile rocks, these men whose fragile flesh is torn to pieces by the hot and ragged steel; they could not accept their death with such good grace if they did not love so deeply and so well—were not determined that love must come alive in the world. What other reason could there be for dying? What other reason for this blood upon your hands?"

Powerful stuff, right?

The Great Disillusionment

While Americans such as Bessie who fought for the Loyalists in the Spanish Civil War remained true to the cause, some who'd once embraced communism came home bitterly disillusioned. Morris Ernst began "correcting" his conception of the Spanish situation, which he had gotten "completely from the American Communist Party." After the war, he found that his criticisms left him ostracized. Brought up on charges of disloyalty to the Party and the Brigade, he found himself described by the head of the Party, Earl Browder (he succeeded Foster after Foster had a heart attack), as "a cunning manipulator who had cultivated a bland exterior to cover up his devious and widespread machinations."

Famed author John Dos Passos went to Spain in 1937 as a committed communist. After observing just as many atrocities committed by the Loyalists as those of the fascists, he came back and quit the Party. By 1964 he'd moved so far away from communism that he was a supporter of Republican Senator Barry Goldwater's candidacy for the presidency. Almost all of those who were in the Lincoln Brigade who'd lived (about half were killed in battles or were captured and executed) ultimately found themselves answering for their actions in the 1950s before a Congressional body that was established in 1938 to investigate "un-American activities."

Something's Troubling Mr. Dies

When 30-year-old Martin Dies of Texas was elected to the U.S. House of Representatives a year after the stock market crash, he became the youngest member of Congress. But Washington, D.C., was not new to him. His father had also represented Texas's Second Congressional District.

Following the arrival of FDR, the Brain Trust, and the New Deal in 1933, Dies was one of their most ardent supporters. But by the start of FDR's second term, the ardor had begun to cool. He found much to dislike in the Roosevelt administration's cozy relationship with organized labor. He looked on with horror at the CIO-led sit-down strikes "sweeping the nation and threatening the very foundations of orderly government."

Dies also suspected that the New Deal was a haven for communists and that "Reds" were infiltrating every aspect of American life. To get proof of the extent and character of these "un-American propaganda activities in the United States," which he said were "instigated from foreign countries or of a domestic origin," he asked the House to establish an investigative committee.

FDR hated the idea and managed to block it, but only for a year. Giving in to Dies's demands in May 1938, the House created the "Special Committee to Investigate Un-American Activities." Its common name at the time was "the Dies Committee."

Timeline _____

HUAC (House Un-American Activities Committee), formed in 1947, was an updated "Cold War" version of the Dies Committee. It became famous (some believe that "infamous" is the proper word) for its investigation of Reds in the movie industry. Its most prominent member in its earliest stage was California Congressman Richard Nixon.

The Chief Inquisitor

It wasn't Dies, but a member of the committee, who took the role of chief inquisitor. He was a New Jersey Democrat by the name of J. Parnell Thomas. Although the committee was authorized to look into the activities of pro-Nazi and other "subversive" groups (see Chapter 15, "Brown Shirts, Black Shirts, No Shirts"), Thomas quickly made it clear that the un-American activities he cared most about were those hatched in the USSR, and carried out by Reds "right in our government."

It was made up of four ultra-conservatives (two were Democrats) and three Democrats who were moderate-to-liberal. One of these was a Californian who'd once joined in Upton Sinclair's EPIC movement, but left it because he believed it had been taken over by communists. His name was Jerry Voorhis. Reluctant to become a committee member, he was persuaded to take the post by Speaker of the House William Bankhead (father of actress Tallulah). Bankhead wanted Voorhis (a liberal) to counterbalance the conservatives.

The Voorhis Act

As a member of the Dies Committee, Voorhis felt that Thomas was mostly ignoring other "subversive groups," such as the Ku Klux Klan and others that we'll learn about later. He remained on the committee until 1943, then voted against continuing to fund it. While on the committee, he won passage of the Voorhis Act (1940). Under its provisions, organizations that represented foreign governments were required to register. But the law did not impose criminal penalties.

In 1946, as the Cold War was taking hold and the country was swept by a wave of anti-communism, Voorhis found himself opposed for re-election to the House by a young ex-naval officer. In a controversial campaign, Richard M. Nixon succeeded in depicting Voorhis as a communism sympathizer. When Voorhis lost, Nixon took his place on the committee. Earning a reputation as an anti-communist by producing evidence that State Department official Alger Hiss was a Soviet agent, Nixon went on to the Senate in 1951, the vice presidency in 1952, and the presidency in 1968, always in the role of the anti-communist.

FDR Looks Overseas

When President Roosevelt sent his annual message to Congress on January 3, 1938, it was, for the most part, concerned with domestic issues. The country was struggling to recover from the 1937 "Roosevelt Recession." Among other proposals was an expansion of the WPA from 1.5 million enrollees to 3 million. The result would be the Emergency Relief Appropriation Act.

But FDR began his message with a reference to the state of the world. With England and France preparing for the likelihood of a military showdown with Hitler's Germany and Mussolini's fascists and with Japan on the march in Asia, the president told Congress and the nation, "We must keep ourselves adequately strong in self-defense."

Three weeks later, he submitted recommendations for increased spending for armaments. He asked for $8 million for anti-aircraft equipment, $6 million to aid certain industries in tooling-up for defense manufacturing, and a 220 percent increase in funds for naval construction.

Who Says When We Should Go to War?

As FDR and others in government anxiously kept their eyes on the events in Europe that might draw the United States into a war, a public opinion poll showed that 73 percent of Americans believed that the question of declaring war should be put before the people in a referendum. Accordingly, Congressman Louis Ludlow of Indiana tried to get Congress to pass such a Constitutional Amendment.

Roosevelt sent a letter to House Speaker Bankhead warning that a change which took the war power from the president and Congress "would cripple any president in his conduct of foreign affairs, and it would encourage other nations to believe that they could violate American rights with impunity."

The Ludlow Resolution was rejected by the House. Forty years later, in the aftermath of the Vietnam War, Congress passed "the War Powers Act" to limit presidential war-waging without the approval of Congress. But the Act has never been tested on the grounds of constitutionality. As you will read later, FDR, with Congressional compliance, would find ways to join the war in Europe without declaring one and to set aside the fears and suspicions of communism that were of such grave concern in the 1930s by providing aid to the Soviet Union.

None of Our Business

As the Ludlow Amendment was being debated, a public opinion poll showed that 75 percent of the people who were questioned approved of limiting the war powers of a president. Their position was based on a historic American distrust of an overly strong federal government, a firm belief in President George Washington's advice to the country to avoid foreign entanglements, and the lingering bitter memories of "the Great War."

Most Americans stood four-square against getting involved in the growing messes in Europe created by the Nazis and fascists and cared little about the adventuring by Japan in the Far East. In a poll taken in 1937, 19 out of 20 people who were asked if the United States should ever enter another war answered "no." That same year, more than half a million college students signed a pledge not to support the United States joining in a European war.

A Country Unready for War

But even if the country had been willing to jump into a war, the chances of the United States having an effect on it were small if any. In 1935, the U.S. Army consisted of 165,000 enlisted men, 67 general officers, a couple of tanks from the Great War, and enough guns to equip just one regiment.

The Navy was so unprepared that the idea of U.S. ships going into action sent shudders through a fleet made up of leftovers of the 1917–1918 war that the United States was permitted under a post-war naval disarmament agreement. Aware of this shortcoming, Congress in 1938 voted money to build a "two-ocean" navy, but over a 10-year period.

A President Caught in the Middle

FDR's policy was to embrace "neutrality." But at the same time, he felt that he had to point out that there were no guarantees that the United States could remain uninvolved.

In a speech at the dedication of a PWA-built bridge in Chicago on October 5, 1937, he warned of a "reign of terror and international lawlessness" that had been unleashed on mankind.

"If those things come to pass in other parts of the world," he said, "let no one imagine that America will escape, that America may expect mercy, that this Western Hemisphere will not be attacked and it will continue tranquilly and peacefully."

Comparing the world situation to an outbreak of sickness, he chose a folksy analogy by stating that "when an epidemic of physical disease starts to spread, a community quarantines the patients. "War," he said, "is a contagion whether it be declared or undeclared." Warning that "it can engulf states and peoples remote from the original scene of hostilities," he pledged that "America actively engages in the search for peace."

Privately, he believed that "as time goes on we can slowly but surely make people realize that war will be a greater danger to us if we close all the doors and windows than if we go out in the street and use our influence to curb the riot."

The Least You Need to Know

◆ Looking for "a better way," millions of Americans thought they saw "the future" in a system built on a "Technocracy," and others turned to the Communist Party.

◆ When a civil war broke out in Spain between backers of the Spanish Republic and fascists led by General Francisco Franco, many Americans enlisted on the Republican side by joining the Abraham Lincoln Brigade.

◆ Alarmed over communist activity in the United States, Congress established a committee to investigate un-American activities.

◆ FDR espoused official American "neutrality" regarding the hostilities in Europe and the Far East but also asked that Congress increase spending for defense.

Chapter 15

Brown Shirts, Black Shirts, No Shirts

In This Chapter

- ◆ Dictatorships in Germany and Italy find sympathizers in the United States
- ◆ A crisis over Hitler's demands for part of Czechoslovakia sets Europe on the road to war
- ◆ As Roosevelt attempts to "purge" anti–New Deal Democrats, Republicans make big gains in Congress
- ◆ The New Deal is pronounced dead
- ◆ FDR proposes a vast reorganization of the executive branch

With dictators in power in Germany and Italy, the British and French governments adopted a policy of appeasing them. It reached a climax in a crisis over Hitler's demands for annexation of part of Czechoslovakia. As the stage was set for the start of what would become the Second World War, Americans demanded U.S. neutrality. Pro-Nazi, pro-fascist, and the militant anti-democracy American "Silver Shirts" and "Christian Front" had an enormous following in the United States.

Furious at opposition to the New Deal by several congressional Democrats, Roosevelt launched a "purge." Republicans made big gains in the 1938 House and Senate elections, and pronounced the end of the New Deal. FDR made sweeping changes in the executive branch of the government's structure.

Triumph of the Will

In 1935 Leni Riefenstahl, a young German woman with a brilliant talent for making documentary films, created one that students of both motion pictures and political history regard as the greatest piece of propaganda of all time. Titled *Triumph of the Will*, it presented, without a word of narration, a gigantic rally of the Nazi party. Held in the city of Nuremberg in 1934, the rally was staged by Hitler's favorite architect, Albert Speer.

The film presented a vivid record of the fervor of thousands of "Brown Shirt" members of the S.A. (*Sturmabteilung*, meaning "Storm Troopers"), black-clad men of the S.S. (*Geheime Staatspolizei*, better known as Gestapo), Hitler Youth, and other groups. Scene after scene of *Triumph of the Will* glorified Germany's charismatic "Führer" (leader) as a strong-willed savior who would avenge the German people's humiliation after World War I.

Famous Faces

Leni Riefenstahl was a talented filmmaker and very ambitious. A former actress and dancer, she got the job because Hitler liked her. It was rumored that she once danced nude for him. After the war she was investigated by the Nuremberg war crimes commission but found innocent because she'd never been a member of the Nazi party. In her 1993 memoir she claimed that it was political ignorance that inspired her wartime activities, not a sympathy for Hitler and Nazidom.

An Austrian-born corporal who had been gassed in that conflict, Hitler had used the Nazi Party to come to power in an election, then consolidated it into a dictatorship, with the intention of "reclaiming" territory that had been taken from Germany. Among Nazi aims was the elimination of Jews, first from Germany, then from Europe, and ultimately from the world.

Later admitting that the party rally "was planned not only as a spectacular mass meeting but as a spectacular propaganda film," Riefenstahl said that "the ceremonies and precise plans of the parades, marches, processions, the architecture if the halls and stadium were designed for the convenience of cameras."

Distinguished American film critic Paul Rotha wrote in 1952 that *Triumph of the Will* "was unique in film history as a dramatized account of a fictional spectacle organized for propaganda," and that it "surpassed any Hollywood super-film."

While the film was lauded as a cinematic masterpiece, one that won the prestigious gold medal at the 1937 Paris International Exposition, it met with protests outside Germany and Italy. And it shocked the world into realizing that Hitler and his minions posed a serious threat to the peace of Europe.

The Man Who Ran Rings Around Hitler

In 1936 Leni Riefenstahl took her camera equipment and crews to the German city of Munich to film the Olympic Games. As head of state, Hitler was the host. He showed up expecting the German athletes to harvest gold medals, thereby validating Nazi theories of the superiority of the Aryan race.

That myth was squashed by a lithe 33-year-old black runner from the United States. Breaking three world speed records and tying another, Jesse Owens won four gold medals. Hitler was so shocked and humiliated that he refused to acknowledge Owens's victories.

An Ominous Balloon with a Swastika

A year after Jesse Owens's triumph of will and skill at Munich, Hitler's pride of the skies, the huge trans-Atlantic dirigible *Hindenburg*, burst into flames as it was attempting to tie up at a "lighter than air" mooring station in Lakehurst, New Jersey. But even if the explosion of the hydrogen-filled airship hadn't put an end to Hitler's dream of German-dominated transocean air travel, the fate of dirigibles was being sealed in the same month as the *Hindenburg* disaster by a U.S. airline, *Pan American*, with a fleet of safe and more roomy air-and-seagoing "Clipper" planes.

Yet for a very brief period in the 1930s, American moviegoers watched newsreels showing dirigibles flying over New York City with the Nazi swastika on them. How many of them noted that if Nazi dirigibles could reach New York carrying passengers, they could also deliver bombs? Probably few, if any.

If the Shirt Fits, Wear It

The truth about almost all Americans in the 1930s is that they couldn't have cared less about what was happening in Europe. The problems they faced here were too important, and persistent, to bother with Nazis in Germany, Mussolini's fascists, a civil war in Spain, and Japanese aggression aimed at taking over Asia and the Pacific in what they called the "greater prosperity sphere of the Empire of the Rising Sun."

Ask most Americans in 1938 about Pearl Harbor, and you probably would have gotten the reply offered by a bewildered would-be actress in 1941, played by Mia Farrow, in Woody Allen's 1987 movie *Radio Days*. When a radio show she was on was interrupted by an announcer with a bulletin that the Japanese had just bombed Pearl Harbor, she asked, "Who's Pearl Harbor?"

Timeline

Like other such groups, the Silver Shirts faded away with the entry of the United States into World War II. Pelley was convicted of treason and sentenced to 15 years in prison. Still assailing FDR in the 1960s as "the forerunner of today's evolving chaos," he died on July 1, 1965, at the age of 75.

While Hitler's Brown Shirts were taking over Germany, and the Black Shirts of Italy were taking orders from Mussolini, shirts of a different hue were being donned by followers of William Dudley Pelley. Operator of a correspondence-course college, the publisher of several papers and magazines, and once a Hollywood screenwriter, he'd launched the "Silver Shirts" on the day after Hitler grabbed power in Germany.

With the formal name "Protestant Militia of America," the Silver Shirts were organized to "save America from a Jewish-sponsored plot." FDR was "a tool in the hands of international bankers." They wore caps copied from those of Hitler's Storm Troopers, blue corduroy trousers, and, of course, silver-colored shirts, each with a scarlet "L," which stood for "Liberation." When the Dies Committee investigated Pelley's "Silver Legion" in 1939, the movement had more than 100,000 followers.

The Christian Front

Remember Father Coughlin, the Radio Priest? By 1939, an army of his followers, the Christian Front, had twice as many "soldiers" as the Silver Shirts. Some 200,000 calling themselves "Fronters" were secretly drilling with rifles and other arms. They roamed New York and other major cities randomly insulting and attacking men and women who looked Jewish or foreign. Their terror sprees naturally had a German name, Propagandamarsch. When the FBI arrested 17 Fronters on January 13, 1940, in New York, agents found arsenals of bombs, the explosive cordite, dynamite, huge caches of ammunition, and an assortment of weapons that had been stolen from National Guard armories.

FBI Director J. Edgar Hoover announced that the Fronters had a plan to "knock off about a dozen congressmen, to assassinate prominent Americans of Jewish extraction, and to seize post offices, the Customs House, and armories in New York City."

In one of the strangest federal trials in U.S. history, despite proof of their plots, the Fronters were acquitted and set free. It turned out that at least one of the jurors was not exactly impartial. She was related to Father Edward F. Brophy, who was the leader of the Front's Eastern Division. The prosecutors had not asked jurors if they had connections to the Fronters.

Meet the American Hitler

Once Hitler and his Nazis had taken over Germany, they took a lead from the Communist International playbook by setting up an operation in America. Founded in 1936 and headed by German-born Fritz Kuhn, it was officially called "The Friends of the New Germany." The name everyone else got to know it by was "Bund." Its headquarters was in a part of the Upper East Side of New York City, known as Yorkville, with a mostly Germanic population.

Facts and Figures

By the end of 1938 there were an estimated 800 American fascist groups. Among the smaller ones were Knights of the White Camelia (West Virginia), Militant Christian Patriots of Los Angeles, and National Gentile League of Washington, D.C.

These American Nazi sympathizers paraded three kinds of uniforms. The rank and file donned black trousers, black caps, and white shirts with swastika armbands. A troop of strong-arm thugs who protected the marchers wore olive drab military-style outfits. The top leaders had actual German uniforms.

Big Noise in the Big Town

One of the Bund rallies, held in Madison Square Garden, attracted 22,000 like-minded nitwits. The main speaker was Herr Kuhn. He roused the faithful by calling FDR "President Rosenfeld." The mayor of New York, whose mother was Jewish, was "the Jew lumpen La Guardia." Racket-busting New York District Attorney Thomas E. Dewey was "Jewey." (Dewey's war with the underworld is discussed in the next chapter.)

An official report of the New York state legislature noted that the Friends of Germany, "chiefly through the stupidity of its leaders, brought a great deal of unfavorable publicity upon the organization. Many of the meetings ended in riot and bloodshed."

At one gathering held on Washington's birthday in 1939, a brave Jewish man, Isadore Greenbaum, broke through the storm troopers and tried to punch out Kuhn. Bund thugs got him before he could land a blow. Newsreel cameras recorded the scene as Greenbaum was beaten and thrown off the stage.

Fritz Goes Up the River

Kuhn had a personal reason for hating La Guardia and Dewey. They had formed an alliance to break up the Bund by lopping off its head, namely Kuhn. But because the Bund's noxious activities had the free speech and freedom of association protections of the

Talk of the Time

The term **up the river** was applied to New York's toughest prison, Sing Sing. It was (and still is) on the west shore of the Hudson River in the town of Ossinning. If you were sent there, you went "up the river."

very Constitution they hoped to scrap, the mayor and D.A. went after the Bund's books. Kuhn was nailed for tax evasion. Indicted on the charge, he was tried, convicted, and sent *up the river* in 1939 for a term of two to five years.

An interesting footnote to all this pro-Nazi stuff was a comment by Hitler's nephew. A resident of New York, William Hitler told the press that his uncle was "a menace."

A Gullible Man with an Umbrella

No, not the movie comedian Charlie Chaplin. This character with an umbrella, and a mustache, was the Prime Minister of Britain, Neville Chamberlain. In 1938, believing that he could do business with Hitler, he went to see the Nazi dictator in Munich, Germany, for the purpose of "avoiding war." But in an age of "shirts," he wound up figuratively losing his. He returned to England waving a paper with Hitler's signature on it.

The agreement gave Germany the slice of Czechoslovakia called Sudetenland. Having gotten this "concession," Hitler promised that he had no more interest in grabbing territory. Chamberlain called it "peace in our time." Others, including Winston Churchill, called it "appeasement." Events would prove the latter right.

Famous Faces

In 1938 the man who would replace Chamberlain after the outbreak of war (September 1939) was out of power and warning England to arm itself. The twentieth century's greatest orator would use his very considerable skill with words to rally the British when they stood alone against the Nazis. Winston Churchill took great delight in calling Hitler "guttersnipe" and "jackanapes." He never said "Nazis." He sneeringly distorted the name and gave it a sinister sound. He always called them "Naaaaahzeees."

FDR Declares War on Democrats

You've read that in 1937 President Roosevelt was so frustrated by rulings of the Supreme Court throwing out large parts of the New Deal that he tried to "pack" it with extra justices who would be favorable to his policies. Well, the "nine old men," as he called them, weren't alone in feeling his ire.

To use a later phrase, Roosevelt was just as "ticked-off" with a group of Southern conservative congressional Democrats. Picking up a name from the Civil War, he called them "*Copperheads*." And he set out to have them defeated in the 1938 elections.

"The issue is not the election of yes-men," said Roosevelt as he declared war on the dissidents, "or men who say they reserve the right to vote their conscience. The issue, in the simplest terms, is the destruction of the New Deal."

Talk of the Time

In the Civil War, **Copperheads** were Northerners who were sympathetic to the South. They belonged to an organization called the "Knights of the Golden Circle of Copperheads."

Here's a Name You'll Recognize

One of the Democrats running for re-election in Texas had FDR's wholehearted support. A lanky political newcomer named Lyndon B. Johnson, he'd been appointed to Congress in 1937 following the death of another representative. In 1938 he was running for the seat in his own right. He had no opposition in the primary, so his return to Congress in a Democrat district was not in doubt.

FDR liked Johnson because he'd headed the Texas branch of the National Youth Administration. As a member of Congress, he'd been four-square behind the New Deal. He'd pushed hard for federal electric projects that would benefit Texas farmers. That was the main reason for the lack of opposition. As vice president of the United States and head of the Space program, Johnson also saw to it that the headquarters of the National Aeronautics and Space Administration (NASA) would be in Houston, Texas. His "War on Poverty" programs as president were patterned on FDR's New Deal.

FDR's "Purge" Backfires

When Roosevelt made it known that he intended to "purge" Congress of Copperheads, he was warned by his closest aides that he was asking for trouble. Vice President John Nance Garner said, "The Boss has stirred up a hornet's nest."

He was right. All the Copperheads won their primaries save one. Congressman O'Connor lost. Recognizing defeat, Roosevelt said, "It takes a long time to bring the past up to the present."

Timeline

FDR's Copperheads were Senators Walt George of Georgia, "Cotton Ed" Smith of South Carolina, Millard Tydings of Maryland, Pat McCarran of Nevada, and Alva Adams of Colorado. John J. O'Connor of New York, chairman of the House Rules Committee, bottled up any New Deal legislation he didn't like.

Roosevelt biographer Nathan Miller wrote of FDR's attempt to oust the Copperheads that by "intruding" into local elections FDR had lost the "moral issue."

All Politics Are Local

One of the men running for office in 1938 (not for Congress, but re-election as Governor of Massachusetts) was a loveable rogue named James Michael Curley. A former member of Congress and mayor of Boston, he'd taken advantage of New Deal programs to build bridges, roads, playgrounds, and hospitals. Free-handed with patronage and political favors, he had preached—and proved—that all politics are local.

Eager to build up a presidential faction in Congress, FDR and his liberal advisers failed to take into account the local nature of American politics. That is, elections of national significance often are decided on strictly local issues. Consequently, FDR witnessed not only the re-election of most of the candidates he'd marked for purging but also a raft of Republicans.

Famous Faces

James Michael Curley lost in 1938 but won election to Congress in 1942 and 1944. Then he was elected mayor again in 1945 (fourth time). Found guilty of fraud and jailed, he remained mayor. Defeated for the office in 1949 and 1951, he quit politics. He died in 1958. If you want a taste of what he was like, read Edwin O'Connor's 1956 novel *The Last Hurrah*, or see the 1958 movie of that title by director John Ford, with Spencer Tracey as the Curley-like "Mayor Skeffington."

A Rude Awakening

When the nation went to the polls in November 1938, they voted for Democrats marked for purging, and a bunch of new Republicans. Among the GOP victors were Robert A. Taft, son of President Taft, sent to the Senate from Ohio; and 31-year-old Harold Stassen as governor of Minnesota. Both would go on to be major figures in the Republican Party long after FDR's death.

The Congress that FDR got was still controlled by Democrats, but the Republicans had scored their biggest gains since 1928. The 76th Congress would consist of:

Senate: 69 Democrats

23 Republicans (a gain of seven)

2 Farmer-Labor

1 Progressive

1 Independent

House: 262 Democrats

    170 Republicans (a gain of 81)

       1 Farmer-Labor

       2 Progressives

Did the Election Sound the Death Knell for the New Deal?

Was the 1938 election a repudiation of FDR and the New Deal? It was seen that way by many, especially by Republicans. But a poll taken by *Fortune* magazine in 1939 found that 60 percent of those questioned approved in some way of both. And the Democrats could point out, as they did, that not since President James Monroe's day had a party kept control of Congress in a mid-term election in a president's second term.

To Preserve Our Reforms

When Roosevelt did not present Congress with a batch of proposals for economic and social reforms, political pundits pronounced the death of the New Deal. And FDR appeared to agree. In his annual message, sent to Capitol Hill on January 4, 1939, he declared, "Our full energies may now be released to invigorate the process of recovery in order to preserve our reforms, and to give every man and woman who wants to work a real job at a living wage."

To accomplish this, Roosevelt requested increased funds for the WPA. When Congress denied him all the money he wanted, WPA rolls were slashed. This caused WPA workers to go on strike, with the result that many WPA employees were fired.

The WPA took another hit in the form of the Hatch Act. Angry that WPA workers in Kentucky, Tennessee, and Maryland had engaged in political activity in the 1938 elections, Congress banned federal employees who were not involved in policy-making from engaging in political campaigns. Political parties were also prohibited from soliciting funds from relief workers. The law also set limits on campaign spending by political parties ($3 million a year) and by individuals ($5,000).

Reshuffling the Executive Branch

While Roosevelt failed to get more money for the WPA, he fared better with proposals for changing the way the executive branch was structured. The Executive Reorganization Act was aimed at increasing government efficiency by regrouping and simplifying federal agencies, boards, commissions, and other bodies that had been in existence for half a century. The result was creation of the institution that we know today as "The Executive Office of the White House."

To help manage it, the president was authorized to appoint six administrative assistants. The reorganization also removed the Budget Office from the Treasury Department and made it a division of the White House. The Act also created the Liaison Office for Personnel Management, Office of Governmental Reports, Office for Emergency Management, and National Resources Planning Board.

Mr. Ickes Says Good-Bye

Another step taken by Roosevelt in reshuffling the Executive Branch was to take the Public Works Administration (PWA) out of the Interior Department. Since 1933, the head of the Interior Department had been Harold Ickes. With the loss of the PWA, he decided to leave government. When the day came (June 26, 1939), his former employees gave him a plaque. Reading like an obituary for the New Deal, it said:

> You drew the thousands of us from all walks of life, from all corners of the country, and you have wielded us into a vital organization of which we are all proud. You have shown neither fear nor favor; you have neither asked nor tolerated any bending of the knee or any concessions to undue influence; and you have asked of us only one thing: that our job be well and truly done for the good of the Nation.

Summing up the demise of the New Deal, Great Depression historian T. H. Watkins wrote, "An era that had discovered hope in the wreckage of the Depression was passing away now, and another was taking its place, one that would be influenced less by the domestic winds of economic trouble than by the even more terrifying uncertainties of a world hell-bent on destruction."

Roosevelt biographer Nathan Miller described FDR at this time as a president "no longer devoting his individual attention" to the domestic concerns that had occupied him for six years, but one who was "absorbed in foreign dangers and American defense."

Bracing for the Gales of War

On January 5, 1939, Roosevelt had asked Congress to authorize $1.3 billion for national defense. In the meantime, he wanted emergency funding in the amount of $300 million for immediate strengthening of air defenses for the continental United States, outlying possessions, and territories. This money would go for a "two-ocean navy," training of civilian pilots, improvement of the defenses of the Panama Canal and Hawaii, and the procurement of military supplies and equipment.

He also requested revisions in the Neutrality Act of 1936. It had banned the United States from granting loans or credits to any nation engaged in belligerent acts. Increasingly worried about the actions of Germany and Italy, he warned that if the terms of the Neutrality Act prohibited him from aiding England, France, and other free nations of Europe, the United States would "be on the side of Hitler."

Hoping for a lifting of the Act's embargo on arms shipments to friendly nations, he ran into opposition from isolationists in Congress. Only after Hitler attacked Poland on September 1, 1939, and Britain and France declared war on Germany, would Congress agree to allow the allies to buy arms on a "cash and carry" basis. But even then, as you will read in Chapter 21, "America First," American involvement in the "European war" would be fiercely resisted not only in the Congress but also by the vast majority of Depression-weary Americans who believed in "America first."

Going Crazy over Royalty

Late in the summer of 1939 as Roosevelt tried to persuade the Congress to clear the way for the United States to aid Britain in becoming a bulwark against Nazism, beneficiaries of the world's first successful colonial revolution suddenly went crazy over the heirs of the monarchy that had been given the boot in 1776. One of the great mysteries of American history is the fact that the people of the greatest democracy in the world have always been fascinated by the British Royal Family. It was manifested first after World War I when the country went into a tizzy over a visit to the United States by a young, dashing Prince of Wales.

They did so again in 1936 when, as King Edward VIII, he gave up the throne to marry the twice-divorced American Wallis Warfield Simpson. Millions of Americans stopped what they were doing to turn on radios to hear his abdication speech in which he tugged at their hearts (or caused them to shake heads in disbelief) when he declared that he could not perform his duties as king "without the help and support of the woman I love."

Six decades later, upon the death of Diana, Princess of Wales, in a car crash in Paris in 1997, the lamenting in the United States was such that you'd have thought that the country was still a British colony. But none of these demonstrations of what's come to be called "the special relationship" between Britain and the United States can match the frenzy with which Americans welcomed a visit by King George VI and Queen Elizabeth in September 1939. The royal pair stopped off in Washington on their way to visit Canada, and to visit the New York World's Fair (see Chapter 20, "World of Tomorrow").

FDR and Eleanor entertained them at a White House state dinner and again at Roosevelt's home in Hyde Park, New York, where the bill of fare for lunch was hot dogs. After a lengthy conversation with FDR on the European crisis, the king asked Canadian prime minister Mackenzie King, "Why don't my ministers talk to me as the president did tonight? I feel exactly as though my father were giving me the most careful and wise advice."

As the royal couple waved good-bye from the rear platform of their special train, Eleanor Roosevelt would record, "One thought of the clouds that hung over them and the worries which they were going to face, and turned away with a heavy heart."

True. But affection for a charming King of England and his wife was not enough to persuade Americans to take up arms to once again save Europe.

Ga-Ga over George

In the 157 years since the American Revolution, there had been 33 presidents of the United States but only 8 monarchs in Great Britain. During that long history, the interests of the two countries had clashed on the western frontier, fought the War of 1812, and had come very close to hostilities over British colonialism in the Western Hemisphere. In 1917 most Americans had come out against the United States "Saving England" by getting into the Great War, and 22 years later, there was very little enthusiasm for getting mixed up in a new European war that a great many Americans believed Britain had helped to bring on by its appeasement of Hitler.

Yet in the face of this history, the people of a country that had fought the first successful war to throw off rule by a British monarch went crazy with enthusiasm over the fact that George VI was the first King of England to visit the land that had been lost by King George III. Preparations for the White House visit had begun six months in advance. White House historian William Seale noted, "The house of Presidents underwent such a cleaning as perhaps it had never known." The executive mansion was so neat and spruced-up that the head housekeeper boasted that it "shone like a brand new stove."

Fit for a King

Having recently hosted George VI at the U.S. legation in Paris, our ambassador to France, William C. Bullitt, thought it would be a good idea to tip off Eleanor Roosevelt about what the British King would expect in the way of accommodations. Among Bullitt's "suggestions for the furnishing of His Majesty's Room" were that there be a large bed with the head against the wall, two pillows with no bolster (the King always brought his own), warm but light blankets with silk covers, and an eiderdown quilt which could be "accordion pleated at the foot of the bed."

In the bathroom or bedroom, and preferably in a window recess, the king required "a dressing table with triple mirror, high enough to enable contemplating oneself when standing," and a "very comfortable settee." His Majesty would bring his own brand of cigarettes, but the White House would have to provide the ashtrays, matches, cigars, and cigarettes "for guests."

Hangers were needed in "great numbers; some of them with wide back slightly curved; others with a double bar for trousers; no special clip for hangers for trousers." The king did not desire a "toweled bathrobe," but he preferred "large bath towels." For the royal visit to the Paris embassy, Bullitt noted, he had bought sheet-sized towels. The desk should be equipped with "an inkstand with two inkwells, one full of blue-black and another of red ink."

No Need for Instructions

The advice from Bullitt was well-intentioned, but Mrs. Roosevelt found it a little presumptuous. Having gone to school in England, she knew the ways of the British. She later told one of her assistants, "I always wanted to ask Mr. Bullitt, whether, when he stayed at the White House, he had not found in the bathrooms such of the things he listed as essential, like soap, a glass, towels, and the like."

The bedroom provided to King George was the one that had been President Lincoln's study and was believed to be haunted by the ghost of the Great Emancipator. Queen Elizabeth was given the Rose Bedroom, just across the hall, but without a ghost.

The royal visit was the last great public event in the White House in the 1930s. The next representative of the British government to stay at 1600 Pennsylvania Avenue would be Prime Minister Winston Churchill, after all American hesitation about the United States getting into the war on England's side went up in the smoke of burning ships of the U.S. Pacific Fleet at Pearl Harbor.

The Least You Need to Know

◆ Pro-Nazi and pro-fascist groups formed in the United States to oppose United States involvement in European affairs.

◆ Following FDR's attempt to "purge" opponents of his policies from the Democratic Party in 1936, the press and political sages pronounced the New Deal "dead."

◆ Congress drastically cut finding for New Deal programs.

◆ Roosevelt reorganized the presidential staff by creating the Executive Office of the White House and making the Bureau of the Budget a division of the White House.

Guys with No Necks

In This Chapter

- ◆ With repeal, ex-bootleggers find new lines of work
- ◆ Cars, interstate crime, and "G-Men"
- ◆ Blazing ends: Dillinger, Pretty Boy Floyd, Bonnie and Clyde
- ◆ Trial of the century: the Lindbergh baby kidnapping
- ◆ The fall of Lucky Luciano

With the repeal of Prohibition, gangsters shifted their criminal activities from bootlegging to gambling, prostitution, extortion, and racketeering. Fast cars provided mobility to crooks. A rash of "interstate crimes" presented a challenge to the Federal Bureau of Investigation. "Public Enemy No. 1" John Dillinger, Pretty Boy Floyd, and Bonnie and Clyde became folk heroes.

All-out efforts to catch them ended in blazes of gunfire. New York City's racket-busting District Attorney, Thomas E. Dewey, brought down the country's top crime boss, Charles "Lucky" Luciano. When Charles Lindbergh's infant son was kidnapped and murdered, the nation's attention was riveted by the crime, the manhunt, and the first "trial of the century."

The Law of Unintended Consequences

During the national debate over amending the U.S. Constitution to outlaw the manufacture and sale of alcoholic drinks, Congressman Fiorello La Guardia of New York declared, "I maintain this law will be almost impossible of enforcement. And if this law fails to be enforced—as it certainly will be, as it is drawn—it will create contempt and disregard for law all over the country."

Famous Faces

Al Capone did time at the Atlanta and Leavenworth federal prisons, then went to the new "escape-proof" Alcatraz. Freed in 1939 on "good behavior," but really because he had incurable syphilis, he lived at his estate in Palm Island, Florida. He died in 1949.

As Prohibition took effect, no one in America benefited from it more than a New York–born, squat, scar-faced thug by the name of Alphonse Capone. Having gone to Chicago to work for his criminal mentor, Johnny Torrio, Al eventually became America's most famous criminal. But on October 24, 1931, he found himself sentenced to 11 years in federal prison on tax evasion charges. Prohibition had made him a multimillionaire, and a folk hero.

When the 18th Amendment was repealed two years after Capone went to prison, it was proof of the law of unintended consequences. That La Guardia had been right could be seen everywhere in the form of bootleggers. Like Capone, they'd become rich, powerful, and plentiful by recognizing that Prohibition was the second most unpopular law in history. (First was the income tax.)

But as the beer and whiskey again flowed legally, gangsters who'd flourished during the "great experiment" had to find other ways to line their pockets. They did so by meeting the public demand for ancient vices that were equal to the thirst for strong drink. Gangs switched to organized prostitution and catering to a desire to strike it rich by betting on "the *numbers*," a racehorse, the turn of a card, the roll of dice, and the whirl of a roulette wheel.

Talk of the Time

Also known as "policy," **numbers** was a gambling system in which a person put money on a number that would be determined by the outcome of a horse race at a designated track. The racket still exists, but it's got competition these days from government-run numbers games known as the Lottery and Lotto.

Lord of the Underworld

Through maneuvers that are too complex to recount here, the early 1930s brought a revolution in the ranks of organized crime that dethroned the founders of the American Mafia. The old "Mustache Petes" who'd come mostly from Sicily were eliminated in a coup masterminded by Charles "Lucky" Luciano.

With the Mustache Petes and Capone out of the picture, Lucky set out to coordinate all aspects of crime on a nationwide basis through a "commission." His efforts resulted in two meetings of the leading crime figures of the country in 1934. And so was born "La Cosa Nostra," meaning "our thing" in Italian.

 Famous Faces

Born in Sicily, Lucky Luciano's real name was Charles Lucania. He got the moniker "Lucky" after he was "taken for a ride" by gangland rivals. The nearly fatal beating left him with a scarred face.

In association with boyhood friends Benjamin "Bugsy" Siegel and a financial wizard named Meyer Lansky (both Jewish), Lucky earned most of his money through prostitution rings. But he expanded his activities into extortion rackets. His men muscled their way into control of labor unions, enabling them to use threats of strikes to shake down legitimate businesses.

Chief lieutenants in the Luciano mob were Frank Costello, Vito Genovese, and Louis "Lepke Buchalter." Costello was in charge of the slot machine racket. Genovese was a killer and in charge of Luciano's brothels and narcotics operation. He fled to Italy in 1937 to avoid a murder rap and then befriend Mussolini. During World War II, he controlled the Italian black market. Lepke moved into the garment business rackets by setting up a corrupt union. He was also chief of the mob's Brooklyn-based killings-on-order outfit known as "Murder, Incorporated."

You Wouldn't Want to Mess with These Guys

Although Luciano was the uncontested head of La Cosa Nostra, he didn't have control over everyone. The rogues gallery of these independent bad guys included:

- **Jack "Legs" Diamond.** Born and raised in Philadelphia, he got the nickname "Legs" because of the speed he showed in escaping cops. He was shot at and wounded so often that he was also known as "the Clay Pigeon." A bootlegger, an owner of speakeasies, and a stone-cold killer, he was rubbed out on December 19, 1931, in an Albany, New York, rooming house, allegedly by hoods acting on orders from Dutch Schultz.

- **Arthur "Dutch Schultz" Flegenheimer.** A bootlegger and Luciano's main rival in the numbers racket, Dutch was a ruthless killer. When he vowed to assassinate New York District Attorney Thomas E. Dewey (see the following section), Luciano ordered him killed. He was gunned down on October 23, 1935, by Charles "the Bug" Workman and Mendy Weiss, in the Palace Chop House in Newark, New Jersey.

- **Francis "Two Gun" Crowley.** A vicious murderer and bank robber, Two Gun killed a police officer and then had a shoot-out with New York cops in what was known as "the Siege of West 80th Street" in 1931. He died in Sing Sing's electric chair a few days before his twentieth birthday.

- **Vincent "Mad Dog" Coll.** The son of Irish immigrants, he was a bootlegger and active in the numbers racket until he shot and killed a five-year-old boy in a botched attempt at a gangland rubout. Dutch Schultz was so angry about the death of the child that he ordered Coll killed. Mad Dog was blasted to kingdom-come in a phone booth in a Manhattan drug store.

The Art of the Stick-Up and Fast Getaway

While Luciano and his henchmen were organizing crime in cities and forming a nation-wide criminal syndicate, out in the wide open spaces in what Lucky and his urban henchmen would disdain as "the sticks" some rugged individualists were busy demonstrating that all you needed to get money was a gun and a speedy car.

Not since the Wild West era of Jesse James, the Dalton brothers, and Butch Cassidy and the Sundance Kid had Americans witnessed such a blizzard of brazen bank holdups. But now the daredevil escapes were made in automobiles that sped the crooks safely out of reach of local cops by crossing state lines.

In 1933 bank robberies were being pulled at the rate of almost two a day. Some were carried out by individuals, but most were the work of gangs of well-armed bandits who rode into town in a car, and sometimes in two or three. They fled via the fastest route to the state line, leaving pursuing cops watching in dismay as they escaped to other jurisdictions.

Federal Law Applies the Brakes

To extend the reach of law enforcement, Congress passed a measure that empowered the federal government to go after anyone who had crossed state lines to avoid prosecution. It was one of nine laws giving the feds, in the words of the Attorney General, Homer Cummings, "control over the unlawful activities of those who deliberately take advantage of the protection presently afforded them by state lines in perpetrating their crimes." The new laws also targeted anyone who drove a stolen car across state lines. Authority to implement the laws was given to the Justice Department's Bureau of Investigation.

Formed on the orders of President Theodore Roosevelt, and later named the Federal Bureau of Investigation (FBI), it had been a rather ineffective and lackluster organization until it got a new director in 1924. He was J. (John) Edgar Hoover. He took over the Bureau with a pledge from President Harding's Attorney General, Harlan F. Stone, that he would be free to appoint agents on the basis of merit. Hoover also demanded that the FBI would function without political influence.

Machine Gun Kelly and the G-Men

Enabled by the "interstate flight" law, FBI agents in 1933 were on the trail of one of the country's worst criminals. A former bootlegger turned kidnapper by the name of George "Machine Gun" Kelly, he was wanted for kidnapping an Oklahoma millionaire oil man, Charles Urschel.

Famous Faces

During the anti-communist "Red Scare" of the years after World War I, J. Edgar Hoover made a name for himself in the Justice Department's Intelligence Division. This resulted in his appointment in 1921 as assistant director of the FBI.

Learning that Kelly was holed up with his wife in a house in Memphis, Tennessee, the FBI and Memphis police swooped down on the hideout in the early morning of September 26, 1933. As the agents burst in, the startled, but unarmed, Kelly pleaded, "Don't shoot, G-Men! Don't shoot, G-Men."

Kelly's fearful plea made for great newspaper headlines, and the name "G-Men" immediately became such a part of the language that it was the title of a 1935 movie starring James Cagney. (More on the gangster movies of the 1930s in Chapter 18, "I Ain't So Tough.") But the event of the 1930s that secured the FBI's reputation for getting its man was really made the year after Machine Gun Kelly gave up to without a shot.

The Last Picture Show

On the night of July 22, 1934, the movie showing at Chicago's Biograph Theater was *Manhattan Melodrama*. Starring Clark Gable, William Powell, Myrna Loy, and Mickey Rooney, it was about two boyhood pals who remained friends while one grew up to be a D.A. (district attorney) and the other a gangster.

Waiting outside the theater as the film played were a team of FBI men led by special agent Melvin Purvis. A cigar smoker, he held an unlighted one. They were waiting to nab "Public Enemy No. 1." As their target came out of the Biograph, Purvis would inform the other agents by lighting up the stogie. The signal to move was to be a certain woman leaving the theater with Dillinger. If all went well, the man accompanying her would be going by the name "James Lawrence." His real name was John Herbert Dillinger.

Timeline

John Dillinger didn't make the FBI's 10 Most-Wanted list. That famous roster wasn't created until the 1950s. "Public Enemy No. 1" was an invention of the Chicago Crime Commission.

Born in Indianapolis in 1903, Dillinger spent some time in the Navy but found a life more satisfying as leader of a gang that included a trio of other desperadoes, Homer Van Meter, Charles "Pretty Boy" Floyd, and George "Baby Face" Nelson.

The FBI's Dillinger "Wanted" poster.

Dillinger earned the dubious title of "Public Enemy No. 1" after leaving a terror trail of ten murders, seven wounded men, four bank robberies, three police arsenals looted, a daring departure from an "escape-proof" jail by using a whittled-wood pistol, and the liberation of men from three prisons. Amazingly, he'd done all of this between September 1933 and July 1934. But the FBI was hot on his trail for none of these crimes. The arrest warrant tucked into Agent Purvis's pocket was for the fact that he'd driven a stolen car across the border of Indiana and Illinois.

The feds almost had him twice. The final break came when a Romanian immigrant and brothel operator, Ana Cumpanas, also known as Ana Sage, struck a deal. If Ana would get a guarantee that she wouldn't be deported, she'd put her dainty finger on Dillinger. Should the FBI stake out the Biograph theater on a certain night, the fellow with her would be Public Enemy No. 1. Purvis wasn't concerned. He'd know Dillinger on sight, even though Dillinger had gotten a facelift and dyed his hair.

While Purvis and a small army of loaded-for-bear G-Men waited for the picture show to end, J. Edgar Hoover sat by his phone at home for word that Dillinger was in custody or, preferably, dead. He soon learned that moments after the country's most dangerous man since Al Capone had ambled from the theater, Dillinger was sprawled dead in an alley. He'd been mowed down by a fusillade of government-issue bullets.

Bye-Bye "Pretty Boy"

With Dillinger relegated to history, the FBI set its sights on Homer Van Meter, Pretty Boy Floyd, and Baby Face Nelson. Homer got his comeuppance on August 23, 1934. Betrayed by friends, he was rubbed out in an alley in St. Paul, Minnesota. A month later (October 22), Melvin Purvis and local cops in Ohio caught up with Floyd in an Ohio field. As he raced away, he was cut down like a stalk of corn by FBI guns. As Floyd lay dying, Purvis sauntered up and lit a cigar. Just to be sure, he asked, "Are you Pretty Boy Floyd?" "I'm Floyd all right," he gasped. "You've got me this time."

Famous Faces

Ana Sage became famous as "the woman in red," but the dress she wore was actually orange. The marquee lights made it appear red. The feds kept their word on not deporting her. But she got the boot in 1947 as an "undesirable."

Facts and Figures

Dillinger got away with a total of $372,500. But the costs of finally getting him came to $595,000.

Getting "Baby Face"

Baby Face Nelson (real name, Lester Gillis) was spotted by a pair of FBI men, Sam Cowley and Herman Hollis, in a car on a country road near Fox Grove, Illinois, on November 27, 1934. They gave chase and caught up with him near the town of Barrington. Machine gun in hand, he charged the agents. Though blasted by Cowley's Tommy Gun, he managed to get away. But not for long. His perforated corpse was found the next day in a ditch near Niles, Illinois.

Two Gun Crowley had given the FBI a colorful synonym in "G-Men," but getting Dillinger, Floyd, and Nelson elevated the Bureau, and its dull dog-face director, to such a legendary position that no president would dare to remove J. Edgar Hoover from his job. He remained "the Director" to the day of his death in 1972.

Bonnie and Clyde

Thanks to the 1967 movie starring Warren Beatty and Faye Dunaway in the title roles, Clyde Barrow and Bonnie Parker became even more famous than they were between 1932 and 1934. A pair of Texas misfits, they never pocketed more than a few hundred dollars in loot at a time.

Like Dillinger and other Midwest-based criminals, Bonnie and Clyde captured the imaginations of a lot of down-and-out, law-abiding Americans who figured that in robbing banks they were turning the tables on institutions that had stolen the land of countless farmers. As if they were mythic heroes, Bonnie and Clyde had a lot of people rooting for them, even though nobody doubted how their lives would end. Part of a song about them went:

> Some day they will go down together,
> And they will bury them side by side.
> To a few it means grief.
> To the law it's a relief.
> But it's death to Bonnie and Clyde.

Their fame came to an end on May 23, 1934, in a Dillinger-like setup arranged by a friend. The result was a cop ambush that the movie *Bonnie and Clyde* depicted far more vividly than words can.

If you think Bonnie and Clyde had to wait 33 years to have their lives immortalized on film, you're wrong. Famed director Fritz Lang adapted their story for the screen in 1937. In *You Only Live Once*, Sylvia Sidney was the loosely based Bonnie character; Henry Fonda provided a sympathetic version of Clyde as the victim of a brutal society.

Crime of the Century

In March of the year that Bonnie Parker decided to add some spark to her dreary existence by running off with Clyde Barrow, and while John Dillinger and his gang were making bank withdrawals at the points of guns, Americans were sickened by the news that the worst possible kind of crime had been committed against the most adored public figure in the country.

On the night of March 1, 1932, Charles "Lucky Lindy" Lindbergh and his attractive, pregnant wife, the former Anne Morrow, were at their home in Hopewell, New Jersey.

Their two-year-old son, Charles Jr., was, they believed, tucked snugly in bed. But in the hours between 8 and 10 o'clock, an intruder had used a makeshift ladder to reach the child's bedroom window, enter, and take him away. Left behind was a note. Written in crude English with no punctuation, it demanded $140,000 dollars in $5, $10, and $20 notes. The kidnapper promised, "The child is in Gut care."

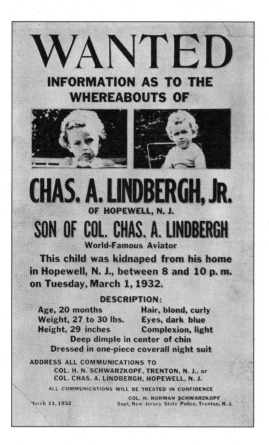

New Jersey police issued appeals for information on the whereabouts of the Lindbergh baby.

Leading the investigation by the New Jersey State Police was its superintendent, Col. H. Norman Schwarzkopf. While he, his police, the Lindberghs, and a shocked nation hoped that the child would be returned safe and sound, Lindbergh paid the ransom through an intermediary. He gave $50,000 to a man who called himself "John." The payment was made in a cemetery in the Bronx. But on May 12 all hope for the baby came to an end. The murdered baby's body was discovered five and a half miles from the Lindbergh house.

Hot Tips, Dead Ends

The most promising clue in the case was the ladder. It had been hammered together in crude fashion from scraps of lumber. An expert on wood analyzed every part of it, including the nails. Alerts were sent out that described the ransom money, which had been paid in gold certificates whose serial numbers had been recorded.

Several promising leads were followed. Possible suspects were questioned. All of these prospects proved to be dead ends. Then, 2 years, 6 months, and 14 days after the kidnapping, the New Jersey State Police, the FBI, and New York City cops got a break in the case. Part of the ransom, a $10 gold certificate, had been used to buy 5 gallons of gas at a Bronx gas station. Fortunately, the attendant jotted down the license plate number of the man's car. It was traced to a German immigrant by the name of Bruno Richard Hauptmann.

Hauptmann denied he was the kidnapper and continued to do so as he was tried. Called "the trial of the century," it became the first media circus as reporters, newsreels, and radio newsmen flocked to cover it from all over the world. Despite overwhelming evidence, including pieces of wood matching that in the ladder that were found in Hauptmann's home, along with ransom money, Hauptmann stuck to his claim of innocence to the moment he was strapped in an electric chair at the New Jersey State Prison in Trenton on April 2, 1936. His widow continued to insist that he was not guilty for the rest of her life.

The Lindbergh Kidnapping Law

The lasting result of the Lindbergh baby kidnapping was passage by Congress of a law that made kidnapping a federal crime. But as sad as the murder of the hero's curly haired child was, it was not the country's only kidnapping. In the 1930s, grabbing people for ransom had become one of the few industries that was growing. So many were taking place that the FBI set up a special phone for people to report them (National 8-7717 in Washington, D.C.).

Major kidnappings of the 1930s were those of:

- ◆ **William Hamm Jr.** June 15, 1933. A millionaire Minnesota brewer was snatched by a gang that included a ruthless killer named Alvin Karpis. Hamm was set free for a $100,000 ransom. Karpis was caught and sentenced to life at Alcatraz.
- ◆ **Charles F. Urschel.** July 22, 1933. As noted earlier, it was the work of Machine Gun Kelly.
- ◆ **Edward G. Brenner.** July 17, 1934. The perpetrators were the "Ma" Barker gang. One of them, "Doc" Barker, took part in the Hamm kidnapping. Ma and another son, Fred, died in an FBI shootout at Lake Weir, Florida, in 1935.

- ◆ **George Weyerhaeuser.** May 24, 1935. The nine-year-old scion of the paper-making company was freed after payment of $200,000. His kidnapper, William Mahan, a department store clerk, got 60 years.

- ◆ **Charles Mattson.** December 27, 1936. The kidnapper of the 10-year-old Tacoma, Washington, boy asked for $28,000, but never tried to collect it. Charles was found dead on January 11, 1937.

- ◆ **Charles S. Ross.** September 27, 1937. A 72-year-old greeting card tycoon, Ross was taken by John Henry Seadlund and James Atwood Gray near Franklin Park, Illinois. A ransom of $50,000 was paid. Seadlund killed both Ross and Gray and buried them in Wisconsin. J. Edgar Hoover called Seadlund "the most vicious killer I ever knew." Seadlund paid for his crimes in the electric chair in Cook County, Illinois, on July 14, 1938.

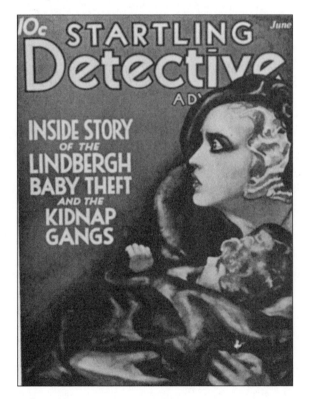

The Lindbergh case and a rash of kidnappings were the subject of many magazine stories.

Tom Dewey Gets Lucky

The FBI's achievements in going after John Dillinger, Pretty Boy Floyd, Machine Gun Kelley, and others were spectacular because of their breathtaking finales of blazing gunfire. Yet none of them surpassed the accomplishment of a soft-spoken district attorney whose only weapon was a New York jury. Fascinated onlookers had not witnessed such a contest since David went up against Goliath.

The modern David was Thomas E. Dewey. Born on March 24, 1902, in Owosso, Michigan, he earned a reputation for crime-busting as an assistant U.S. attorney by putting away one of New York's biggest hoodlums. Going by the name Waxey Gordon, Irving Wexler had been in control of all Prohibition rum-running on the East Coast. His illicit enterprises brought him a profit of $4.5 million in two years, on which he'd paid $2,010 in taxes. He was also directly linked to 16 murders in three months. After hearing Dewey's evidence, a jury took only 51 minutes to convict Gordon.

Elected District Attorney of Manhattan in 1934, Dewey next set his sights on Luciano. Scoffing at such brash impudence, Lucky and his cocky henchmen called Dewey "the Boy Scout." But law-abiding citizens of New York were not in a laughing mood when they heard for the first time, from D.A. Dewey, that crime was "organized," and at the head of this national criminal "syndicate" stood Lucky Luciano.

Facts and Figures

Luciano's estimated "take" per year was $12 million. Lucky used part of it to live in high style at the Waldorf-Astoria Hotel.

Facts and Figures

Each "girl" handed over 2 percent of her "wages" to Luciano. The madam of a "house" paid Luciano half the gross. Multiply that by several thousand bawdy houses, and you can see that prostitution paid Luciano a sizeable income.

"There is today," declared Dewey, "scarcely a business in New York which does not somehow pay its tribute to the underworld—a tribute levied by force and collected by fear."

Knowing that Luciano ran all the prostitution in the city, Dewey began his pursuit by sending teams of raiders to the houses and apartments where Lucky's "girls" worked. Their names were as colorful as any found in the "guys and dolls" stories by Damon Runyon. Trooping into Dewey's office in the Woolworth Building with tales to tell about Luciano were Gas House Lil, Frisco Jean, Nigger Ruth, Polack Frances, Silver-Tongued Elsie, Sadie the Chink, Jennie the Factory, and the one who gave Dewey all the ammunition he needed, a brassy hooker named Cokey Flo Brown.

A One-Way Ticket to a Home in the Sticks

On the basis of Flo's testimony, and on evidence gathered by Dewey's investigators, Lucky Luciano went on trial on May 11, 1936. It lasted until June 7. When the jury came back with a verdict of guilty on all counts, the result was a term of 30 to 50 years for Lucky to spend in the state pen "up in the sticks" at Dannemora, New York. By the autumn of 1937, Dewey and his deputies had chalked up an astonishing record of 72 convictions out of 73 cases tried. The result was the breakup of the big rackets in Manhattan and the imprisonment of numerous gangsters.

Another consequence was that the bosses of organized crime decided to keep a very low profile. They managed to do so fairly well until the 1950s when a Senate committee headed by Estes Kefauver of Tennessee drew back the veil in a sensational televised investigation. The "star" of the show was Frank Costello, who refused to let TV cameras show his face. They zeroed in on another portion of his anatomy, thereby making Costello's hands the most famous bodily appendages since millions of World War II GIs went crazy over movie queen Betty Grable's "million dollar legs."

How's This for an Ironic Twist?

Flash forward to the war years. Concerned about possible Nazi sabotage on the New York waterfront, and knowing that Luciano's mob was still in control of the longshoremen's union, the U.S. Navy asked Luciano for his gang's help in protecting the ships. For cooperating in this way, Luciano was promised that when the war was over, he'd be released from prison and sent back to his native Sicily.

Here's the irony. The governor who had to sign the papers setting him free after serving only 10 years was Thomas E. Dewey. So on February 10, 1946, Luciano departed America's shores. When a reporter found him a few years later and asked if he regretted the life he'd led, Lucky replied, "I'd do the same thing all over again, but I'd do it legal. I learned too late that you need just as good a brain to make a crooked million as you need to make an honest million. These days you apply for a license to steal from the public. If I had my time again, I'd make damn sure that I got that license."

While some Americans looked at Bonnie and Clyde, John Dillinger, Pretty Boy Floyd, Machine Gun Kelly, Lucky Luciano, and other headline-grabbing criminals as folk heroes, most people saw them for what they were. Yet there's no getting away from the fact that the way they thumbed their noses at the government struck at least a momentary sympathetic chord in millions of ordinary men and women who often wondered where they'd get the money to put food on their tables. One can only wonder just how many of them might have thought about sticking up a bank.

Timeline

Lucky Luciano died of a heart attack in Naples, Italy, in 1961. Thomas Dewey ran unsuccessfully for president in 1944 and 1948, and died in 1971.

The Little Flower and the Slots

A significant ally for Dewey in the war against gangsters was the Mayor of New York, Fiorello "the Little Flower" La Guardia. With characteristic vigor and appreciation of the political value of a good picture in the newspapers, he personally went on the attack against all kinds of gambling, but especially the corner-store "one-armed bandit" in the form of the slot machine.

People who happily dropped coins in slot machines were "boobs." With dripping scorn he said of one, "Does he use his last two bucks to buy his kids food? This boob pays it over to some tinhorn bookie. Some boob."

The chief of all the city's bookmakers was Frank Costello. Born Franceso Sergilia in Calabria, Italy, in 1893, he was brought to the United States as a child shortly after his birth. At an early age he was running with a street gang in East Harlem. In the 1920s he ran rum for a criminal outfit overseen by Arnold "Mr. Big" Rothstein. When Rothstein was rubbed out, Costello inherited the gambling operations as an associate of Luciano. The year before La Guardia became mayor, "Uncle Frank," as he was known in the underworld, raked in more than $37 million from "mom and pop store" slot machines estimated at 25,000 in the five boroughs of the city.

Just as bad was "policy," a racket in which the "boobs" put their money on picking the day's "number," a figure derived through a formula based on the outcome of daily horse races at a particular New York track. This wagering was in addition to actual betting on the horses that went on in "bookie parlors" all over a city that never turned the lights out, a city in which the people had a yen for striking it rich in a horse's dash to the finish line, a roll of the dice, a turn of card, a spin of a roulette wheel, and dropping the kids' milk money in a slot.

On the basis of a section of the Penal Act, La Guardia's cops were sent on raids to confiscate slot machines. They were put on a barge on the Hudson River, then towed to deep waters of Long Island Sound. Surrounded by police, reporters, and photographers, the mayor grabbed a sledgehammer and began flailing away at piles of them. "These machines," he said, pausing to catch his breath, "were controlled by the most vicious of criminal elements."

No more indelible popular image of Mayor Fiorello H. La Guardia exists in the memory of the people who were alive then, and in the history of the La Guardia years, than that of the tubby, shirt-sleeved, sweaty, fiercely expressioned warrior against organized larceny swinging a sledge hammer in the midst of a small mountain of slot machines. When he was through and cameramen had scores of pictures, the battered devices were dumped into the ocean.

One can only wonder what La Guardia would think, and say, if he could come back to life, look around his city, and find that "policy" has become "the lottery," run not by crooks, but by the state of New York with "tickets" on sale everywhere, even sold in vending machines. And that any New Yorker who desired to put a bet on a horse running anywhere in the country could do so in city-owned Off Track Betting rooms, complete with food, drinks, comfortable chairs, and color TV screens showing the races.

The Least You Need to Know

- When Prohibition was repealed, gangsters concentrated their illegal activities on gambling, prostitution, loan-sharking, and taking over legal businesses through intimidation and violence.
- The criminal "boss of bosses" was Charles "Lucky" Luciano.
- FBI agents got the name "G-Men" as they took on gangsters such as John Dillinger, Machine Gun Kelly, and Baby Face Nelson.
- The "crime of the century" was the kidnapping and murder of the two-year-old son of aviation hero Charles A. Lindbergh.

Part 5

Better Tomorrows

This section examines the societal and cultural effects of the Depression on the American family. Mom, Dad, and the kids find escape from cares together by tuning in their favorite radio shows, going out to the movies, and cheering for the greatest stars of the "national pastime," Babe Ruth and Lou Gehrig. "Big Bands" set the younger set dancing to the new rage in popular music called "Swing."

Cars, trains, airplanes, buildings, and almost everything else become "streamlined" in the "Art Deco" style. A taste of the ideal "world of tomorrow" is displayed at the decade's biggest extravaganza, the New York World's Fair of 1939. Americans' hope that they can stay out of the conflicts in Europe and Asia is dashed on "a date that will live in infamy," December 7, 1941. As the country goes to war, the longest and worst economic depression in history comes to an end.

Chapter 17

Dimples and the Hoofer

In This Chapter

- The Great Depression and the average American family
- A movie-crazy country goes nuts over a dimple-cheeked, curly haired, tap dancing and singing tot on the silver screen named Shirley Temple
- Mickey Rooney and Judy Garland become teenage role models in "the golden age" of the movie musical
- There's laughter aplenty in "screwball comedies"
- Horrors of the real world are shown in documentaries and the newsreels

This chapter deals with the American family during the years of the Great Depression. Seeking an escape from their cares, the average family tuned their radios to their favorite shows. They also flocked to the movies.

Radio and films presented personalities that the country took to its heart. They included radio's Jack Benny, film moppet Shirley Temple, Mickey Rooney and Judy Garland, Jean Harlow, and W. C. Fields. In sports, Americans hailed Babe Zaharias, Babe Ruth, and Lou Gehrig.

A Week with Mr. and Mrs. Average American

On Monday mornings in the 1930s, most of the houses all across the country smelled of soap and bleach being churned in big tubs of water that contained the previous week's dirty clothes. Sorted by "Mom, "Ma," or "Mother" into "white" and "colored" heaps as they waited their turn to go "in the wash," the garments were put in "labor-saving" washing machines that more than likely had been bought on the install-ment plan. Later, as "Dad," "Pa," "Pop," "Father," or "the Old Man," if he was lucky enough to still have a job, went off to work and the kids went to school, Mom carried the wash out to the back yard and hung it on a clothesline to dry.

Tuesday, in most homes, was ironing day. With no such thing as "drip and dry," "wash and wear" clothing, or "wrinkle-proof" fabrics, every home had an ironing board. Those who could afford an electric iron had it. But plenty of "housewives" continued to use a heavy black "flatiron." It was heated atop the kitchen's coal stove.

In the case of Mrs. Thomas Jeffers, mother of the author of this book, the Monday-is-wash-day ritual was once moved to a Sunday (November 18, 1934). Because she was pregnant with me, as she told me when I inquired into the circumstances of my birth, she "knew something was going to happen that day" that would keep her from doing the wash on Monday. So she decided that she had better get it out of the way. But my appearance as the fifth child of Tom and Margaret Jeffers did not keep her from doing the ironing on Tuesday. Because it was a time before hospitalization and medical coverage, and given the fact that the Jeffers family had very little in the way of money (Dad worked in a small steel plant), I was born at home. It was no big deal. Giving birth at home was a common thing.

Whether Mom was in a mood to listen to the radio on that Sunday evening I don't know. If she did, one of the shows certainly would have been *The Jell-O Program*. It starred an ex-vaudeville comedian named Jack Benny. By the end of the decade, he was the king of Sunday nights. If you could have traveled instantly from coast to coast at 7 P.M., you would have heard his voice coming out of practically every radio. Starting in March 1937, you would also catch the gravelly tones of Eddie Anderson as "Rochester."

Timeline

The *Rochester* show's writers made the main character a former Pullman porter. His full name was "Rochester Van Jones." Anderson, the actor who played Rochester, was a Broadway and movie actor who'd starred in the 1939 all-black film *The Green Pastures*, based on the Broadway play of that title. He's also the fellow holding a hatchet as he chases a scrawny chicken that's earmarked for dinner at "Tara" in the movie *Gone with the Wind*.

Now a Word from Our Sponsor

As noted earlier, radio had been envisioned as a music box in the home that would stimu-late sales of phonograph records. Within a decade, it was selling almost everything anybody could want. In 1937 manufacturers loaded the nation's airwaves with as many "commercials" as networks and stations allowed. Among the most familiar phrases Americans heard on the air during a week were "brought to you by" and "now a word from our sponsor."

The most frequently advertised products, in order of sales, were as follows:

- Home-remedy drugs and toiletries
- Foods, especially breakfast cereals
- Coffee and soft drinks
- Cars
- Cigarettes
- Laundry soaps

Almost all radio shows were "owned" by sponsors. This meant that Jack Benny's show was *The Jell-O Program*. When ventriloquist Edgar Bergen went on with his alter-ego dummy "Charlie McCarthy," his program, sponsored by a coffee firm, was called *The Chase and Sanborn Hour*. Sponsored by a chain of food markets, popular singer Kate Smith starred on *The A&P Bandwagon*. Makers of Lux Soap presented dramatizations of current hit movies on *The Lux Radio Theater*, hosted by film director Cecil B. DeMille.

The Soap Opera

Picture "Mrs. Average Housewife" doing the wash, ironing, and all her other daily chores. On the radio to keep her company from 10 in the morning to 4:30 in the afternoon are people on such shows as *The Romance of Helen Trent*, *John's Other Wife*, *Stella Dallas*, *Ma Perkins*, and the comfortingly titled *Life Can Be Beautiful*.

Because the daytime programs were sponsored by makers of the things every housewife needed on a Monday, they became known as "soap operas." Along with following the travails of characters on the programs, women were informed that for "cleaner, whiter, and fresher" clothes she should use Duz, Rinso, Chipso, Oxydol, and other detergents. All promised, and sometimes guaranteed, that they would leave her hands soft and pretty.

Something for the Kiddies

At half-past four, Monday through Friday, as women got the supper ready, radio kept the kids out of her way by presenting adventure shows. Usually 15 minutes long, the thrilling fare included "Hop Harrigan," "Smilin' Jack," "Flash Gordon," "Dick Daring," "Bobby Benson's Adventures," "Sky King," "Tom Mix," and a hero who was "faster than a speeding bullet" and able "to leap tall buildings with a single bound." If you don't know his name, what planet did you come to earth from? Certainly not from "Krypton."

A mainstay of these kids' shows was known in the radio business as "the premium." You could get rings, toys, and badges just by sending in a product's box top and sometimes by also enclosing a nickel or a dime.

A "kids'" show that the whole family listened to was *The Lone Ranger*. First heard in 1933 on Detroit station WXYZ, the tales of the masked ex-Texas Ranger and his "faithful Indian companion Tonto" soon went nationwide. Because it was on the air at 7:30 P.M., three days a week, it rapidly became a staple of family radio listening.

Facts and Figures

For a Shredded Wheat box top and "ten cents in coin," a kid got a "Tom Mix Horseshoe Nail Ring." This was the first kids' premium.

The initial sponsor was Silvercup bread. The premiums kids could send for included a "silver bullet" and cowboy belt. Before long, Lone Ranger items were on sale in stores. For not a lot of money a kid could buy (or ask Mom and Dad to buy) Lone Ranger pistols, holsters, outfits of white hats and masks, and lunch boxes with pictures of the Lone Ranger and Tonto on them.

Downtown on Saturday Night

It's Saturday evening in the small steel town of Phoenixville, Pennsylvania. This Philadelphia suburb is served by two rail lines, the Pennsylvania and the Reading, with steam locomotives. Population, about 12,000. The town's men are employed by the steel company. It makes structural beams. Orders have been slow in coming since 1929.

It's a typical American town. The main drag is Bridge Street. On every Saturday night it seems as lively as New York City's Times Square. The good people of Phoenixville who've come there call it "going downtown." Families who have the money might have supper at Buster's restaurant. It stands between the Newberry's five-and-ten-cent store and the much bigger Woolworth's. Shoulder to shoulder on both sides of the street are locally owned stores: shoes, men's clothes, women's attire, sporting goods, "variety" stores, and a music and record shop.

At a time when a factory worker earned $16.89 a week, a cook made $15, and a doctor brought in $61, typical prices are as follows:

- Woman's winter coat: $28.00
- Man's overcoat: $18.50
- Man's broadcloth shirt: $1.00
- Table lamp: $1.00
- Washing machine: $33.50

- Flexible Flyer sled: $3.95 to $8.95
- Doll: $1.95
- Boy's wind-up toys: 3 for 59 cents

For a dime, you can have a milk shake at Feicht's Drug Store. A penny will get you a bag of freshly roasted peanuts at a stand next to the town's main movie theater, the Colonial. There's another theater on Main Street. Named the Rialto, it's where kids go for a double bill of a cowboy picture and a mystery, plus a "serial" with a "cliffhanger" to make sure you come back next week for the next "exciting episode." Its youthful patrons have their own name for it: the Rat Hole.

On Saturday nights, the Colonial shows new movies that are for the entire family. The walls are gilded. There's a huge chandelier. Off to the side down front is an organ, left over from the era of silent films. The seats are plush. The screen is behind a gold-colored curtain. As the chandelier dims, the curtain parts and opens. And in that instant, whatever had been worrying you a moment before is gone.

A Miraculous Silver Screen

When Will Rogers joked about the American people going to the poor house in an automobile, he also could have said that those who didn't own cars escaped the Great Depression blues by going to the movies. Those years provided an amazing roster of films that are now considered classics. Because the people were looking for escapist fare, hardly any of the features dealt with themes of the Great Depression. What you got for your quarter or less were family-oriented pictures, screwball comedies, big costume dramas, westerns, and lavish musicals.

 Famous Faces

One of the founders of the famed circle of literary wits known as "the Algonquin Round Table," Robert Benchley was middle-aged and portly, with a small mustache. He wrote and performed in satirical shorts that included "How to Be a Detective," "How to Sleep," "How to Raise a Baby," "How to Break 90 at Croquet," and "How to Figure Income Tax." Benchley also appeared in features in comedic supporting roles. His son Nathaniel's book *The Off Islanders* was the basis of the 1966 film *The Russians Are Coming, The Russians Are Coming.* Grandson Peter wrote the novel that became the 1975 movie blockbuster *Jaws.*

Americans in the 1930s also delighted in the antics of a cartoon mouse named Mickey. Created by Walt Disney, he was the first of an array of characters that included Pinocchio and Snow White. Along with the main attraction came a newsreel (more on these later), a cartoon, previews of coming attractions, and selected short subjects. Among the latter were the *Three Stooges*; *Our Gang* and *Little Rascals* featuring small kids; "follow the bouncing ball" sing-alongs; travelogues, *Popular Science*; the antics of a hapless bungler named *Joe Doakes*; and "lectures" by Robert Benchley.

America's Little Darling

Her name, as if you didn't know, was Shirley Temple. When she was talked about (and was she talked about!) it was a gushing stream of adjectives: "America's Little Darling," "bundle of sweetness," "Little Miss Curly Locks," and "pint-sized stick of dynamite."

 Famous Faces

After making several films as a teenager, Shirley Temple gave up movies. In 1958 she attempted a comeback on TV, but then she turned her attention to government. She served as a U.S. representative at the UN, then as ambassador in Ghana and Czechoslovakia in the administrations of presidents Nixon and George Bush (the first).

Said FDR about Shirley Temple in 1935, "During this Depression, when the spirit of the people is lower than at any other time, it is a splendid thing that for just 15 cents an American can go to a movie and look at the smiling face of a baby and forget his troubles."

And what a talented baby she was! She acted, she sang, and she danced. And not just by herself. Her little tapping feet kept pace with two of the movies' best hoofers. She was a partner of tall, lanky, and rubber-legged Buddy Ebsen, and when she danced with the country's most famous black dancer, Bill "Bojangles" Robinson, the pair did more for racial tolerance than any of the words of W.E.B. DuBois and other black leaders at the time.

 Timeline

Popular Andy Hardy films during the Great Depression included:

- *Judge Hardy's Children* (1938)
- *Love Finds Andy Hardy* (1938)
- *Out West with the Hardys* (1938)
- *The Hardys Ride High* (1939)
- *Andy Hardy Gets Spring Fever* (1939)
- *Judge Hardy and Son* (1939)
- *Andy Hardy Meets Debutante* (1940)

The cover of a Shirley Temple book.

Shirley also earned her movie studio, 20th Century Fox, more than $5 million a year, saving the studio from bankruptcy. When a grateful Hollywood presented her with a tiny special Academy Awards "Oscar," the inscription credited her with "bringing more happiness to millions of grown-ups than any child of her years in the history of the world."

As Shirley turned out four pictures a year, the country bought up Shirley Temple dolls and other items marketed with her name and picture on them. Her smiling face was on countless magazines and children's books.

America's other movie sweethearts were soprano Deanna Durbin, Gloria Jean (teamed with W. C. Fields), and Judy Garland. A few years older than Shirley Temple, Judy made 11 features in the 1930s, but was best known as Mickey Rooney's co-star in "Andy Hardy" pictures. Her skyrocket to fame came in 1939 as Dorothy Gale in *The Wizard of Oz*.

An ad for 1940's Andy Hardy Meets Debutante, *starring Mickey Rooney and Judy Garland.*

Life with the Hardy Family

One of the most popular movie series of all time was the *Hardy Family*. Starring Mickey Rooney as typical-teenager Andy, and set in the fictional small town of Carvel, the films presented family life as every American imagined (and wanted) it to be. The head of the family was Judge Hardy, played by Lewis Stone. Made by MGM, the films were recognized with a special Academy Award for their "achievement in presenting the American way of life." The series ran between 1937 and 1946.

Toe-Tapping, Twirling, and Plenty of T and A

Hooray for Hollywood! Hooray for the 1930s movie musical! Not for no reason are the 1930s remembered as Tinsel Town's Golden Age. The movies appeared to have gotten more out-of-work dancers back on their feet than all of the New Deal's "artists" employment programs put together. Lavishly staged, with casts of hundreds of singers and dancers, they cost a bundle to make, but they raked in much, much more. If Hollywood was a dream factory, studios that made musicals were production lines of pure fantasy.

Into Depression grayness they brought a glitz, glamour, and gaiety unavailable anywhere else. Women audiences sighed over the gowns and romantic stories with plenty of handsome guys. The men got a chance to ogle beautiful, busty, and leggy gals long before TV producers coined the term "T and A." (If you don't know what that means, you've obviously never watched *Charlie's Angels.*)

Busby's Girls and Boys

King of the movie musical was Busby Berkeley. The son of a stage director and stage and film actress, he was named after turn-of-the-century star Amy Busby. With 21 Broadway musicals in his credits, he went out to Hollywood in 1930 to direct for Samuel Goldwyn. But it was for Warner Bros. that he scored his first huge successes as a stager of musical numbers in *42nd Street* and *Gold Diggers of 1933.*

Famous Faces

Busby Berkeley was responsible for many innovations in movie-making. He invented a monorail to give the camera greater mobility. His "Berkeley top shot" had the camera placed above dancers as they formed intricate patterns. Another sensational innovation was a shot in which the camera passed through a tunnel of women's legs.

Ad for Gold Diggers of 1933.

Sex, Sex, Sex, and More Sex

From today's "anything goes in the movies" perspective, it seems rather a quaint idea that there should be a board of censors to tell movie-makers what they couldn't show on the silver screen. But in the 1930s, Hollywood was a pretty prissy place. All the studios produced films under the watchful eyes of the Motion Picture Producers and Distributors Association.

Known as "the Hays Office," after its head, Will Hays, who'd been Postmaster General in the Harding administration, it created a "code" that dictated "acceptable" material. Most strictures had to do with sex. One of them required that no one, not even married couples, could be shown together in a double bed. And if a man and woman were depicted on a bed together, one of them had to have a foot on the floor. Many states also had their own censorship boards.

Hollywood actress Jean Harlow in 1937.

(AP Photo)

The Screen's Sexiest Gal

Her name was Jean Harlow. In the movies since 1928, she really took the country by storm starting in 1931 opposite James Cagney in *The Public Enemy* (more on this in Chapter 18, "I Ain't So Tough"), and in a movie that gave her the nickname Platinum Blonde. Breathtakingly gorgeous and with a mane of platinum hair, she was usually in the role of an ambitious young woman who took stock of her situation, planned her strategy, and wound up doing okay. Her type of film became known as "screwball comedy." She invariably had a string of wisecracks to deliver, most often at "the other woman," or a gold digger.

Here's a classic Harlow moment in 1933's *Dinner at Eight* that is the essence of Harlow characters. She tells the hostess (Marie Dressler) that "machinery is going to take the place of every profession." Doing a marvelous double-take, Dressler gives her a head-to-toe appraisal and retorts, "Oh, my dear, that's something you'll never have to worry about."

How Can You Hurt a Watch by Dipping It in Molasses?

While mothers went crazy over Shirley Temple to the point of dressing-up their little girls just like her, and men of all ages mentally lusted after Jean Harlow, more than a few husbands who went to the movies in the 1930s found inspiration in a bulbous-nosed, cranky, twangy-voiced, and bibulous rebel against wives, kids, and all forms of authority: the one and only W. C. Fields.

An ex-vaudeville juggler and silent-film comedian, he laced the years of the Great Depression with comedies that are as funny now as they were then. Trapped in a marriage with a nagging wife and disrespectful children, on the run from the sheriff, or a victim of circumstances, he had audiences laughing (and men nodding their heads in sympathy) as he battled everyone, especially kids. In *The Old Fashioned Way*, after an infant Baby Leroy dropped his pocket watch into a bowl of molasses, and the kid's mother said, "I hope he hasn't hurt your watch," Fields replied, "Oh, no. How can you hurt a watch by dipping it in molasses?" Later, to the secret delight of who-knows-how-many-fathers, he got even by giving Baby Leroy a well-deserved kick in the ass.

Timeline

The first drive-in movie opened on June 6, 1933, in Camden, New Jersey.

W. C. Fields in a publicity photo for the 1940 film The Bank Dick.

(AP Photo)

A Dose of Reality

Although movies of the Great Depression generally avoided dealing with the nation's economic woes, the moviegoer got a dose of the realities outside the theater through newsreels. Invented at the time of the Spanish-American War, these weekly summaries of the news of the nation and world would remain an important facet of the movie-going experience until they became outmoded by daily newscasts on television.

Usually shown at the start of an evening's screenings, they were produced by all the major film studios. In addition to clips of news events, they often included human interest items, fashion reports, and sports. One of the most popular of the light-hearted features was a story about animals. Narrated by Lew Lehr, they ended with him declaring, "Animals are the craziest people."

The March of Time

Launched by the magazine *Time* in 1935, these monthly "screen magazines," produced by Louis de Rochement, ran between 15 and 25 minutes. Originally presenting several news events, *The March of Time* eventually dealt with one subject. One that had a profound effect on Americans' turning away from isolationism was *Inside Nazi Germany*, presented in 1938. Another dealt with Huey Long and went a long way in discrediting him.

The style consisted of dynamic editing, use of music, and a powerful narration. *The March of Time* became so ingrained in the movie-going experience that when Orson Welles produced *Citizen Kane* in 1940, the fictionalized biography of newspaper tycoon William Randolph Hearst began with a *March of Time* parody.

Three Landmark Documentaries

Although the American movie business has never been big on the documentary, the Great Depression produced three landmarks of the genre. *The Plough That Broke the Plains* was commissioned by the Roosevelt administration in 1936. Made for $20,000, it dealt with the Dust Bowl. Despite Hollywood's opposition, the film was shown in thousands of theaters. It was made by director Pare Lorentz, with music composed by Virgil Thompson. Lorentz also made *The River* (1937), a panoramic history of the Mississippi River basin. He wrote a treatment, but did not direct, a cinematic portrait of New York, *The City*.

Sundays in Great Depression America

As noted earlier, the Great Depression didn't bring with it an upsurge in church membership. People still went to services, especially women, but the advent of the automobile introduced a new activity for the whole family—the Sunday drive. Dad, Mom, and the kids piled into the car and went for "a ride."

These sojourns into the countryside often included stopping for a picnic, or pausing at a roadside dairy for ice-cream cones. In the summertime, the outing might extend to visiting an amusement park. People from Pennsylvania and New Jersey trekked to Atlantic City to spend the day strolling the Boardwalk while chewing on saltwater taffy, going into the water, or taking in the stage show on the Steel Pier, famed for "diving horses" that plunged headlong from the pier into the Atlantic Ocean. On summer Sundays New Yorkers went to Coney Island. Los Angelenos had numerous parks, Alligator and Ostrich farms, maps to show them where to find homes of movie stars, and, of course, beaches.

The Funnies

Whatever you did on Sunday, you started the day with the Sunday newspaper. Although the Depression caused some papers to fold or merge, Americans could still rely on having one to read with breakfast or later in the day. They all had "funnies."

For laughs, or at least a chuckle, you turned to *Blondie*, *L'il Abner*, *Joe Palooka*, *Maggie and Jiggs*, *Katzenjammer Kids*, and others. If it was an adventure you wanted, there were *Dick Tracy*, *Terry and the Pirates*, *Tarzan*, *Prince Valiant*, and *Steve Canyon*. And there was a girl with bushy red hair and eyes with no pupils named Little Orphan Annie, and her dog, Sandy, whose bark came out "arf."

Two Babes and an Iron Man

If you kept up on sports during the Great Depression, you would have seen golfer Bobby Jones attain the Grand Slam by winning both amateur and open championships in the United States and England in 1930. If you were a smart bettor, you'd have put money on Gallant Fox to take racing's Triple Crown—and won.

In 1932 Los Angeles hosted the Olympics. Among the American competitors was a 19-year-old Texan named Mildred Didrikson, known to friends, competitors, and sportswriters as "Babe." Running the 80-meter hurdles, she won the gold medal. She also set a world record in the javelin throw. She could also play basketball, tennis, pool, and billiards; throw a baseball and football; and burn up the golf links. Sportswriter Paul Gallico asked her, "Is there anything you don't play?" Babe answered, "Dolls."

> **Famous Faces**
>
> Future Boston Red Sox star Carl Yastrzemski was born on August 27, 1939.

> **Facts and Figures**
>
> Babe Ruth's home run tally in the 1930s:
> - 1930: 49
> - 1931: 46
> - 1932: 41 (two in the World Series)
> - 1933: 34
> - 1934: 22
> - 1935: 6 (with Boston Braves)

In 1938 she married wrestler George Zaharias. With George's encouragement, she took up golf and went on to capture the U.S. Women's Open Championship three times. Back then, no one had seen anyone like her. We still haven't.

The Other Babe

As a baseball fan, you would have observed superstars Dizzy Dean, Jimmy Foxx, Carl Hubbell, Bob Feller, and two greats of the New York Yankees: Babe Ruth and Lou Gehrig. George Herman Ruth was tubby. He loved to eat and drink. "Sultan of Swat" for the New York Yankees, he was arguably the best baseball player ever.

The Iron Man

From June 2, 1925, to May 2, 1939, Lou Gehrig played in 2,130 consecutive baseball games. During his career, he averaged 147 RBIs (runs-batted-in) per season. On June 3, 1932, he became the first American Leaguer to hit four home runs in a game. In the 1934 World Series he batted .361, with 10 homers, 8 doubles, and 25 RBIs.

Stricken with a neurological disease that has since been named after him, he provided the 1930s with one of its most emotional moments as he said goodbye to 61,000 fans in Yankee Stadium.

Babe Ruth hugs Lou Gehrig on the day Gehrig retired from baseball on July 4, 1939.

Memorable Movie Lines

The decade in which millions of Americans had sought escape from the tribulations of the Great Depression in movies ended with a cinematic bang. The silver screen in 1939 offered some of the finest films in Hollywood history: *Mr. Smith Goes to Washington; Goodbye, Mr. Chips; Of Mice and Men; Wuthering Heights; Babes in Arms; Dark Victory; Beau Geste; Juarez; Ninotchka; Stagecoach;* and two with memorable lines at the end.

In *Gone with the Wind*, Clark Gable as Rhett Butler gazed hard at Vivien Leigh's Scarlett O'Hara and spoke a word that had never been spoken on the screen. Audiences gasped as he said, "Frankly, my dear, I don't give a damn."

Far more acceptable, and in keeping with America's mood, were Judy Garland's words at the end of *The Wizard of Oz.* You would have been hard-pressed to find in Depression America anyone who didn't believe, despite all the hardships of the past 10 years, "There's no place like home."

Judy Garland portrays Dorothy in The Wizard of Oz.

Depression? What's That?

Thanks to the need of Americans to escape their Depression woes, at least for a couple of hours, two groups were spared the hard times. Professional athletes and people employed in the movie industry got paid for working as usual. When a sports writer pointed out to Babe Ruth that the "Sultan of Swat" earned more in a year as a baseball player than

Herbert Hoover got as president of the United States, the Babe replied, "Yeah, but I had a better year than he did."

But when it came to escaping economic doldrums by filling seats with people who were looking for a respite from their day-to-day gloom, Hollywood beat the owners of ball teams hands down. In the depths of the Depression, in the year 1935, the movie business took in at the nation's box offices an average of $20 million a week. For people lucky enough to be working in movies, the words "Hooray for Hollywood" were more than a song title.

Hollywood pages of the *WPA Guide to California* noted that the movie capital attracted "more types and nationalities than any city of its size in the world," and that about 75 percent of the population was connected in some way with motion pictures. At the very top were the moguls who owned or ran the studios and the men, women, and children to whom they'd granted both "stardom" and immunity from the Great Depression.

"In the first flush of cinema prosperity," noted the writers of the *WPA Guide*, "Hollywood society went in for extravagance and informality, evidenced by carefree parties and sporty cars. Now top-flight movie society affects white ties and evening gowns, with the accent on dignity and position, but the yardstick of eminence is still the number of digits in the salary."

But why not flaunt it? The movie-going audience demanded that the people whose giant faces they admired on the screen be just as oversized off-screen, oozing glamour and living in a magic world that the audiences dreamed of having for themselves. In an age of soup kitchens and bread lines, who wouldn't, if you had the money, dress-up and go out to eat at the Brown Derby?

Leafing through a movie fan magazine while worrying about how you were going to come up with your rent, you could only admire—not envy, mind you, but admire—the splendid homes of movie stars. If Edward G. Robinson was worth a quarter to watch in a movie, who could begrudge him his two-story English-type white brick house in Beverly Hills, surrounded by low walls, and containing his collection of modern French paintings and a magnificent library? Or Joan Crawford's Colonial style home in Brentwood Heights; the field-stone house of Ginger Rogers, set in landscaped grounds at the highest point in Beverly Hills; and even the young Freddie Bartholomew's place on a quiet avenue shaded by silk oak trees?

Why, with fare for a Greyhound bus you might find yourself at the Union Bus Terminal and being "discovered" as the next big star, like the girl played by Janet Gaynor in *A Star Is Born*. As the song said, if you went out to Hollywood to try your luck, you might become as famous as Donald Duck. But if you didn't have the bus fare, or lacked the nerve, you could go to a movie and dream.

The Least You Need to Know

◆ Motion pictures provided millions of Americans an escape from their Depression troubles.

◆ America's "Little Darling" of the screen, Shirley Temple, earned $5 million a year, while her films saved 20th Century Fox studios from bankruptcy.

◆ The king of the movie musical was director Busby Berkeley.

◆ New York Yankees baseball player Lou Gehrig played in 2,130 consecutive games, then was forced to retire by a neurological condition that is now known as "Lou Gehrig's Disease."

I Ain't So Tough

In This Chapter

- Communists and "Fellow Traveler" sympathizers use the New Deal's Federal Theater Project to present propagandistic plays
- Communists in Hollywood attempt to control motion picture craft unions
- Gangster films portray criminals as anti-establishment heroes and victims of capitalism
- The CBS radio drama *The War of the Worlds* scares a nervous country into believing Martians have invaded
- Congress ends the Federal Theater Project

With creation of the Federal Theater Project (FTP) and other agencies to assist people in creative arts, communists and sympathizers grabbed the opportunity to promote a "new American Revolution." Numerous plays had anti-capitalist themes. Novelists such as Ayn Rand who did not go along with the Red line, or who criticized communism, were subjected to vicious criticism. Eventually, an investigation by the Red-hunting Dies Committee forced the end of the FTP.

Communists in Hollywood sought to control unions of screenwriters, actors, and other motion picture crafts. A string of gangster movies, depicting outlaws as heroic figures and victims of a capitalist society, made stars of

Edward G. Robinson, James Cagney, and Humphrey Bogart. After Orson Welles caused a national panic with *The War of the Worlds*, he went to Hollywood to write and direct *Citizen Kane*.

We Are All Soldiers

When the New Deal sought to provide assistance to the unemployed people in the arts (writers, actors, musicians, painters, and so on), one of the most successful results was the FTP. Suddenly available federal funds stimulated the formation of numerous theatrical groups across the country. Among them were the New Theatre Players of Hollywood, Negro Peoples' Theatre of the South, the Chicago Group Theater, and the Group Theatre of New York.

Recognizing a rich opportunity to push its agenda, the Communist Party of the United States jumped onto the bandwagon. Thus was born in April 1932 the American section of the Moscow-run International Union of Revolutionary Theaters. The U.S. outfit was the League of Workers Theatres. Its unifying entity was a magazine, *Workers' Theatre*, which was renamed in 1934 as the un-communist-sounding *New Theatre*.

The next year brought a summons to the like-minded to a "Congress of American Revolutionary Writers." It was held in New York City at the New School for Social Research on April 24 through 27, 1935. The main speaker was Earl Browder. (You remember him, the head of the CP-USA.) Giving marching orders to the faithful, he proclaimed, "We are all soldiers, each in our own place, in a common cause. Let our efforts be united in fraternal solidarity."

In noncommunist language, he meant, "Get out there and pitch the Party line." In short order, a National Council was up and running to coordinate action. There was no lack of "soldiers."

The Group Theater

Inspired by the Russian director Konstantine Stanislavski, the Group Theater was founded by Harold Clurman, Lee Strasberg, Cheryl Crawford, and Luther and Stella Adler. In Clurman's words, its goal was to "make the theater vitally expressive of the American scene, of the life of the times." Translated, the goal was to blame "the American way" for the Depression, racism, and oppression of "the worker."

With a grant of $1,000 from the Theater Guild, the merry band of young "idealists" (average age: 25) trooped off to Brookfield, Connecticut, to fashion their version of a socially conscious theater. Returning to New York, they had a success with their first production (*The House of Connelly*, by Paul Green, in 1931). Subsequent ventures, Paul

Sifton's *1931*, Maxwell Anderson's Night Over Taos, and John Howard Lawson's *Success Story*, did not fare so well. They did better with Sidney Kingsley's hospital drama, *Man in White*.

Then along came "Lefty."

No More Craven Servitude

One of the most fervent figures in the theater of propaganda was an actor turned playwright named Clifford Odets. The authority on the subject, Harold Clurman, saw Odets as "the central figure of the Left movement" in the theater of the 1930s whose writing had a fervor "derived from the hope and expectation of change and a desire for it."

The title of Odets's magnum opus left no doubt where he expected the change to come from. Its title was *Waiting for Lefty*. The "Lefty" was a taxi driver, but the message of the play was "the impediment to that full life for which youth hungers" that could be removed only by Marxist revolution. Inspired by a New York City taxi drivers' strike, the play was a "call to join the good fight for a greater measure of life in a world free of economic fear, falsehood, and craven servitude to stupidity and greed." It ends with cries of "Strike! Strike!"

Produced by the Group Theater, it gave Odets, in Clurman's view, "a platform and loudspeaker" to speak to "a vast population of restive souls" that was "unaware of its own mind, seeking help."

Timeline ───────────────────────────────

Other leftist plays included Odets's *Awake and Sing* (1935), *Golden Boy* (1937), and *Rocket to the Moon* (1938), as well as Maxwell Anderson's *Winterset* (1935), Lillian Hellman's *The Children's Hour* (1934) and *The Little Foxes* (1939); Sidney Kingsley's *Dead End* (1935); and Robert E. Sherwood's *The Petrified Forest* (1934), *Idiot's Delight* (1936), and *There Shall Be No Night* (1940).

Black, White, and Red All Over

Another manifestation of U.S. writers rallying to the Red flag was a national network of "clubs" named in honor of John Reed.

The John Reed clubs were not exactly literary discussion groups. Controlled by the CP-USA, scores of them existed to further the Red cause. They turned their ire on any writer who didn't toe the Party line. One of the victims was Ayn Rand. A young woman writer who'd fled the Communist Revolution in Russia with hopes of becoming a screen-writer, she published an anti-communist novel, *We, the Living*. When it came out in 1936, she immediately found herself being blasted by communists and Fellow-Traveler writers and literary critics.

Famous Faces

An American writer of the 1920s, John Reed actually went to Russia to help the Bolsheviks organize their proletarian utopia. He was honored with a tomb in the Kremlin Wall. Reed was por-trayed by Warren Beatty in the 1981 movie *Reds*.

Famous Faces

Fierce opponent of "collec-tivism" and exponent of individu-alism, Ayn Rand scored her greatest success with a novel, *The Fountainhead*. It was made into a movie starring Gary Cooper.

Rand wasn't alone. Also savaged for their anti-communism were John Dewey, Max Eastman, John Dos Passos, Edmund Wilson, Andre Gide, and James T. Farrell. Black-balled-by-the-Reds journalist Eugene Lyons observed, "For a 'renegade' to crash one of the cultural Federal projects—literary, theater, art—was a feat more difficult than a camel passing through the eye of a needle."

Communism with Two Butlers and a Swimming Pool

The Red tide also flowed on the West Coast. While writers for the stage championed a left-wing American Revolution, so did many of the writers and directors of movies. The editor of *Screen Guild Magazine*, William Bledsoe, wrote in an article for the American Mercury that Hollywood in the 1930s became a city of "unhappy successful people" who found in communism "a reason for living and an alibi for living so absurdly well." It was a communism "with two butlers and a swimming pool."

When attempts were made to organize motion picture studio unions, the painters union enlisted in the cause, but the Screen Actors Guild managed to stave off a takeover by communists and their "progressive" sympathizers. The richest pickings in Hollywood were among individuals. Movie stars lent their prestige to gala cocktail parties, rallies, and meetings at which millions of dollars were raised for communist activities.

Many of these people later found themselves summoned before congressional committees investigating communist influence in Hollywood. Some would claim that they had been "duped," and no doubt many of them were. But others knew precisely what they were doing. Known as "The Hollywood 10" they assumed the role of martyr by refusing to answer questions and by wrapping themselves in the Constitution of the country they'd sought to subvert. The truth is that more than a few people in movies in the 1930s believed that communism was the wave of the future.

The Gangster as Society's Victim

While many movie-makers flirted with communism and movie-goers were flocking to see the comedies and musicals discussed earlier, Hollywood film factories took note of the country's fascination with the likes of Al Capone, John Dillinger, the Barker family, and other outlaws. In 1931 alone they cranked out more than 50 pictures about gangsters.

A common theme of these films, especially in the first half of the decade, was that the gangster was a product of all the ills of society. He was a man for whom "the American dream" became a nightmare. It was a feeling shared by millions of out-of-work people. Typical was a James Cagney character who was hailed as a hero in World War I. When he couldn't get a job when he returned home, he took up crime ... and succeeded.

In picture after picture, the true villains were the politicians, landlords who made it rich owning slums, bankers, prison guards and wardens, and "high society." Criminals were individualists who found that the only way to survive in such a cruel system was to defy the law.

One example was *Dead End* (1937). Based on Sidney Kingsley's hit Broadway play, it portrayed slum dwellers living in the shadow of a posh New York East Side apartment house. The hero of the "Dead End Kids" was a former denizen of the neighborhood who had become a crook known as "Baby Face" Martin, played by Humphrey Bogart. The point the movie made was that poverty, broken homes, bad parents, and corrupt institutions, such as government, bred criminals.

Facts and Figures

Total movie attendance in 1930 was about 60 million, down from 110 million in 1929. The average weekly attendance in the decade was 85 million. The population of the United States in the 1930s was about 125 million.

Talk of the Time

Teenagers Leo Gorcey, Huntz Hall, Gabriel Dell, Bobby Jordan, and Bill Hallop were in the play and movie. They enjoyed continued success well into the 1950s as basically good-hearted kids as "the **Dead End Kids**," "the East Side Kids," and "the Bowery Boys."

The Big Three of Cinematic Crime

If you don't know by now that they were Edward G. Robinson, James Cagney, and Humphrey Bogart, where have you been? They created characters who on their own terms attained all the symbols of success: power, money, fame, and status. By overcoming the odds, they came out on top. "Their energy, dedication, and ingenuity make us admire [them]," wrote gangster-film historian John Gabree, "and in some films even love him."

Who doesn't feel a little pang of sympathy for Robinson as "Rico" in *Little Caesar* as he falls, pumped full of cops' bullets, into a gutter and gasps, "Is this the end of Rico?" And Cagney as he dies with the exclamation, "I ain't so tough."

Edward G. Robinson as
"Rico" in Little Caesar.

Classic Cagney, Robinson, and Bogart Films of the 1930s

The movie gangster was a tragic figure, but a romantic one whose life and inevitable doom in a blaze of gunfire was an indictment of the modern world. The Big Three played the role to rave reviews throughout the 1930s in films including the following:

- 1930: *Doorway to Hell* (Cagney), *Little Caesar* (Robinson)
- 1931: *Blonde Crazy* (Cagney), *The Public Enemy* (Cagney)
- 1932: *The Hatchet Man* (Robinson)
- 1935: *G-Men* (Cagney)
- 1936: *Bullets or Ballots* (Robinson), *The Petrified Forest* (Bogart)
- 1937: *Dead End* (Bogart), *The Last Gangster* (Robinson)
- 1938: *Angels with Dirty Faces* (Cagney), *Crime School* (Bogart), *I Am the Law* (Robinson), *Racket Busters* (Bogart), *A Slight Case of Murder* (Robinson)
- 1939: *The Roaring Twenties* (Cagney and Bogart)

Dames, Molls, and Whores with Hearts of Gold

Other victims of society in gangster movies were women. They were a criminal's broken-hearted mother, Mae Clark having a grapefruit shoved into her face by James Cagney in *The Public Enemy* (1931), or Sylvia Sidney as a movie version of Bonnie Parker in *You Only Live Once*. They played "dames," "gun molls," and mistresses. All of them were gals with hearts of gold who'd been led astray.

James Cagney with Meryl Mercer as his mother in The Public Enemy.

If a woman took to the streets or was kept by a wealthy man, she did so to get food for her child, an education for a sister, or medicine for her husband. If it was beauty that killed the beast in *King Kong*, it was poverty and desperation that set a woman on the wrong path. In their own way, noted the distinguished film critic Arthur Knight, these women "were merely confirming the gangster theme that the only escape from Depression-bred despair was to live outside the law."

Women's Pictures

That idea of a woman struggling against circumstances also showed up in romances that were made primarily for women. Starring Bette Davis, Joan Crawford, Greta Garbo, Norma Shearer, Merle Oberon, Katharine Hepburn, Tallulah Bankhead, Marlene Dietrich, Irene Dunne, or Barbara Stanwyck, these films were categorized as "women's pictures." They were judged by how many handkerchiefs were wet by female tears, as in "a three-hanky picture."

Typical "three hanky" pictures were films such as:

+ *Morning Glory*, 1933, Katharine Hepburn is stage-struck.
+ *Barrets of Wimpole Street*, 1934, Norma Shearer as lovesick poet.
+ *The Dark Angel*, 1935, Merle Oberon, pre–World War I tragic love.
+ *Dark Victory*, 1939. Bette Davis bravely goes blind.

Going Ga-Ga over Gable

Women loved Clark Gable. Men wanted to be like him. When he took off his shirt in *It Happened One Night* and had nothing on under it, women were thrilled and sales of undershirts plummeted. It was said that if Gable hadn't shown up in Hollywood, the movie industry would have had to invent him. He was described as the first great anti-hero of the movies who took no bull from any man, saw a lady in a whore, and found the whore in every woman.

Between 1930 and 1939, he made 39 movies. He did melodrama, two-fisted action pictures, screwball comedies, romances, and even a musical. Between 1931 and 1939, he went from a cowboy in his first film, *The Painted Desert*, with William Boyd (future *Hopalong Cassidy*), to a gangland boss, several reporters, a villainous chauffeur, gambler, lawyer, minister, doctor, plantation owner, theatrical producer, ship captain, miner, Fletcher Christian in *Mutiny on the Bounty*, cabaret owner in earthquake-stricken San Francisco, prizefighter, Irish revolutionary, and Rhett Butler in *Gone with the Wind*.

As noted earlier, the last movie seen by John Dillinger was a Clark Gable picture. When columnist Ed Sullivan organized a nationwide contest in which movie fans were asked to vote for the King and Queen of Hollywood, they picked Gable and Myrna Loy. MGM immediately teamed them in *Too Hot to Handle*. In the 1938 drama, Gable played a character based on daring real-life men who were bringing an increasingly perilous world to the attention of the American movie audiences through newsreels.

Orson Welles Says "Boo!"

With Nazis and Italian fascists making trouble in Europe, and the Japanese on the march against China, Americans who went to the movies in 1938 could count on getting a summary of world events in newsreels. But they were also getting almost daily doses of unsettling news out of radios in the form of something new. More and more programs were being cut off for the news "bulletin." They often came directly from a network's "man on the scene" of the latest crisis.

Usually in restrained tones, but occasionally in voices brimming with urgency, "commentators" became almost as familiar as Jack Benny, crooners Rudy Valley and Bing Crosby, Burns and Allen, Amos and Andy, and FDR's fireside chats. Voices of "news" were those of H. V. Kaltenborn, Lowell Thomas, Boake Carter, Edwin C. Hill, and William Hard. Consequently, on the night of October 30, 1938, as millions of radio listeners had become accustomed to having their favorite programs interrupted with news bulletins, a young theatrical producer, Orson Welles, and his group of actors known as "The Mercury Theater" went on the air on the CBS network with an updated, Americanized version of an H. G. Wells science-fiction novel in which planet Earth was invaded by creatures from Mars.

Talk of the Time

The Mercury Theater company included Joseph Cotten, Agnes Moorhead, Ray Collins, Everett Sloan, George Coulouris, Ruth Warrick, William Alland, Paul Stewart, and Erskine Sanford. You can see all of them in *Citizen Kane*.

If you were tuned in for the start of the program you would have heard this announcement: "The Columbia Broadcasting System and its affiliated stations present Orson Welles and the Mercury Theater of the Air in *The War of the Worlds* by H. G. Wells." But if you turned on the radio right after that, you heard a weather report, then an announcer saying that the program would continue from a New York hotel, with dance tunes. This certainly was not unusual. Orchestras were common fare.

Then you would have heard a "flash." A professor in New Jersey, declared an excited voice, had just noted from his observatory a series of explosions on Mars. Other bulletins followed in rapid succession. Next, "on the scene" reports came in. A meteor had hit near Princeton, killing 1,500 people. But wait! It was not a meteor. It was a metal cylinder out of which came ugly looking Martians equipped with death rays. The world was being invaded! These things were plopping all over the place! They'd been seen in Grover's Mill, New Jersey, and near Phoenixville in Pennsylvania.

Head for the Hills!

Well, if this was on the radio, it had to be true, right? A lot of scared folks thought so in Newark, New Jersey. More than 20 families rushed from homes with wet handkerchiefs and towels over their heads and faces. A man in Pittsburgh came home to find his wife in the bathroom with a poison bottle and screaming, "I'd rather die this way than like that!" In New York's Harlem, 30 men and women ran to the nearest police station in panic. Similar scenes unfolded all across the country.

Meanwhile in the studio, even though police and CBS executives were rushing in, Welles and his actors went on with what Welles thought would be an amusing way on the night before Halloween to say "Boo!" When the show was over, he learned what had happened.

Sorry About That, Folks

Looking haggard and bewildered the next day, he apologized. "Far from expecting the radio audience to take the program as fact," he explained, he supposed "that the special nature of radio, which is often heard in fragments, or in parts disconnected from the whole, had led to this misunderstanding."

Said *The New York Times*, "Common sense might have warned the projectors of the broadcast that our people are just recovering from a psychosis brought on by the fear of war." *The New York World-Telegram* found it "strange and disturbing that thousands of Americans, secure in their homes on a quiet Sunday evening, could be scared out of their wits by a radio dramatization."

One of the paper's columnists, Heywood Broun, joked in print, "I'm still scared." He hadn't heard the broadcast, and he doubted that he would have called up the police to complain merely because he'd heard that men from a strange machine were knocking the daylights out of Princeton. But he lived "in terror that almost any time now a metal cylinder will come to earth and out of it will step fearsome creatures carrying death-ray guns."

While Orson Welles may have wondered if his career was over, he needn't have worried. Hollywood was soon knocking on his door. The deal he struck with RKO studios gave him a blank check. He used it to co-write and direct a movie that most film experts consider the finest picture ever made, *Citizen Kane*.

NEW YORK, MONDAY, OCTOBER 31, 1938.

Radio Listeners in Panic, Taking War Drama as Fact

Many Flee Homes to Escape 'Gas Raid From Mars'—Phone Calls Swamp Police at Broadcast of Wells Fantasy

A wave of mass hysteria seized thousands of radio listeners throughout the nation between 8:15 and 9:30 o'clock last night when a broadcast of a dramatization of H. G. Wells's fantasy, "The War of the Worlds," led thousands to believe that an interplanetary conflict had started with invading Martians spreading wide death and destruction in New Jersey and New York.

The broadcast, which disrupted households, interrupted religious services, created traffic jams and clogged communications systems, was made by Orson Welles, who as the radio character, "The Shadow," used to give "the creeps" to countless child listeners. This time at least a score of adults required medical treatment for shock and hysteria.

In Newark, in a single block at Heddon Terrace and Hawthorne Avenue, more than twenty families rushed out of their houses with wet handkerchiefs and towels over their faces to flee from what they believed was to be a gas raid. Some began moving household furniture.

Throughout New York families left their homes, some to flee to near-by parks. Thousands of persons called the police, newspapers and radio stations here and in other cities of the United States and Canada seeking advice on protective measures against the raids.

The program was produced by Mr. Welles and the Mercury Theatre on the Air over station WABC and the Columbia Broadcasting System's coast-to-coast network, from 8 to 9 o'clock.

The radio play, as presented, was to simulate a regular radio program with a "break-in" for the material of the play. The radio listeners, apparently, missed or did not listen to the introduction, which was: "The Columbia Broadcasting System and its affiliated stations present Orson Welles and the Mercury Theatre on the Air in 'The War of the Worlds' by H. G. Wells."

They also failed to associate the program with the newspaper listing of the program, announced as "Today: 8:00-9:00—Play: H. G. Wells's 'War of the Worlds'—WABC." They ignored three additional announcements made during the broadcast emphasizing its fictional nature.

Mr. Welles opened the program with a description of the series of

Continued on Page Four

The New York Times story *on* The War of the Worlds *scare.*

The Curtain Comes Down on the Federal Theater

Imaginary hostiles from the red planet were one thing. Earthly Reds were quite another. Discerning the pink tint of the Federal Theater Project, Congressman Martin Dies declared that the FTP and the Works Projects Administration were "doing more to spread communist propaganda than the Communist Party itself." He opened hearings on the matter.

Along with House Un-American Activities Committee Chairman J. Parnell Thomas, Dies enlisted the help of the House Subcommittee on Appropriations in seeking to end FTP funding. Its chairman, Representative Clifton Woodrum, held his own hearings. The result was legislation that was part of the overall Emergency Relief Appropriations Act for 1940.

The measure stripped the WPA of $125 million. All its workers who'd been on the federal payroll more than 18 months were given their walking papers. Future WPA people would be required to sign a loyalty oath. While the Federal Writers Project, Federal Arts Program, and the Federal Music Project survived, they would have to get state sponsorships or cease to exist. The deadline set was September 1, 1938.

The FTP got no such consideration. Once FDR signed the bill, it would be history. Faced with a virtual ultimatum in the form of a bill he couldn't veto if he wished to continue other programs, he signed. The death knell for the FTP sounded on June 30, 1938.

At New York's Ritz Theater, FTP actors appearing in a production of *Pinocchio* changed the ending of the play to turn the boy back into a puppet. Placing it in a casket and tearing down scenery in view of the audience, they chanted, "So let the bells proclaim our grief that his small life was all too brief." Placed on the casket was a printed epitaph: "Killed by Act of Congress."

In the FTP's four years of existence, the estimated audiences for its productions came to approximately 30 million. Its members saw the FTP as a way of presenting "free, adult, uncensored" drama. Its critics believed it was a brazen attempt to "Russianize" the American stage. Both sides were to some extent right.

Mysterious Stuff

In 1930 a tall, slender, good-looking young woman with long legs, narrow feet, and red hair walked into the San Francisco offices of the private detective firm of Spade and Archer. Her hat and dress were two shades of blue. Her name, she told the secretary, Effie Perine, was Miss Wonderly. Because Miles Archer was not in, she spoke to Samuel Spade. She expressed concern for her younger sister's involvement with a man named Floyd Thursby. Spade didn't believe a word of it. He eventually learned that Miss Wonderly was really Bridgid O'Shaughnessy, and that what she wanted was protection from a fat cat named Gutman in an intricate scheme involving a valuable black statuette of a bird.

When famed literary critic Alexander Woollcott, self-proclaimed expert on crime, true and fictional, read Dashiell Hammett's detective novel, he extolled *The Maltese Falcon* as "the best detective story America has yet produced."

This was high praise for Hammett, but not a lot of praise for the state of mystery writing in the United States. The plain fact was that Americans with a zest for the "who done it" were more likely to turn the pages of thrillers written by British authors, such as Agatha Christie, Dorothy Sayres, and Sir Arthur Conan Doyle, the masterful creator of the "world's first private consulting detective," Mr. Sherlock Holmes of 221 Baker Street, London, and his companion in crime-solving, Dr. John H. Watson.

Not until 1934, with publication of Rex Stout's *Fer-de-Lance*, would America get to know a fat, orchid-growing detective by the name of Nero Wolfe who came anywhere near Sherlock Holmes in criminological brilliance. (The first book by Raymond Chandler, with a hard-boiled private eye named Philip Marlowe, didn't make an appearance until 1939.)

Other popular writers of "whodunnits" in the 1930s were Anthony Abbot, Earl Derr Biggers ("Charlie Chan"), Nicholas Blake, Leo Bruce, John Dickson Carr, Leslie Charteris ("The Saint"), John Creasy, R. Austin Freeman, David Frome, Philip MacDonald, Ngaio Marsh, Barry Perone ("Raffles"), Sax Rohmer ("Dr. Fu Manchu"), Georges Simenon ("Maigret"), S. S. Van Dyne ("Philo Vance"), and Louis Joseph Vance ("The Lone Wolf").

The Genuine Article

That Sam Spade's sleuthing had an authenticity came from the fact that his creator had been a gumshoe for the Pinkerton Detective agency, whose symbol, a wide-open eye, and its motto, "We never sleep," gave us the term "private eye." In the 1920s, Hammett had drawn on his detective experiences in writing short stories for a popular pulp detective magazine called *Black Mask*.

Following *The Maltese Falcon* in 1931 with a less successful yarn (*The Glass Key*), Hammett came up with Nick and Nora Charles in a mystery tale titled *The Thin Man*. The husband-and-wife team was so entertaining that they became stars of a wildly successful series of movies, with suave William Powell as Nick and Myrna Loy as the vivacious, wisecracking Nora.

The Real Nick and Nora

What most Americans didn't know as they watched Nick and Nora on their movie screens was that the characters had been based on Hammett's relationship with one of the nation's most successful playwrights, Lillian Hellman. At Hammett's suggestion, she had written a play about a schoolgirl's lies concerning a lesbian relationship between two teachers. *The Children's Hour* proved to be a sensation on Broadway, running for 86 weeks.

A 1936 drama about labor strife, *Days to Come*, failed, but in 1939 another hit, *The Little Foxes*, a scathing indictment of greed and materialism in a southern family, put Hellman right in line with the leftist wave in American drama. Her work, and a trip to the Soviet Union, eventually made her a prime target of the House Un-American Activities Committee in the 1950s. Refusing to provide information on other people, she declared, "I can't cut my conscience to fit this year's fashions."

When Hammett was called to testify about his own political views by Senator Joseph R. McCarthy, he invoked the 5th Amendment's protection against self-incrimination. For this he was sentenced to six months in federal prison for contempt of Congress.

Doyle Is Dead, Sherlock Isn't

As previously noted, in the year that Hammett published *The Maltese Falcon* (1930), the most popular mysteries were those written by Agatha Christie and Sir Arthur Conan Doyle. While Christie would turn out best-selling yarns for the next four decades, the creator of the Sherlock Holmes stories published his final collection in 1927. He died on July 7, 1930.

If Americans thought that was the last they'd hear of Holmes, they were mistaken. On June 5, 1934, at Crist Cella's restaurant in New York City, eight literary men got together to delight in each other's company and to ensure that no one would ever forget Sherlock Holmes. When they met a second time, they found that an uninvited guest was Alexander Woollcott. In an essay for *The New Yorker* of December 29, 1934, he gave the group a name: "The Baker Street Irregulars." The group, greatly increased in size, and with members from all over the United States and the world, continues to meet annually in January to celebrate Holmes, Dr. Watson, and other aspects of "Sherlockiana" with a dinner, toasts, learned papers, and other suitable ceremonies.

Worthy members of the BSI receive an "investiture" in the form of a name of a character, or a place, and sometimes a physical description, contained in the Holmes *Canon*. (The "Titular Investiture" of the author of the book that you're now reading is "Wilson Hargreave," who was a member of the "New York Police Bureau.")

The Least You Need to Know

- Communists and "Fellow Traveler" sympathizers saw in the Federal Theater Project an opportunity to promote what they called a "new American Revolution."
- Hollywood gangster films made stars of Edward G. Robinson, James Cagney, and Humphrey Bogart.
- Orson Welles's 1938 radio play *The War of the Worlds* caused a nationwide panic.
- Congress shut down the Federal Theater Project and began an investigation of "un-American activities" in the arts, theater, and motion pictures.

Don't Mean a Thing If It Ain't Got That Swing

In This Chapter

- The Federal Music Project scores a huge success
- Duke Ellington, Count Basie, and Benny Goodman teach the country how to swing
- The Big Bands, jitterbugging, jukeboxes, and radio's *Your Hit Parade*
- Pinball machines, chain letters, roller skating, and other national crazes
- America falls in love with the Dionne quintuplets

Through the Federal Music Project, millions of Americans who went to thousands of free concerts learned to appreciate classical music. New symphony orchestras formed in cities and towns. More than 13 million people enrolled in music classes.

The introduction of swing by Duke Ellington, Benny Goodman, the "Big Bands," the jukebox, and radio's *Your Hit Parade* set the nation's youth dancing the jitterbug and speaking in "boogie woogie" slang. It's the era of the "five-and-dime store," Bingo, bridge-playing, comic books, "Big Little" books, chain letters, pinball machines, and roller rinks.

The birth of the Dionne quintuplets in Canada sent the United States into its biggest tizzy over a foreign event since the abdication of England's King Edward VIII.

America's Music Teacher

After reading about the House Un-American Activities Committee's obsession with "Russianization" of the United States by people in the arts, you might think that the mere mention of the name of the man chosen to be the director of the Federal Music Project would send Martin Dies and J. Parnell Thomas off the deep end.

But the only purpose of Nikolai Solokoff as he gave up conducting the Cleveland Symphony Orchestra to take the FMP post was to show Americans that if they would just open their minds, they'd learn to love classical music as passionately as he did. But make no mistake about it, he declared, the FMP was not going to include "popular music." The Music Project would have no place for anyone interested in "playing stupid things," such as "dance music." To equate dance tunes to good music, he said, was like "comparing the funny papers to the work of a painter."

As if Maestro Sokoloff's conductor's baton were a magic wand, the country saw an explosion in its number of symphony orchestras, chamber groups, and choruses.

"Good Music" on Radio

With the enthusiastic support of the FMP, radio networks added symphony orchestra programs to their schedules. The combined listenership of the NBC Symphony, the New York Philharmonic, the *Ford Sunday Evening Hour*, and *The Voice of Firestone* surpassed 10 million a week.

Facts and Figures

In 1935 the United States had 11 symphonies. At the end of 1936 there were 34 more. By 1939 they numbered nearly 300.

Timeline

Located in what was then called the RCA Building (now owned by General Electric) in Rockefeller Center, Studio 8H is now the home of TV's *Saturday Night Live*.

For NBC the real coup was getting the services of the world's greatest conductor, Arturo Toscanini. He led the NBC Symphony in the largest radio studio in the world. It had been constructed on special shock-absorbers to prevent the studio from being shaken by the subways that ran beneath the building. To keep down the noise of people handling programs, the pages were satin cloth.

When NBC aired a *Music Appreciation Hour*, with famed conductor Walter Damrosch, it was primarily directed to schools. In 1938 more than seven million kids were getting lessons in music in 70,000 schools. The adult audience was estimated at four million.

A classical-music innovation of the 1930s that is still on the air is a Saturday afternoon broadcast of the Metropolitan Opera of New York. Sponsored for many years on NBC by Texaco, the programs are now carried by New York's "classical music" radio station, WQXR. Owned by *The New York Times*, it began broadcasting "good" music in the 1930s.

What About the Low Brows?

The problem in vowing to keep the FMP a highbrow operation was that the cultural brows of the majority of the people whose taxes paid for the FMP, and other New Deal arts projects, were somewhat lower. As a result, Maestro Sokoloff resigned himself to FMP programs including marching bands, "hillbilly" performers, folk singers, jazz and blues, gospel groups, Indian, Latin-American, and Mexican music.

An important part of the Federal Music Project's work was the collection and preservation of America's musical heritage. FMP workers ventured everywhere to record and write down the songs of the people of Appalachia, the music of Southern blacks, and other examples of music that originated among the common folk.

Beginning in 1938, the FMP organized a nationwide, three-day American Music Festival to coincide with Washington's birthday. The programs included traditional forms of popular music, from Negro folksongs, "down home" country fiddlers, banjo pickers, performances of Woody Guthrie tunes, and jazz combos to music that suddenly had become all the rage among the nation's younger generation—"Swing."

The Duke, the Count, and the King

The Duke was Edward Kennedy Ellington. Born in Washington, D.C., in 1899, he remains one of the seminal figures in popular music. Asked to define Swing, he explained that it was filled with the sudden turns, shocks, and swift changes of pace of jazz "that serve to remind us that the world is ever unexplored, and that while a complete mastery of life is mere illusion, the real secret of the game is to make life swing."

He provided a shorter version of his definition in the title of one of his hit songs: "It Don't Mean a Thing If It Ain't Got That Swing." Social historian Frederick Lewis Allen noted that a good swing band "smashing away at full speed" had its trumpeters and clarinetists rising in turn to "embroider the theme with their several furious improvisations and the drummers going into long-drawn-out rhythmical frenzies."

Facts and Figures

These are some other Ellington classics:

- ◆ "I Got It Bad"
- ◆ "I'm Beginning to See the Light"
- ◆ "In a Sentimental Mood"
- ◆ "Do Nothing Till You Hear from Me"
- ◆ "Mood Indigo"
- ◆ "Solitude"
- ◆ "Sophisticated Lady"
- ◆ "Take the A Train"

A prime example of Swing form was the music of William "Count" Basie. Born in Red Bank, New Jersey, in 1904, he set up his piano and band in New York's Roseland Ballroom in 1937 and took the city and country by storm. One jazz historian wrote that Basie's orchestra had "a powerful drive that used crescendos of riffs interspersed with blazing solos, all of it further propelled by the best rhythm section in the business."

The Count's 1937 hit and theme song, "One O'Clock Jump," ranks high on lists of all-time great Swing numbers. New Yorkers who wanted to hear the Count and his band flocked uptown to the Savoy Ballroom in Harlem or to the Famous Door on the block of West 52nd Street known as "Swing Street."

But the musician who put Swing into the national mainstream was a young, Jewish, white man with horned rim glasses and clarinet. His name: Benny Goodman. Born in Chicago in 1909, he'd made his debut at age 12 in an amateur contest. After playing with several noted jazz bands, he formed his own. On December 1, 1934, Benny Goodman and his orchestra were hired to play on a three-hour Saturday night NBC radio show, *Let's Dance*, sponsored by the National Biscuit Company. The program featured two other bands. Xavier Cugat's offered jazz with a Latin twist. Kel Murray's was "sweet." The difference between them and Benny Goodman, said critic George Simon, was "downright thrilling."

When *Let's Dance* went off the air after a six-month run, Goodman and the orchestra appeared at the Palomar Ballroom in Los Angeles in August 1935. The audience went crazy for them. It was at that instant, music historians agree, that the "Swing Era" was born. By the late 1930s Goodman's recordings and radio appearances had crowned him the "King of Swing."

Pandemonium at the Paramount

If you'd been passing through New York's Times Square at six in the morning on March 3, 1937, you would have had to make your way through 3,000 teenagers waiting for the Paramount Theater to open its doors. When it did so at eight o'clock, there were so many people trying to get in that mounted police had to be called out to prevent a riot.

The King of Swing, Benny Goodman.

None of the 3,364 kids who found a seat were there for the movie. They'd come to swing to the music of the country's most popular orchestra. Unless you were a Swing fan yourself, you probably would have wondered what language the kids were speaking. You'd have heard them saying "in the groove," "hipster," "hepcat," "jive," "spank the skin," "killer-diller," "jam session," "they really send me," and "get off." (The term was not used in its later sexual meaning.)

A Royal Jam at Carnegie Hall

On the night of January 16, 1938, the royalty of Swing gathered at New York's most esteemed musical venue. In a two hour concert, *Benny Goodman at Carnegie Hall*, the King of Swing shared the stage not only with his orchestra, but also with Duke Ellington and Count Basie. It was a singular turning point in jazz and Swing and not just because it was an unprecedented jam session by jazz's best. It was momentous in that it shattered the racial barrier. The integrated orchestra, trio, and quartet included Goodman, Basie and Ellington (black), Gene Krupa on drums (white), Lionel Hampton (black) on the "vibes" (vibraphone), and members of the Basie and Ellington bands.

Goodman's Carnegie Hall concert program.

> **CARNEGIE HALL PROGRAM**
>
> SEASON 1937-1938
>
> FIRE NOTICE—Look around *now* and choose the nearest exit to your seat. In case of fire walk (not run) to *that* Exit. Do not try to beat your neighbor to the street.
>
> John J. McELLICOTT, *Fire Commissioner*
>
> CARNEGIE HALL
>
> Sunday Evening, January 16th, at 8:30
>
> S. HUROK
>
> presents
>
> (by arrangement with Music Corporation of America)
>
> # BENNY GOODMAN
> and his
> # SWING ORCHESTRA
>
> I.
>
> "Don't Be That Way" .... *Edgar Sampson*
> "Sometimes I'm Happy" (from "Hit the Deck") .... *Irving Caesar & Vincent Youmans*
> "One O'clock Jump" .... *William (Count) Basie*
>
> II.
>
> TWENTY YEARS OF JAZZ
> "Sensation Rag" (as played c. 1917 by the Dixieland Jazz Band) .... *E. B. Edwards*
>
> PROGRAM CONTINUED ON SECOND PAGE FOLLOWING

To preserve the concert for a posterity that proved grateful, to say the least, Goodman arranged to have three microphones on the stage so it could be recorded on 41 12-inch 78 RPM acetate discs at a studio in the RKO Building at Rockefeller Center. It's safe to say that no one lucky enough to be in Carnegie Hall on that occasion could imagine that the music would be available more than six decades later on small round things called "CDs."

Carnival of Swing

Nowadays, rock stars make headlines by performing before throngs of fans in huge stadiums and arenas. Their shows are glitzy and often enlivened by the boisterous enthusiasm of fans. But none of them can match an amazing "Carnival of Swing" that was held in the summer of 1938 on Randall's Island in New York's East River.

It lasted six hours and featured 25 bands. A crowd of 25,000 that got in for free was so caught up in the Swing that the police and park officers had their hands full protecting the musicians from what a *New York Times* reporter saw as threat of "destruction from admiration."

America's youth got caught up in the Swing mania through the two means of mass communication in the home that came of age in the 1930s: radio and phonograph records.

Swinging at 78 Revolutions per Minute

When Thomas A. Edison invented the phonograph in 1877, the device on which voices and music were recorded was a cylinder with a thin coating of metal. Soon, the recording machine's needle was cutting grooves into a wax veneer. A flat disc appeared in 1904. With one song per side and revolving 78 times a minute, it would remain the standard speed until the introduction of the 45 RPM and 33⅓ "long playing" record in the 1950s.

Records were purchased in shops that specialized in phonographs, and in "five-and-ten-cent" stores, such as Woolworth's, Kresge's, and J. J. Newberry. Popular music could be heard in diners and soda shops by dropping a nickel into a "jukebox." The "platters" were stacked in a huge lit-from-within machine with a Bakelite front and side panels and strips of bubble lights. By 1940 half a million jukeboxes were taking in half a billion dollars a year.

Facts and Figures

Record sales between 1933 and 1938 rose 600 percent.

The Big Bands

Of course, 78 RPM records at home or on a jukebox were heard by only a few people, one side at a time. Radio had the potential of bringing Swing to millions of fans all at once, and with no need for anyone to flip to the other side or change records. A radio station or network could carry Swing bands without interruptions, except for the occasional commercial, by setting up microphones when they performed in ballrooms and dance halls. Such broadcasts were "band remotes." Without them, it's unlikely that the 1930s would be remembered, and venerated, as the era of the "Big Band."

With a twist of the radio dial on a Saturday night, a Swing fan was transported to the Glenn Island Casino, "the mecca of music for moderns" in New Rochelle, New York; the Meadowbrook at Cedar Grove, New Jersey; Grand Terrace, Chicago; the Reno Club, Kansas City; and many others. The Big Band remotes originated in hotel ballrooms, mostly in New York. One of Glenn Miller's orchestra's biggest hits even took its title from the Pennsylvania Hotel's phone number: Pennsylvania 6-5000.

The remotes usually came on at 10 or 11 on Saturday night and ran four hours, generally with a different band each half-hour. One avid listener depicted the experience as "a huge and marvelous musical bazaar—a bubbling, exciting mixture of places, names, melodies, and events, coming right into your living room from one after another of America's great dance floors." Dancing to the Big Bands was called "jitterbugging." Those who did so were "jitterbugs." Why? Because their lively antics made them look like a swarm of jittery bugs, at least to the eyes of the older generation.

Facts and Figures

These were some of the other music shows popular in the Big Band era:

- ◆ *The Camel* [cigarettes] *x*
- ◆ *Chesterfield [cigarettes] Time* (Glenn Miller)
- ◆ *Kay Kyser's Kollege of Musical Knowledge*
- ◆ *Let's Dance* (Goodman)
- ◆ *Paul Whiteman's Kraft Music Hall*
- ◆ *Saturday Night Swing Club*
- ◆ *Sensation* [cigarettes] *and*

During the week, radio carried band shows during hours that today we call "prime time." Between seven and 10 or 11 o'clock, the listener had a choice of programs featuring the big names in pop music. Many of the shows were sponsored by cigarette makers. The show that had the greatest influence was *Your Hit Parade*. When it made its debut on April 20, 1935, the orchestra leader was Lennie Hamilton, but soon the show had "visiting" bands that included Goodman. What made the program unique was that the songs were given a numerical ranking of hits, 1 to 15, hence "hit parade." The result was a new phrase for the American language: "Number One on the hit parade."

One of the singers eventually featured was a skinny youth with a bow tie, blue eyes, and silky voice from Hoboken, New Jersey, by the name of Frank Sinatra.

The Five-and-Dime Store

Also called the "five-and-ten," these "anything you could ever want" emporiums in nearly every small town and city in the United States offered a vast variety of items. The "five-and-ten" actually had goods that cost as much as a dollar. But on a Saturday night in one of them, one could buy candy, toys, clothing, kitchen items, dishes, "Depression glass" for a nickel that in today's antique shops and flea markets can cost you hundreds of bucks, Shirley Temple Dolls, lipstick, Burma-Shave cream, and virtually every product anyone wanted or needed.

In 1929 the grand-daddy of the five-and-ten, F. W. Woolworth, had 2,100 stores. By 1933 the chain had added 395. Its founder and namesake made so much money in nickels and dimes that he built the world's tallest building. Opposite New York's City Hall, the "cathedral of commerce" remained the globe's highest skyscraper until the Chrysler Empire State buildings left it in the shade. One of the Great Depression's most popular songs was "I Found a Million-Dollar Baby in a Five-and-Ten-Cent Store."

A Few Fads and Nonmusical Crazes

The 1930s were a decade of fads and crazes. They included:

- **Big Little books.** Small, thick, children's books with pictures. Cheap then; highly collectible and costly today.

- **Comic books.** The first genuine American comic book, *Funnies on Parade*, appeared in 1933. It was followed by *Superman* (1938) in *Action Comics Number One, Captain Marvel, Mary Marvel, Wonder Woman, Green Lantern, Daredevil, Bullet Man, Hawk Man, Blue Bolt*, and *The Flame*.

- **Chain letters.** Starting in Denver in 1934, they soon crossed the country like wildfire. If you got one, you crossed out the first name and sent that person a dime, then mailed out copies with your name at the top, hoping that your mail box would soon be full of dimes. Theoretically, you'd get $1,562.50. Of course, the only person who profited was the one who started the letter on its way.

- **Pinball machines.** Introduced in Chicago in 1932. Some government officials, especially New York's Mayor La Guardia, saw the "slot machine" as a cruel device that robbed families of money. A 1938 Gallup Poll found that 29 percent of Americans had put money into some kind of slot machine.

- **Bingo.** One pastime the government couldn't touch was gambling in a house of worship in the form of Bingo and other lotteries. The same Gallop Poll discovered that about a third of the population had attended a church Bingo party, or taken part in a lottery run by their parish or congregation.

- **Bridge.** When the Lynds (Remember them?) checked up on the people of "Middletown" in 1935, they discovered a huge increase in the number of bridge players. But what was new was that many of them weren't just using the card game for after-supper amusement. They were placing bets.

- **The Irish Sweepstakes.** When the Irish Sweepstakes was held in 1933, 214 of the 2,404 people who had won in a drawing of 6.5 million tickets were Americans.

- **Punchcards.** Available in stores everywhere, they were cards with holes to be punched out in the hope of winning money. Millions of Americans were left holding a worthless slip of paper.

- **Jar games.** People guessed how many marbles, jellybeans, or other items were in a jar. Few winners claimed the prize in the two million such jars on store counters between 1933 and 1939.

- **Roller rinks.** The nation's 3,500 skating rinks drew as many as 7,000 people per rink per week. People didn't just roll around the rink. They danced on skates to waltzes and fox trots. Only the most daring tried jitterbugging on skates.

- **Softball.** By 1939 there were five million players of all ages and half a million teams.

- **Golf.** Earlier you read about a craze for miniature golf, but the full-scale game also thrived. Thanks to federal funds through the various work projects, 576 municipal courses were opened in 1935 alone. Thousands of private clubs also opened.

- **Skiing.** Not affordable by most Americans, a passion for swooping down a snowy slopes by the rich resulted in ski resort building in California, Colorado, New England, and New York. Skiing and ice-skating got a boost from the 1932 Winter Olympics, held in Lake Placid, New York.

- **Goldfish swallowing.** The fad lasted a very brief period in 1939 on college campuses. In started at Harvard with a $10 bet. In keeping with the nutty mood, other students formed Societies for the Prevention of Goldfish Eating. The record tally of goldfish swallowed was 210, set by a sophomore.

- **Dish nights.** To entice women into movie theaters during the week, operators picked a particular day to give every woman who came in a plate, bowl, cup, or saucer. If she come back often enough, she would have a complete place setting.

- **Knock-knock jokes.** Yes, even way back then. Example:

    "Knock knock."
    "Who's there?"
    "Freda."
    "Freda who?"
    "Freda you, but five bucks to someone else."

Call for Philip MAW-RISSS

You've read that several music shows on radio were sponsored by cigarette companies. Aside from the fact that the programs had a huge young audience of present and potential smokers, the tobacco companies of the 1930s were locked in a war for domination of the market.

The main contestants in the struggle were the big three: Camel, Lucky Strike, and Chesterfield. But vying against them were such new names as Ramrod, Bright Star, One-Eleven, Black and White, Sunshine, Golden Rule, Avalon, Revelation, Wings, Parliament,

Viceroy, Raleigh (you got a coupon in a pack that you traded in for merchandise), Spud, Fatima, Pall Mall, Kool, and Sensation. (The sponsor of Sammy Kaye's band on *Sensation and Swing*.)

Since there was little difference, if any, between the brands, success depended on advertising. Companies also sought to have a distinctive packaging. The Camel pack had a camel (actually it was a dromedary). Chesterfield was an elegant white. Luckies had a green pack with "Lucky Strike" in black against a red circle. A pack of "Philip Morris," made by the same firm as Luckies (the American Tobacco Company), was brown with a regal-looking crest. The cigarette was also available in "king size." To market the brand on radio, the firm's advertising agency came up with one of radio's distinctive ad campaigns.

Hired for the job was Johnny Roventini. He was a midget. (It's a politically incorrect word today, but that's what "little people" were called then, as you know from *The Wizard of Oz*, about which you'll read more later.) A former page at the New Yorker Hotel, he had the perfect voice for commercials in which he was heard paging, "Call for Philip Morris." The Morris was protracted into "MAW-RISSS." The commercials were part of a campaign of billboards, newspaper, and magazine ads. Together, they garnered sales that moved the brand into fourth place in popularity, even though Philip Morris cigarettes cost more per pack than the top three brands.

Facts and Figures

The combined total of all brands of cigarettes sold in 1939 was 180 billion. The three top brands claimed 89 percent of the market. By the end of World War II 400 billion cigarettes were being turned out. Cigars sold in the United States in 1939: 5 billion, a per capita decline since 1930 from 48 percent to 39 percent.

Papa Dionne Hands Out a Bunch of Cigars

Giving out cigars, of course, has long been a tradition for a man who's just become a father. Usually, the blessed event involves one baby. But on May 28, 1934, from a small town in Canada, news flashed around the world that 24-year-old Mrs. Oliva Dionne had given birth to five. Having babies wasn't unusual for her. She was already the mother of six. But quintuplets? And all of them doing well? That was an event to throw the whole world into a tizzy, and no place more so than in the United States. Few Americans couldn't tell you the names of the girls: Emilie, Marie, Cecile, Annette, and Yvonne.

Quick Way to a Fast Dollar

By Friday, five days after the birth of the Dionne "quints," as they would ever after be known, the town of Corbeil was up to its elbows in more reporters, photographers, and newsreel cameras than Papa and Mama Dionne were in diapers. Along with the press came a horde of "promoters" with eagle eyes ablaze with schemes to cash in. So many hoped to knock on the Dionnes' door that a police guard had to be posted.

Made wards of the Ontario government, the sisters were put on display for as many as 6,000 people a day to watch as they played behind a one-way screen. The place established by authorities across from their house was named "Quintland." Under the direction of the doctor who delivered them, Allan Roy DaFoe, a commercial enterprise had them endorsing hundreds of products. Hollywood gave them a movie contract for $250,000 for a movie based on them. Eventually, three films were made.

Famous Faces

Only two of the famous five Dionnes are alive at this writing. Emilie died in 1945 at age 20 of an epileptic seizure. Marie died at home at age 36. In 1998, Yvonne, Cecile, and Antoinette were awarded $4 million in compensation by the Ontario government. Yvonne died of cancer on June 23, 2001. The two survivors live near Montreal.

The Rest of the Story

After a nine-year legal battle by Papa Dionne, they were returned to their parents in 1943. Years later, three of the surviving sisters published a book, *We Were Five*. They then revealed in 1995 that the five girls had been sexually abused by their father for years. Papa Dionne had died in 1979. In 1994, CBS ran a made-for-TV that placed most of the blame for the way the quints were treated like commercial products on Dr. DaFoe.

A Big Boom in War Toys

A child going into a five-and-dime during the later years of the 1930s found the toy department as heavily armed as the troops of the Nazis and Italians who had Europe and the rest of the world feeling jittery about the prospects for another war. So many war toys were on sale that *Fortune* magazine took notice. Counters of chain stores, the magazine reported, "are overflowing with tanks and soldiers and cannons."

While toy makers and stores had war on their minds, so did the president of the United States. As the country heard reports on the radio of the mounting tensions in Europe, FDR was reading messages from U.S. diplomats that reminded him of events that had preceded the "Great War" of 1914 to 1918 that before long would have the Roman numeral "I" after the words "World War."

During that conflict, Roosevelt had been Assistant Secretary of the Navy. Now he admitted to "a strange feeling of familiarity." Each day at 2:45 P.M., he listened to Army and Navy intelligence officers as they briefed him on developments. As he listened, he thought back to a telephone at his bedside with a direct wire to the Navy Department. Then, the same messages were sent around, the same lights snapped on in the nerve centers of the U.S. government.

At three in the morning of September 1, 1939, FDR's phone rang. On the line was the American ambassador in Paris, William Bullitt. The news was very bad. Ignoring a British-French warning that a German attack on Poland would mean an automatic declaration of war, the Nazis had unleashed a Blitzkrieg. Several divisions were already deep inside Poland. The Second World War had begun.

Wild Bill

One of the heroes of the Great War was a U.S. Army battalion commander by the name of William J. Donovan. A winner of the Congressional Medal of Honor for leading a charge against German lines, he earned the nickname "Wild Bill." Hoping to convert his fame into a political career, he ran for governor of New York in 1932 but lost to Democrat Herbert Lehman in the landslide that put Franklin D. Roosevelt in the White House.

You'd think that the election campaign would have meant an end to Donovan's future in government service. But as Roosevelt looked at the growing crisis in Europe, he realized that if the United States were to be ready for war, there was a need to know what the Nazis were up to. Learning that Donovan had made valuable contacts in the German government and that he'd had a meeting in England with Winston Churchill, FDR recognized that when it came to the security of the United States, politics took a back seat.

Churchill had been so impressed with Donovan that he'd sent a cable to FDR saying that Donovan "has carried with him throughout an animating, heart-warming flame." Churchill's confidence paid off when Donovan urged FDR to provide aid to Britain by swapping 50 aging U.S. destroyers for leases on British bases located in the western Atlantic and Caribbean. Roosevelt saw in Donovan the very man who might be needed, should it become necessary, to set up an American system for collecting intelligence.

Having traveled widely since his service in the Great War, he'd been a careful observer of the social, political, and military conditions. As a lawyer, he'd demonstrated competence on behalf of corporate clients. As an Army officer, he'd proved his ability to lead and inspire.

Other People's Mail

It's hard to believe today that when FDR came into office in 1933 there was no American system for keeping an eye on what possible future enemies were up to. Indeed, when the

Secretary of State, Henry L. Stimson, learned of the existence of a small military intelligence unit known as the Black Chamber, he ordered it shut down with the remark, "Gentlemen do not read each other's mail."

By 1940, according to a senior diplomat, Robert Murphy, the U.S. intelligence organization was "primitive and inadequate" and was "timid, parochial, and operating in the tradition of the Spanish-American War."

Determined not to be left in the dark on the growing crisis in Europe, FDR saw the need for the United States to get back in the spying business. Because his new Secretary of the Navy, Frank Knox, had been a classmate of Donovan at Columbia University's Law School, Knox proposed that Donovan be put in charge of coordinating the gathering of "strategic information." Despite opposition from J. Edgar Hoover of the FBI, who feared such an organization would step on the FBI's toes, Roosevelt authorized a secret fund for the operation. Donovan would report directly to the president "and to no one else."

More Letters in the Alphabet Soup

Donovan's new title was "Coordinator of Information." As "COI" joined the list of "alphabet soup" government agencies, Donovan's task was to "collect and analyze all information and data, which may bear upon national security; to correlate information and data, and to make such information available to the president and to such departments and officials of the government as the president may determine; and to carry out, when requested by the president, such supplementary activities as may facilitate the securing of information important for national security not now available to the government."

Assuring J. Edgar Hoover and nervous men in the Army and Navy that as COI he would not interfere with their organizations, Donovan made it clear that he saw himself as someone who would coordinate, classify, and interpret "all information from whatever source obtained." He noted, "We have, scattered throughout the various departments of our government, documents and memoranda concerning military and naval and air and economic potentials of other nations which, if gathered together and studied in detail by carefully selected trained minds, with knowledge of both of the related languages and technique, would yield valuable and often decisive results."

When the Germans learned of Donovan's new job, they saw Donovan "brewing a Jewish-Democratic crisis." The main points of the "Roosevelt-Donovan program," said the Nazis, were "terroristic attempts, acts of sabotage, revolts, corruption, and bribery."

Except for the junk about the COI being connected to a Jewish conspiracy, they were close to the mark of what the COI would become during the Second World War as the Office of Strategic Services (OSS). With Wild Bill Donovan at its head, it became a full-scale spy agency that did, indeed, carry out sabotage, try to stir up revolutions, and undermine enemy officials through bribery. With the war over, and the Cold War taking shape, OSS would be replaced by the Central Intelligence Agency.

While the Germans were alarmed over the creation of the COI, Donovan's new job received little attention in the American press and even less among the American people. To the majority of them, Europe was far away, and what was happening over there was not the main business of a country with enough problems of its own.

In 1940 the unemployment rate stood at 14.6 percent, with 8.1 million people still out of work. Based on 1929 national income figures, between 1930 and 1938 the national income had declined $132 billion. And the country remained divided into two classes. In a public opinion survey conducted at the end of the decade, Americans believed by a two-to-one margin that there was "too much power" in the hands of "a few rich men" and corporations.

The Least You Need to Know

- The Federal Music Project introduced millions of people to symphony orchestras and appreciation of "classical" music.
- "Big bands" drew audiences in person, by records, and on the radio to a new style of popular music called "Swing."
- Fads and crazes included bingo, pinball machines, bridge, dish nights at the movies, and knock-knock jokes.
- Concerned about the possibility of the United States getting drawn into war, FDR created an intelligence office known as the Coordinator of Information.

Chapter 20

World of Tomorrow

In This Chapter

- The ultra-modernistic Art Deco style takes over industrial design and architecture
- Just about everything goes "streamlined"
- The United States puts on four "international expositions"
- The New York World's Fair of 1939 raises the curtain on the promised glories of "the world of tomorrow"
- America is woefully unready for war

Following the 1926 International Exposition of Decorative and Modern industrial Arts in Paris, American designers went crazy for "Art Deco" styling. Suddenly, "streamlining" was introduced in automobiles, airplanes, ocean liners, buildings, fashions, and the movies. Five American cities—Philadelphia, Chicago, San Francisco, San Diego, and New York—find reasons to host a "World's Fair." The hands-down biggest and best was New York's in 1939 and 1940.

Who the Devil Is This Guy Named Art Deco?

Four years before the collapse the world's economies, the city of Paris invited artists and designers from all over the globe to come to "The City of Light" and have a look at its Exposition International des Arts Decoratifs et Industriels Modernes. The purpose of the 1925 extravaganza was to encourage a "common aesthetic" among leaders of the world of decorative arts and architecture. While this seemed like a fine idea to the French, many nations were absent, including the United States and the rest of the Western Hemisphere. Because of lingering resentment over the recent Great War, Germany was not invited.

Shorthand for the dramatic, sleek, new style introduced in Paris was "Art Deco." It was controversial, and some leading designers denounced it. But before long, the Art Deco influence would be seen everywhere and nowhere more than in the United States.

If It's for Sale at Macy's, It Must Be Okay

Although the United States was not a part of the Paris exposition of 1925, Americans who went on behalf of two of New York's top department stores, Lord & Taylor and Macy's, were impressed with the new modern-design concepts. To test the waters and to see if American housewives might be willing to jump in, the firms held separate special show- ings of Art Deco furnishings in 1928. Macy's added a distinguished co-sponsor to its Art Deco display in the form of the Metropolitan Museum of Art. The following year, the stately institution on Fifth Avenue held its own showing of room interiors, "The Architect and Industrial."

In 1934 the Art Deco ball was really rolling in art museums. The Metropolitan spot- lighted work of designers Lee Simonson, William Lescaze, and a man who would be regarded as the leading exponent of the bold new style, Raymond Loewy (more coming up). Presenting an exhibition called "Machine Art," the Museum of Modern Art put on display a wide range of Art Deco–style household wares, from bathtubs to kitchen appli- ances, lamps, toasters, and dustpans.

Form Follows Function

The ruling concept in making art of the ordinary was as simple as the style: The function of the object dictates its form. A chair, therefore, must fit the human shape. A handle, whether on a car door or a suitcase, should look good but be comfortable in the hand. Above all, there was no reason why the form that fit the function couldn't make an artistic statement. Industrial designer Walter Dorwin Teague put it this way in the design magazine *Art and Decoration:* "Painting and sculpture are art, but so is the making of kitchen sinks and pickle bottles."

In a process in which function determined the shape of objects, new materials were needed. The result was a flood of items made from synthetics that included Bakelite, Formica, Lucite, Catalin, Celluloid, Beetleware, and other plastics. Industrial designers turned them into dishes, cutlery handles, toothbrushes, plates, soap dishes, ashtrays, clocks, lamps, telephones, jewelry, and cases for table-model radios. The term for these artful designs was "streamlining."

Mr. Breer's Brainstorm

One day in 1927, goes a story that was told around water-coolers in Walter Chrysler's elegant, new, spire-topped, Art Deco–style headquarters building at 42nd Street and Lexington Avenue, car-designer Carl Breer saw a flight of Army Air Corps planes zooming overhead. Admiring how easily they plied the sky, he wondered if Chrysler automobiles could be designed in an "aerodynamic" way. To find out if it was possible, he consulted with engineers Fred Zeder and Owen Skelton, and designer Oliver Clark to produce a sleek-looking prototype. By putting the engine directly over the front axle, and with the body a modified tear-shaped silhouette, they produced the eight-cylinder, roomy Chrysler "Airflow."

Facts and Figures

In 1936 a Chevy, Ford, or Plymouth was priced around $750. The luxurious Cadillac V-16 was $3,500 without "extras." The average-priced car was $580. Americans liked to drive the Pontiac, Dodge, Chevrolet, Ford, Cadillac, La Salle, Buick, Plymouth, De Soto, Nash, Chrysler, Oldsmobile, Lincoln, Hudson, Packard, Willys, and Studebaker.

When the Airflow appeared on the market in 1934 as Chryslers and De Sotos, the age of square auto bodies was over. Other automakers rushed into streamlining. The American auto now sported sloped radiators, curved windshields, and backswept fenders. With the sleek shapes came higher speeds. The 1935 Auburn was clocked at 100 miles an hour.

America's movie-darling Shirley Temple gave her endorsement to the 1936 Dodge, made by Chrysler.

Streamlining Takes to the Rails

Although better cars and new and improved roads had Americans taking to the highways more than ever, the preferred means of long-distance travel was the train. There's no telling how many people listened to the distant whistle of a train in the night and imagined themselves on it. Poet Edna Vincent Millay spoke for almost everyone when she wrote, "There's not a train I wouldn't take, no matter where it's going."

If a person had the money and the time, he could step on board the New York Central Railroad's "20th Century Limited" at Grand Central Terminal, or the Pennsylvania's "Broadway Limited" at Penn Station in New York, and be in Chicago the next day. Then he could hop onto the Union Pacific's "Super Chief" and three days later step off in Los

Angeles, where as the song "Hooray for Hollywood" proposed, with a little luck he might be "discovered" and become as famous as Donald Duck.

Since the invention of trains in the nineteenth century, locomotives were big, steam-powered, smoke-belching, noisy, and bulky black Goliaths. Passenger cars were generally rattling boxes with hard seats. But in 1934 a designer for the Pullman Car Company, Otto Kuhler, created the first high-speed "streamliner." Built for the Union Pacific, the egg-shaped train, painted brown and yellow, was named "City of Salina." Union Pacific promoters called it "Tomorrow's Train for Today."

When the 600-horsepower train with its sleek, air-conditioned cars rolled into Washington, D.C., on a 22-state tour, it was given an approving inspection by FDR himself. Arriving in Chicago for the "Century of Progress" World's Fair (more on this in a later section), more than two million people flocked to look it over. Also on display was the Burlington Zephyr. The first train to have cars with an exterior of gleaming aluminum, built by the Budd Company of Philadelphia, it won the fair's design competition.

Mr. Loewy Jumps on Board

Deciding to streamline its trains, the Pennsylvania Railroad hired the top man in industrial design. French-born Raymond Loewy came to the United States in 1919 after studying engineering and physics in Paris. He'd made his name in 1929 by redesigning the Gestetner duplicating machine. Deciding to update its trains, the Pennsy asked Loewy to redesign the workhorse of its line, the S1 locomotive. He also fashioned the "6100." The largest locomotive ever built by the Pennsy's shops in Altoona, Pennsylvania, it was 149 feet long and weighed 526 tons. To show it off, the railroad placed it on a continuously running, 60 mph roller bed at the New York World's Fair. Loewy is the acknowledged "father of modern industrial design."

All Aboard for Art Deco Luxury

The streamlined trains offered more than flashy looks and swift travel. Advertisements promised, and the trains delivered, the height of luxury. One settled into seats as roomy and comfy as his favorite armchair. Art Deco lounge and "observation" club cars served cocktails. Chefs in the dining car prepared superb meals served on fine china. Porters looked to everyone's comfort. And if a person was speeding across the continent, he went to bed in an upper or lower berth, or settled down in a private "roomette" or "compartment," all of which was air-conditioned.

Timeline

Among Raymond Loewy's other designs were the Coca Cola bottle, a streamlined Greyhound bus, the Electrolux cylinder vacuum cleaner, and the radical 1945 Studebaker. During the Kennedy administration he designed the presidential plane, *Air Force One*.

The Pennsylvania Railroad's streamlined "6100" engine, designed by Raymond Loewy, at the 1939 New York World's Fair.

A person didn't just get on a train. He boarded one with a name that was romantic and enticing: Blue Comet, Hiawatha, Silver Meteor, Electroliner, Sunset Limited, Super Chief, the Powhatan Arrow, Rock Island Rocket, and Silver Streak.

Up, Up, and Away

All through this exploration of the 1930s, the general theme has been the movement of the federal government into almost every aspect of American life. But in February 1934, the Postmaster General, James A. Farley, shocked the nation by announcing that the feds were getting out of the business of carrying the mail on government airplanes. In a story that's too complicated to tell here, the result was the birth of transcontinental commercial airlines.

First to take off was American Air Lines, founded in April 1934. By the end of the year, the company was looking for a new plane that would allow it to carry not just mail from coast to coast, but people as well. American bought a modification of Douglas Aircraft Company's DC-2. Lengthened and fitted with 21 seats that could be converted to beds, it was named the DC-3. It allowed American to introduce, on July 15, 1936, "Giant Flagship Non-Stop Service" between New York and Chicago.

Lining Up on the Runway

Other airlines followed suit, giving passengers the choice of American, TWA, and United. By 1940 the DC-3 was used in 80 percent of domestic flights. Other smaller airlines were soon plying the skies to provide regional services.

With so many in business, the federal government got back into the act in order to regulate the burgeoning industry. It did so on June 23, 1938, when FDR signed the Civil Aeronautics Act. It created the Civil Aeronautics Authority (CAA). It was empowered to certify airlines and their routes and to establish safety regulations.

Three months after the CAA was established, President Roosevelt authorized construction of an airport for the nation's capitol. Just across the Potomac River in Virginia, it was named National Airport. When it opened six months before the Japanese attack on Pearl Harbor plunged the country into World War II, it quickly became one of the busiest in the country.

Not to be outdone, Mayor Fiorello La Guardia, who'd been an Army pilot in the First World War, used New Deal money to build the biggest airport anywhere. With the longest runway in the world, it was immediately named (by New York's City Council) La Guardia Airport. It started operating just in time for the opening of the greatest international exposition ever held.

Facts and Figures

In November 1939 the United States had 645 municipal airports and 455 commercial airports. There were 29,513 licensed pilots and 27,691 student pilots.

Time Out for a Flashback

To appreciate why the United States went wild for having world's fairs in the 1930s, we have to know a bit of pre-Depression history. The country's experiences in hosting international expositions had started in 1876. The Philadelphia Centennial Exposition was a salute to 100 years of U.S. independence. On 465 acres of the city's vast Fairmount Park, stood 249 buildings in the Queen Anne variation of Victorian Gothic. Everyone who went loved it.

Pleased with the outcome, Philly threw another fair 50 years later. Held for the same reason, it was called the "Sesqui-Centennial International Exposition." Its grand entrance was an 80-foot replica of the Liberty Bell. Lest some prankster try to put a second crack in the real bell, it was kept inside the Old State House, best known as Independence Hall. The celebration was another whopping success.

Ticket to the Philadelphia World's Fair of 1926.

One Good Turn Deserves Another

Between the Philadelphia expositions came the 1893 "Columbian Exposition" in Chicago. It marked the 400th anniversary of Christopher Columbus's voyage to the New World. Of much more interest to the fair-goers was a new thrill called "riding the Ferris Wheel."

Mr. Ferris's invention was part of an entertainment area. The first fun-and-games section at a world's fair, it was known as the Midway Plaisance, hence the "midway" at fairs, circuses, and carnivals ever since. Chicago's midway drew throngs of men to watch "Little Egypt" shed layers of see-through veils as she did the "hootchie kootchie."

Right Here in Our Home Town

If you've seen the Judy Garland movie *Meet Me in St. Louis* (silly me; of course you have), you know something about the "Louisiana Purchase Exposition" held there in 1903. Yes, people back then did go around singing the song that became the movie title. They also had iced tea for the first time, along with the hot dog and the ice-cream cone.

With the successes of these previous U.S. world's fairs and the Art Deco fair in Paris in 1925, American cities that had never had a fair figured that by putting on an international exposition they would give a boost to their Depression-plagued economies. As a result of this optimism, there were five fairs held, in Chicago again, in Dallas, two in California, and the biggest of them all, in New York City.

The Century of Progress

The purpose of Chicago's 1933 "Century of Progress" exposition, according to its president, Rufus C. Dawes, was to show to the world "the spontaneous expression of the pride of citizenship of Chicago." To do this, the city created its third world's fair on 400 acres of landfill on the edge of Lake Michigan.

Poster for the 1933 Chicago World's Fair.

It opened on April 19, 1933. Everyone had such a good time that its run was extended to October 31, 1934. Its many exhibits were intended to "demonstrate to an international audience the nature and significance of scientific discoveries, methods of achieving them, and changes which their application has wrought in industry and living conditions." It attracted more than 38 million people to look at the Windy City's glories on its hundredth anniversary.

Meet Me in San Diego

The "California Pacific Exposition" opened shop in San Diego on May 29, 1935. Greetings on the gala occasion came from FDR over the phone. His words were boomed to the crowd by loudspeakers, and to a national radio audience tuned to CBS. FDR attended the fair on October 2, 1935. In his speech to 60,000 people inside and 15,000 outside San Diego Stadium, he praised "the products of American artistic and mechanical genius." He then attributed the success of the Exposition to individual effort which policies of his New Deal were "created to promote." (No one said that FDR didn't know how to toot his own horn.)

Former president Herbert Hoover paid a visit on June 18. If the namesake of countless Hoovervilles had been there a week sooner, he might have met the one and only Mae West. The buxom star of stage, movies, and the sexy wisecrack arrived wearing a black dress that clung to her hourglass figure.

At the "Midget Village" she tempted one of the diminutive men with her trademark query, "Why don'tcha you come up and see me sometime?" Told that if she had come to the fair the next day she would be surrounded by 58,000 sailors of the U.S. Pacific Fleet, she disappointed no one with, "I'm sorry I didn't know. I certainly would have come down to see them. I'm very patriotic that way."

Famous Faces

Born Aimee Elizabeth Kennedy in Canada, "Sister Aimee" in her heyday, starting in the 1920s, used huge tent revivals, radio, and her "Four Square Gospel" church to become the most famous Christian evangelist since St. Paul. Sinclair Lewis's novel *Elmer Gantry* and the 1960 movie starring Jean Simmons and Burt Lancaster were based on Aimee.

When evangelist Aimee Semple McPherson was invited by "Queen Zorina" to visit the nudist colony at the fair, Sister Aimee politely declined. To dispel any misunderstanding, Zorina quickly explained, "I didn't expect her to take off her clothes. I only invited her to tea." Sister Aimee told a crowd of 20,000 at the fair's Amphitheater that the cure for the Depression and all the woes of the nation was for Americans to "go back—back to the faith of the religion of our fathers."

Among other fair attractions were a Children's Day in which Joe Louis was referee of boxing bouts with midgets in Midget City; a birthday party for Buddha, held by 8,000 Japanese Americans (most of whom would find themselves locked into detention camps during World War II); a National Negro Day for which 20,000 blacks showed up; Nickel Days (kids got in for a nickel instead of the usual quarter); a bicycle-riding chimpanzee named "Duke of Wellington"; an appearance by the kids from the popular *Our Gang* movies; and 132 concerts paid for by the Ford Motor Company.

During the fair's first year, 4,784,811 people attended. But the number was less than half of what had been expected. Year two of the exposition was more disappointing. Only two million came. The second year of the fair suffered because many of its main exhibitors, such as Ford, turned their attention to another fair in Dallas, Texas. It opened on June 6, 1936. The Texas Centennial Exposition marked the 100th year since the Lone Star State won its independence from Mexico. Along with a smaller event in Fort Worth, it was minor compared to Chicago's, drawing about seven million visitors.

But Dallas department store owner Nieman Marcus judged it a success because "the rest of America discovered Texas." It seems to have worked. Four of the next nine U.S. presidents were officially Texans: Dwight Eisenhower (born in Denison), Lyndon Johnson (near Stonewall), and the two George Bushes (New Englanders, but transplanted to Houston and Midland).

Open Up Your Golden Gate

In 1939, it was pretty hard for Americans not to think about San Francisco. First, they'd gotten a lesson in the history of the *City by the Bay* in a 1936 Clark Gable movie. Co-starring Jeanette MacDonald and Spencer Tracy, San Francisco reached its climax in a recreation of the earthquake that had flattened and burned the place in 1906. Having seen the movie, one was likely to leave the theater singing the words of the film's big hit song, "San Francisco, Open Your Golden Gate."

Three years later, that's just what the folks of San Francisco did. Their world's fair was the "Golden Gate Exposition." Built on 400 acres of landfill named "Treasure Island,"the extravaganza celebrated the construction of the Golden Gate Bridge, as well as the Oakland–San Francisco Bay Bridge. The island itself was quite an achievement. It was the largest man-made island in the world.

The theme of the Exposition was "A Pageant of the Pacific." It offered exhibits of 30 foreign nations and nearly 300 industries. The plan envisioned keeping three of its structures to serve as a terminal for trans-Pacific flights, including the Pan American Airways' China Clipper "flying boat."

Admission to the fair was 50 cents for adults and 25 cents for kids. The 1939 *WPA Guide to California* described an "illusion of magnitude and splendor" that was "heightened by the use of flaming banners, huge cylindrical lanterns, translucent glass fabric pillars, and pylons with torchieres streaming flames of vapor." Built in Art Deco style, the buildings at night created a "magic city in amber, white, and pastel shades of shimmering light, floating in the Bay."

Timeline

The ribbon opening the Golden Gate Bridge was cut on May 27, 1939. To mark the occasion, the city held a seven-day "Golden Gate Festival." The highlight was 250,000 people walking across the bridge from Marin County to the city side.

Producers of the *Charlie Chan* series of mystery movies were so enthralled by the Exposition that they filmed one of them there. Starring Sidney Toler, a white man in the role of the oriental sleuth, the plot involved a magician (Cesar Romero) helping Chan to unmask a fake psychic who blackmailed gullible clients. It was a pretty good movie, but it also provided glimpses of the fair to moviegoers who couldn't afford a trip to San Francisco.

Chicago's Columbian Exposition had shocked some people with the antics of Little Egypt. The San Francisco World's Fair caused eyes to pop with strip-teaser Sally Rand, famed for feathery fans and a giant bubble. While laws kept Sally from showing all of her attributes, she sill managed to titillate the men. She also was in charge of a "nude ranch" where 74 pretty "cowgirls" played horseshoes and rode burros. The gals wore 10-gallon hats, boots, and G-strings.

The Biggest and Best

The gates of the New York World's Fair opened on April 30, 1939. By day's end, 198,791 people had paid to get in (adults: 75 cents, kids under 14: a quarter). Its single-busiest day would be August 26, when admissions totaled 306,408.

Financial planners estimated its turnstiles would turn four times a second, amounting to 60,000,000 revolutions in the first year, for a projected $1 billion in overall business for the city. Built on a reclaimed city dump, the fair covered nearly two square miles of ground and extended a mile and a quarter across at its widest point. It had six main zones: Government, Transportation, Communications, Food, Community Interests, and Amusement.

The centerpiece was "the Perisphere and Trylon." The former was a mammoth globe containing an exhibit called "Democracity." This was a diorama depicting a future idyllic city and countryside. Inside a space as large as Radio City Music Hall, fair-goers were transported on two "magic carpets" (revolving platforms) to gaze in wonder, as the advertising said, "as if from Olympian heights to pierce the fogs of ignorance, habit, and prejudice that envelope everyday thinking, and gaze down on the ideal community that man could build today were he to make full use of his tools, his resources, and his knowledge."

Aerial view of the New York World's Fair.

The enlightening experience in the Perisphere lasted six minutes, after which the observers exited by way of a bridge, the Helicon, connecting the huge globe to the Trylon. It was a three-sided, upward tapering shaft reaching 750 feet in height. Cost to build: $1.7 million. Together, the Trylon and Perisphere became the dominant symbol of the Fair.

They were sold in miniature as paper weights, ash trays, key chain fobs, pins, postcards, hair pins, money clips, and anything else souvenir entrepreneurs could think of for fair-goers to take home. In memory of the sesquicentennial of the swearing-in of the first president of the United States, a colossal image of Washington stood in a semicircular "Washington Square" to dominate a mall between the Tyron and Perisphere and a Lagoon of Nations with flags of members of the League of Nations flapping in breezes wafting off Flushing Bay.

A page of a New York World's Fair guidebook, with the Trylon and Perisphere.

Portending an America that would continue to take to the highways and make the United States the biggest buyer and maker of cars in the world was the second-most popular area, the Transportation Zone. Within it, General Motors presented a picture of a country on wheels, speeding along super-highways without red lights from coast to coast. Its Highways and Horizons "Futurama" was "a world of tomorrow." GM's rival, Ford, offered "The Road of Tomorrow," viewed from spiral ramps. Available to ride in were Ford V-8s and Lincoln Zephyrs.

Surpassing the automotive shows in the public's approval was the Amusement Zone. The Chicago Fair of 1893 introduced the Ferris Wheel. The New York World's Fair of 1939's breathtaking ride was the parachute jump. It gave the brave and hardy the "experience of all the thrills of bailing out, but without any of the usual hazards or discomforts of actually parachuting. Permanently opened chutes (11) with two side-by-side seats were attached to wires. They were lifted to the top of the tower and released to fall (held by the wires). They came to a stop with a bounce.

Timeline

The Parachute Jump ride was so popular that when the World's Fair closed in 1940, it was moved to Coney Island. Its tower is still there, but not operating. It's a rusted derelict and a reminder of a more innocent time.

Another successful entertainment was found daily at the Fountain Lake Amphitheater. It had 10,000 seats for watching a spectacular "Aquacade" of swimmers and water ballets staged by one of New York's legendary showmen, Billy Rose. The star of this "girlie extravaganza," as the show was known by some, was the swimming champion Eleanor Holm. Every night of the Fair at 9:30, fireworks lit up the sky above the Lagoon of Nations. It was followed at 10:30 by pyrotechnics above Fountain Lake that were described as "the nearest approach to chaos that man can contrive" for "sheer entertainment."

Sallying forth each day from an office on the fairgrounds, Mayor La Guardia greeted celebrated visitors and ordinary, startled fair-goers. He accepted for display from England the genuine Magna Carta. When King George VI and Queen Elizabeth came to take in the show, he escorted them in an open car, then told reporters that the royals were "easier to entertain and live with for a day than many other great guests we've had."

At the official opening, 150 years to the day after Washington's inauguration, FDR formally pronounced the fair "open." When La Guardia's turn to talk came, the mayor of New York said, "May I point to one exhibit that I hope all visitors will note, and that is the city of New York itself."

By any measure, the New York World's Fair of 1939 and 1940 was the biggest and best ever presented. When it closed its two-year run on October 27, 1940, 44,990,000 Americans and other visitors had been given a taste of "The World of Tomorrow." Unfortunately, not everything that was promised became reality.

Amusement Parks

The American "amusement park" traced its beginnings to the 1893 Chicago World's Fair, where the world was introduced to an area of fun and games called "the Midway." The "hit" of the fair was the Ferris Wheel. In 1919 there were 1,500 such parks. But at the time of the stock market crash in 1929, the number had declined to only 400. A decade later, there were less than 300.

Timeline —————

Buildings from the New York World's Fair of 1939 became the first home of the United Nations.

Almost all big cites had one, or were close to one. People who lived north of New York City had the Rye Playground. Just across the Hudson River, there was Palisades Park; Philadelphians had Woodside Park. Bostonians could drive down the coast a way to Revere. Pittsburgh had Luna Park. Dayton, Ohio, offered Lakeside Park. In Kansas City, Missouri, the resort was Electric Park. In Chicago, it was Riverview Park. San Diego, California, provided thrill-seekers Mission Beach.

Biggest and Best

By all accounts, the greatest of the amusement parks was along a stretch of beach in Brooklyn, New York, named Coney Island. Its ads proclaimed it "the world's largest playground." Made more reachable by an elevated subway line in 1920, it had a six-mile-long beach, a boardwalk, cheap amusements, and what the *WPA Guide to New York* called "a plague of hot dog stands," the most famous of which was Nathan's.

The *WPA Guide* noted, "From the boardwalk the whole beach may be viewed: bathers splash and shout in the turgid waters close to the shore; and the sand, children dig in the sand, young men engage in gymnastics and roughhouse each other, or toss balls over the backs of couples lying amorously entwined."

Each season (May 30 to the second week after Labor Day) brought millions of New Yorkers and people from cities and towns all over the northeast. Tourists to New York City counted a visit to Coney Island as essential as seeing the Statue of Liberty and going to the top of the Empire State Building.

Having been to Coney Island as a child in the early 1940s, I can attest that the builder of Steeplechase Park, George Cornelius Tilyou, was right when he declared, "If Paris is France, then Coney Island between June and September is the world." The *WPA Guide* put it this way in 1939: "From early morning, when the first throngs pour from the Stillwell Avenue subway terminal, humanity flows over Coney seeking relief from the heat of the city. Italians, Jews, Greeks, Poles, Germans, Negroes, Irish, people of every nationality; boys and girls, feeble ancients, mothers with squirming children, fathers with bundles, push and collide as they rush, laughing, scolding, sweating, for a spot on the sand."

If the beach wasn't your cup of tea, you could spend an entire day in the boardwalk's two vast entertainment areas, Luna Park and the Steeplechase (with 31 rides). You could wander from a "Chamber of Horrors," to the "fun house," a spinning circular floor that sent you flying off it, a huge revolving barrel that dared you to stay on your feet, huge slides that you took by sitting on a slick carpet (only the most daring went zooming down it headfirst), and a ride with wooden horses on undulating tracks of an outdoor "steeple-chase" race track.

Hanging On for Dear Life

And there were the roller coasters: the Thunderbolt, built in 1925, the Tornado in 1926, and the Cyclone. Opened in June 1927 at a cost of $146,000 and built by the National Bridge Company, it climbed 86 feet, then dropped the riders at an 53-degree angle on its way to a system of dips, rises, and sharp turns that Charles Lindbergh described as a thrill "greater than flying an airplane at top speed." (The Cyclone is still there, as popular as ever, and even in the age of higher and faster roller coasters, it is still regarded by coaster experts as the wickedest of all.)

The Resort of the Monopoly Board

While millions of Americans in the years of the Great Depression didn't have the money to go to the second-greatest amusement area on the east coast, they knew a great deal about Atlantic City, New Jersey, from playing "Monopoly." As noted earlier, the most popular game board, after Checkers and Chess, used Atlantic City real estate as the properties to be bought, sold, mortgaged, or lost to one's opponent. Just as "Boardwalk" was the most costly place on the board, the real Boardwalk of the seaside resort and its accompanying beach and amusements was the source of Atlantic City's wealth and fame.

It was in Atlantic City in 1882 that the first ocean amusement pier was built. "Ocean Pier" proved so successful that in 1906 it was joined by the "Million Dollar Pier," and, in 1925, the most famous and successful of all, the "Steel Pier." Extending far out over the ocean, it had six theaters that offered the most famous entertainers of the 1930s and all the big swing bands. It also staged some spectacular stunts that included Alvin "Shipwreck" Kelley setting a world record by sitting atop a flag pole for 49 days in 1930 (the record stood until 1964).

Queen of Resorts

A popular attraction was the "diving horse." It plunged 50 feet from a tower into a salt-water tank. People who wanted to know what it was like to be deeply submerged in the ocean paid to go down in a diving bell. There was also a "Dip of Death" taken by a dare-devil cyclist who rode around the inside of a 360-degree track, then flew off into the air and into the sea. The Steeplechase Pier (built by George Tilyou of Coney Island fame) provided thrills in the form of the Sugar Bowl Slide, the Mexican Hat Bowl, and the Flying Chairs that swung riders out over the ocean.

People who went to Atlantic City invariably went home with boxes of saltwater taffy and fond memories of being pushed along the Boardwalk in "rolling chairs." They held two people. (To assure that the rides were smooth, the planks of the Boardwalk were laid lengthwise.) While one side of the Boardwalk offered views of the beach and the Atlantic Ocean, the other, as in Coney Island, was lined with stores offering food, beverages, souvenirs, and photo shops where a person could get a picture of himself with his head stuck through a hole above a painted figure in an old-fashioned bathing suit.

If one wanted people at home to know about his visit to the "Queen of Resorts," he had a choice of "Atlantic City" postcards to send. Indeed, the city claimed to have been the birthplace of the picture postcard.

There She Is

Americans who lived too far away from Atlantic City in the 1930s knew all about it, not only through post cards they might have gotten from a friend, but also from two annual events that made their way onto the nation's movie screens in newsreels. One was the Easter Parade on the Boardwalk. The other was the selection of "Miss America." The first of these "beauty pageants" had been held in 1921, with seven contestants, on the Garden Pier. (The winner was Margaret Gorman of Washington, D.C.)

Staged by the Atlantic City Chamber of Commerce the week after Labor Day in hopes of extending the season by a week, the pageant was held until 1927, when it lost its financial backing. After a try at a comeback in 1933, it was revived for good in 1935.

For the record, here's who claimed the title "Miss America" in the 1930s:

- 1933: Marion Bergeron, Connecticut
- 1935: Henrietta Leaver, Pittsburgh
- 1936: Rose Coyle, Philadelphia
- 1937: Betty Cooper, Bertrand Island, New Jersey
- 1938: Marilyn Meseke, Ohio
- 1939: Patricia Donnelly, Michigan

It wasn't until 1938 that rules required that Miss America be unmarried (and not divorced), and be between the ages of 18 and 28. The crowning anthem, "There She Is, Miss America," wasn't sung until 1954, by which time the pageant had become an extravagant TV show.

A Park for the Sweet-Toothed

While seaside playlands attracted millions of people seeking a respite from the summer heat of cities, a different environment was available in the cool, rolling hills of eastern Pennsylvania in a town that existed only for the making of chocolate candy. It was a gem of an amusement park that was created primarily for people who worked for Milton Hershey. Developed as an integral part of the factory town named for its owner, Hershey Park attracted thousands of visitors with rides, a famous carousel, swimming pool, amphitheater, picnic grounds, and a ballroom featuring the top big bands.

What Hershey Park had that no other amusement park could claim was the smell of chocolate being made and an opportunity to tour the factory and go home with free helpings of candy bars that got broken in the manufacturing process.

The Least You Need to Know

- The 1930s was the decade of a form of modern design known as "Art Deco" as automobiles, trains, household utensils, and furniture were designed to look "streamlined."
- There was a rapid growth of airlines and air travel.
- Of four "world's fairs" held in the 1930s, the biggest and best was the New York World's Fair of 1939.
- Millions of Americans sought a break from Depression woes by flocking to amusement parks and riding roller coasters.

Chapter 21

America First

In This Chapter

- ◆ In 1939 Hollywood produces an amazing array of movies that are to become classics
- ◆ FDR makes presidential history by winning a third term
- ◆ Charles A. Lindbergh spearheads the isolationist "America First" movement to keep the United States out of the war in Europe
- ◆ Japan's attack against the United States brings the rapid conversion of industries to wartime footing and the mobilization of men for the armed forces ends unemployment
- ◆ Might there be another Great Depression?

After a nationwide poll of movie fans chose Clark Gable to play Rhett Butler in the movie of Margaret Mitchell's novel *Gone with the Wind*, a search was launched to fill the role of "Scarlett O'Hara." Despite public sentiment in favor of Shirley Temple to be "Dorothy" in *The Wizard of Oz*, MGM gives the part to Judy Garland. Were the movies a metaphor for America in the 1930s?

In the presidential election of 1940, pitting Roosevelt against Wendell Willkie, the dominant issues were a question as to whether FDR deserved an unprecedented third term and a movement led by Charles Lindbergh to "isolate" the United States from the war in Europe. When the Japanese sneak attack on Pearl Harbor plunged the country into the Second World War, "mobilization" of industries and men brought the Great Depression screeching to an end. Could it happen again?

Who's Scarlett?

In 1937, a book about the Civil War, a first novel by a lady in Atlanta named Margaret Mitchell, swept the nation the way General William Tecumseh Sherman's Union soldiers had stormed through the South in 1865. Everyone who read *Gone with the Wind*, especially women, saw no one but Clark Gable playing the dashing rogue Rhett Butler in the inevitable movie. Launching one of the smartest publicity gimmicks in history, the film's producer, David O. Selznick, announced a worldwide search for a woman to play the novel's heroine, Scarlett O'Hara.

Believe It or Not

Almost every established star, from Bette Davis to Jane Wyman, vied for the part. To everyone's surprise, it went to an English actress, Vivien Leigh.

Famous Faces

An established star in England, Vivien Leigh had made nine films before *Gone with the Wind*, including the following:

◆ *Things Are Looking Up*, 1934
◆ *Look Up and Laugh*, 1935
◆ *Fire Over England*, 1937
◆ *A Yank at Oxford*, made in the United States and United Kingdom, 1937
◆ *St. Martins Lane*, 1938

According to the story that went around, Selznick made the choice when Leigh was introduced to him with the words, "Here's your Scarlett." They were spoken by his father-in-law, Louis B. Mayer, head of MGM, during filming of the scene depicting the burning of Atlanta. Whether the tale was true or not didn't matter. It helped to hype the film. So did the fact that he used 15 screenwriters and three top directors. *Gone with the Wind* became one of Hollywood's most profitable pictures. Many film critics and historians still rank it as the best movie ever made.

The Envelope, Please

On the night Hollywood handed out the Academy Awards for 1939, Selznick won for Best Picture, Victor Fleming for direction, Sidney Howard for screenplay, Lyle Wheeler for art direction, Vivien Leigh for best actress, and Hattie McDaniel for supporting actress. For her role as "Mammy," McDaniel was the first black actor to be so honored. She was also the first black person to be nominated in any category and the first black ever invited to an Academy Awards ceremony.

Special Oscars were also presented to William Cameron Menzies for "colorful" art direction and to the Technicolor Company for the most spectacular film yet made in that process. Best Actor went not to Gable, but to Robert Donat for the title role in *Goodbye, Mr. Chips*.

In a year that was regarded as the pinnacle of quality movies made in Hollywood, *Gone with the Wind* was up against *Mr. Chips*, *Dark Victory* (brave Bette Davis goes blind), *Ninotchka*, *Love Affair*, *Of Mice and Men*, *Wuthering Heights*, and director John Ford's *Stagecoach*, which was John Wayne's breakout film. Although Thomas Mitchell had been in *Gone with the Wind* as "Mr. O'Hara," he earned a Supporting Actor Academy Award for his role as the boozy doctor in *Stagecoach*.

The other major 1939 film, also directed by Victor Fleming, was MGM's extravagant musical version of a classic children's book by L. Frank Baum.

Where's Dorothy?

At long last in this book, I am able to provide my eyewitness certification of a major Great Depression event. I was five years old in 1939 when the Jeffers family went to the Colonial Theater in my hometown to see *The Wizard of Oz*. To this very day, I am terrified of witches and tornadoes, and my favorite song is "Over the Rainbow."

I'm also bowled over every time I see the movie by the amazing acting job delivered by Dorothy's "little dog" Toto. The next time you watch it, pay attention to him as he leaps from Miss Gulch's basket; follows the yellow brick road; escapes from the Wicked Witch's castle; and leads Tin Man, Strawman, and the Cowardly Lion to the rescue. You'll see what I mean. That dog should also have gotten an Oscar.

Although most Americans at that time wanted, and expected, the part of Dorothy Gale to go to Shirley Temple, it went, as you well know, to Judy Garland. Having read about the nation's odd fascination with midgets in the 1930s, you can see why MGM cast scores of them to populate "Munchkin Land."

So why all this attention in a book about the Great Depression to a couple of movies that were made when it was close to over? I don't believe I'm reading something bizarre into

Gone with the Wind and *The Wizard of Oz* in noting that each is a metaphor for the 1930s as a decade of hope against despair that ended as the films did, with a loss of innocence and the shattering of the established order. Scarlett's former civilization was gone with wind, and so was Dorothy's, blown away in a tornado. Both of these plucky characters ended up affirming a good old American conviction. Whether it's Tara or a Kansas farm, "There's no place like home."

This looks like Dorothy's home in The Wizard of Oz, *but it's a Dust Bowl farm in Boise City, Oklahoma, in a photo taken on April 15, 1935.*

(AP Photo)

It's not too much of a leap to suppose that a lot of Americans in 1939 thought that they saw in the miracle-working Wizard of Oz the president they'd all come to call by his initials.

That SOB in the White House

While Americans were buying tickets to see *Gone with the Wind* and *The Wizard of Oz* in the autumn of 1939, they did so with encouraging words from FDR that their country could avoid getting mixed up in the fighting in Europe. On the night of the day that England and France went to war officially with Nazi Germany (September 3), Roosevelt said in a fireside chat, "I hope the United States will keep out of this war. I believe that it will. And I give you assurance and re-assurance that every effort of your government will be directed toward that end. As long as it remains in my power to prevent, there will be no black-out of peace in the United States."

As he spoke to the nation, another question on the minds of his countrymen was whether he would break with the tradition set by George Washington that a two-term president should not seek a third term. That Americans appeared to agree with this unofficial rule had been proved in 1912 when voters rejected a bid for a third term, though not a consecutive one, by Theodore Roosevelt.

On the "third term" issue, one could have made a good bet either way. He could wager "no" on the basis that FDR would not run again because Congress had let the air out of the New Deal, and that Roosevelt could leave office knowing that his policies had prevented a revolution. Some said that the New Deal had, in fact, saved capitalism.

A reasonable wager could also be made on "Yes, he will run." For him not to do so, said people in this category, was not in FDR's character. According to those with this point of view, Roosevelt was a power-hungry egomaniac incapable of folding his tent and retiring quietly to Hyde Park. For these people—and there were a lot of them—FDR was "that SOB in the White House" who had his heart and mind set on getting the United States into the war.

The Health of Ostriches

As you read earlier, Roosevelt had asked Congress to repeal the Neutrality Act so that the United States could sell arms and other war materiel to Britain and France. The request had caused a storm of opposition to "cash and carry" from the Committee for the Defense of Constitutional Rights and from such influential leaders of the Senate as William Borah, George Nye, Robert M. La Follette, and Hiram Johnson. Also joining the chorus against aid to Britain was Father Coughlin. These "isolationists" claimed that FDR's policy was the first step on a slippery slope to war.

Roosevelt replied in his State of the Union message on January 4, 1940, "There is a vast difference between keeping out of war and pretending that war is none of our business." He added, "I hope we shall have fewer American ostriches in our midst; it is not good for the ultimate health of ostriches to bury their heads in sand."

A Birthday Poem

AS FDR turned 58 on January 30, 1940, members of his staff held a birthday party for him in the White House. His long-time personal secretary, Grace Tully, offered a poem based on the song "My Rosary." It dealt with the question of a third term:

> The hours I spend with thee, dear boss,
> Are like a string of pearls to me.
> I count each hour a gain and not a loss,
> A faithful gal, that's me!
> Each hour I've toiled I've said a prayer,
> I've prayed you'd think my job well done,
> Oh, tell me, must this be the end,

Or what about forty-one?
I do not know which way to turn.
I cannot longer bear this cross,
I'd give my head if I could learn
Who'll be my boss next year,
Who'll be my boss!

My Conscience Will Not Let Me

During the first six months of 1940 the country debated "Will he or won't he?" Some Democrats who thought he wouldn't thought of themselves as his successor. When the Democratic convention met in Chicago on July 15, delegates received a message from FDR in which he said he had no desire to be a candidate. In terminology of a later time in politics, the statement contained a great deal of "wiggle room." Cynical observers in Chicago saw through the words and found FDR telling the convention that what he really wanted was to be asked to run again. In fact, FDR had more than enough votes for the nomination even before the convention met.

After listening to himself being nominated on radio, Roosevelt took a little time "to freshen up," then delivered his acceptance speech from the White House. With the most familiar voice in the country booming from loudspeakers, the conventioneers heard him declare, "Lying awake, as I have on many nights, I have asked myself whether I have the right, as Commander-in-Chief of the Army and Navy, to call men and women to serve their country or to train themselves to serve, and at the same time decide to serve my country in my own personal capacity, if I am called upon to do so by the people of my country. Today, all private plans, all private lives, have been in a sense repealed by an overriding public danger … I have made plans for myself, plans for a private life … but my conscience will not let me turn my back on a call to service."

Barefoot Boy from Wall Street

Before June 28, 1940, not a lot of Americans had heard of a man named Wendell Willkie. But on that day, he'd pulled off a kind of miracle at the Republican National Convention in Philadelphia by beating Thomas E. Dewey and Ohio Senator Robert A. Taft for the GOP presidential nomination.

A big man in a rumpled-looking suit, a gruff voice, and an unruly shock of dark hair, Willkie came across as a simple country boy from Indiana. He was, in fact, a shrewd Wall Street lawyer who'd been president of the giant Commonwealth and Southern public utility company. He'd also been a Democrat, had voted for FDR in 1932, and once flirted with socialism. On that period of his life he'd said, "Any man who is not something of a

Socialist before he is forty has no heart; any man who is still a Socialist after he is forty has no head."

Not all Republicans embraced Willkie. Conservative GOP Senator James Watson wise-cracked, "I don't mind the church converting a whore, but I don't like her to lead the choir the first night." Other disgruntled Republicans called Willkie the "barefoot boy from Wall Street," and the "rich man's Roosevelt."

Old Campaigner and America's First Dog

Plunging into the campaign, Roosevelt exclaimed, "I'm an old campaigner, and I love a good fight." He made an issue of three GOP leaders, House Speaker Joseph Martin; New York senatorial candidate Bruce Barton; and conservative New York congressman Hamilton Fish. With great delight, FDR said in a scornful sing-song chant, "That great historic trio ... Martin, Barton and Fish." Soon, all he had to say was "Martin" to bring his audience to its feet to chime in with "Barton and Fish."

For the first time in American political history, a president's dog took center stage. After Republicans claimed that FDR had realized he'd left his Scottish terrier, Fala, in Alaska, and had sent a Navy destroyer to pick him up, Roosevelt brought the house down when he told a campaign crowd that he (FDR) didn't resent GOP attacks, and that his wife Eleanor didn't really resent such attacks, "But Fala does resent them."

Famous Faces _____

In 1952 Democrats accused GOP vice presidential nominee Richard M. Nixon of having a secret "slush fund" and taking expensive gifts. Going on TV and radio to answer the charge, Nixon said he'd accepted a gift of a spotted cocker spaniel puppy that his two daughters named Checkers. "Well, no matter what they say about him," Nixon said, "we're going to keep him."

Carried on against the backdrop of war in Europe and Japanese aggression in Asia, the campaign was fiercely fought. Willkie often made 15 speeches a day. Roosevelt acted pres-idential. Willkie promised that if he won, no sons of American mothers would go to war. FDR told a Boston and radio audience, "Your boys are not going to be sent into any for-eign wars."

When the last vote was counted, FDR had 27,444,160. Willkie had 22,305,198. The rest had gone to socialist Norman Thomas, Earl Browder on the communist line, Roger Babson of the Prohibition Party (they never give up), and Socialist Labor's John W. Aiken. Roosevelt carried 38 states, with 449 electoral votes; Willkie 10 states, with 83 electoral votes.

The Four Freedoms

Speaking to Congress on January 6, 1941, Roosevelt delivered a State of the Union address containing a stirring explanation of American idealism that remains the foundation of U.S. foreign policy to this day. FDR said:

> In the future days, which we seek to make secure, we look forward to a world founded upon four essential human freedoms. The first is freedom of speech and expression, everywhere in the world. The second is freedom of every person to worship God in his own way, everywhere in the world. The third is freedom from want, which, translated into world terms, means economic understanding which will secure to every nation a healthy peacetime life for its inhabitants, everywhere in the world. The fourth is freedom from fear, which, translated into world terms, means a worldwide reduction of armaments to such a point and in such a thorough fashion that no nation will be in a position to commit an act of physical aggression against any neighbor, anywhere in the world.

Arsenal of Democracy

Eight days before he gave the Four Freedoms speech, Roosevelt had a fireside chat (December 29, 1940) in which he defined the role of the United States as he saw it at that moment. "We must be," he said, "the arsenal of democracy."

Among the steps he took toward that goal was to release to Britain in May and June of 1940 surplus and outdated U.S. stocks of arms, munitions, and airplanes. More than $43 million worth were sent in June alone.

This aid was known as "Lend-Lease." It was a clever disguise by which the United States would supply the stuff of war to the British by either sale, transfer, exchange, or lease. It raised the "installment plan" to the level of foreign policy, but in this case, no one expected money "down" or repayment of the rest over a specified period.

Facts and Figures

The initial appropriation authorized by Congress for Lend-Lease was $7 billion. During the course of the war, the amount came to more than $50 billion. Churchill called Lend-Lease the most unselfish act by one nation to help another in the history of the world. On November 6, 1941, the United States granted $1 billion in Lend-Lease credit to the Soviet Union.

A Great Hour to Live

In August, under the cover of taking some time off to go fishing, FDR met secretly with Britain's Prime Minister Churchill on the U.S. Navy cruiser *Augusta* off the coast of Newfoundland. "At last," he said, "we have gotten together." They agreed on a blueprint for the defeat of the dictatorships and a plan for post-war peace called the "Atlantic Charter."

The meeting ended with FDR, Churchill, their aides and members of the crews of the Anglo-American ships singing the hymns "To Those in Peril on the Sea" and "Onward Christian Soldiers." Churchill later recalled, "Every word seemed to stir the heart. It was a great hour to live. Nearly half those who sang were soon to die."

A result of the alliance was secret talks between the British and American military staffs in January 1941. It was agreed that the strategy, once the United States got into the war, would be to defeat the Germans first, then take on Japan.

This Dabbling in Europe's Wars

As everyone knows, the 1960s went into the history books as a decade of dissent against the war in Vietnam and that much of the opposition sprouted first on campuses. Back then it seemed to be a dramatically historic thing for college kids to do. It was filled with drama, and it certainly made history, but it wasn't the first time that collegians organized to resist a government war policy.

In July 1940 a student and football star at the University of Michigan, and future U.S. president, by the name of Gerald R. Ford was one of a group of college kids who formed a committee called "America First." Seed money came from Chicago textile manufacturer William H. Regenery. The adult chairman was General Robert E. Wood. Another grown-up who lent support and a famous name was Alice Roosevelt Longworth, daughter of Teddy Roosevelt and wife of a late, legendary Speaker of the U.S. House, Nicholas Longworth.

But the personality who emerged as the chief spokesman for the organization was America's greatest, and most sympathetic, hero, Charles A. Lindbergh.

The Saga of Lucky Lindy

As you've read, Lindbergh had become a tragic figure with the kidnapping and murder of his two-year-old son in 1932. To get away from relentless publicity, he took his family to live in England. In 1936, at the request of the U.S. government, he'd accepted an invitation from the head of the Nazi air force, Hermann Goering, to inspect Germany's military aviation program.

America First anti-war poster saying, "There is still time to keep out."

He also went to the 1936 Olympics as Goering's guest. Impressed with Germany's industry and orderly society under Hitler, he even contemplated living there. As war loomed, he returned to the United States, but not before Goering presented him with the Nazi Service Cross of the German Eagle for his contributions to aviation.

Poster Boy for Isolationism

Lindbergh also brought home with him a belief that the United States must not be drawn into a war to save England nor come to the aid of the primary victims of Nazi persecution, the Jews. Compared to the "vitality" and "efficiency" of Germany, he said, England and the other democracies offered only "impotence" and "degeneracy."

Unwilling to keep these views to himself, he praised the cause of "America First" in headline-making speeches in Des Moines, Iowa, Washington, D.C., and in New York's Madison Square Garden. His main theme was that because of U.S. military unpreparedness, the Germans had "armies stronger than our own."

Aviator Colonel Charles A. Lindbergh speaks before major radio network microphones in Washington, D.C., on September 15, 1939. He is urging Americans to keep out of the war in Europe.

(AP Photo)

Claiming the United States was weak and that "we have divided our own people by this dabbling in Europe's wars," he said that when history was written, "the responsibility for the downfall of the democracies of Europe will rest squarely on the shoulders of the interventionists who led their nations into war uninformed and unprepared." While the nation should have been "concentrating on American defense," he said, "we have been forced to argue over foreign quarrels."

Calling on Americans to "turn our eyes and our faith back to our own country before it is too late," he continued, "That is why the America First Committee has been formed—to give voice to the people who have no newspaper, or newsreel, or radio station at their command; to the people who must do the paying, and the dying, if this country enters the war."

The Fat Lady Sings

Since March of 1931, Americans had been tuning in their radios to the programs starring a fat lady with an amazing vocal talent. They knew that when Kate Smith came on the air with her theme song, "When the Moon Comes Over the Mountain," they were in for a half-hour of not just great singing, but entertainment from guest stars. They included Bud Abbott and Lou Costello, corny jokes by Henny Youngman, and comedy skits with Ezra Stone playing a squeaky-voiced teenager named "Henry Aldrich." (The sketches became so popular that Stone got his own hit show, *The Aldrich Family*.)

A song introduced by Kate Smith was guaranteed to climb high on the Hit Parade, and often to Number One. She was so well known in 1939 that FDR invited her to come to the White House to sing "A Nightingale Sang in Berkeley Square" for the King and Queen of England before they went up to New York for the World's Fair and then to Hyde Park for hotdogs.

In 1938, the nation's top songwriter, Irving Berlin, asked Kate Smith to introduce a new song on her Armistice Day radio show (November 11). It began with a verse about "storm clouds" gathering "far across the sea." It asked Americans to "swear allegiance to a land that's free," and "lift our voices in a solemn prayer."

From that moment on, "God Bless America" became, in effect, our second national anthem. Kate Smith's is still the definitive rendition.

 Timeline

The original version of "God Bless America" was written during the summer of 1918 at Camp Upton, Yaphank, Long Island, for a soldier show called "Yip, Yip, Yaphank." Berlin decided that the solemn tone of the tune was out of keeping with the more comedic elements of the show, so it was dropped. A Jewish immigrant who was aware of what was happening in Nazi Germany, Berlin, revised it in 1938.

The End of Isolationism

On May 27, 1941, President Roosevelt signed a document stating that "an unlimited national emergency confronts this country." It required "its military, naval, air, and civilian defenses be put on the basis of readiness to repel any and all acts or threats of aggression toward any part of the Western hemisphere."

The attack came not on the American mainland, but against the U.S. Pacific Fleet and Army and Air Force installations in the Hawaiian Islands on December 7, 1941. On the day that FDR branded "a date that will live in infamy," a place called Pearl Harbor was added to the roster of "Remember" slogans that rallied Americans to recall and avenge two other outrages, "the Alamo" and "the *Maine*."

Japan's "dastardly" attack, to quote FDR, followed by declaration of war against the Axis Powers in Europe, served to accelerate the rate of growth of already-mobilizing industries. By mid-1941, more than two million jobs had been created, with thousands more being opened every day. With paychecks came a surge in buying. Retail goods were moving by 16 percent more than in 1939. Auto sales jumped 40 percent. Dollars were flowing into cash registers at a clip that hadn't been seen since the Roaring Twenties. The longest and cruelest Depression in American history was over.

> **Timeline**
>
> The unlimited national emergency proclaimed by FDR in 1941 was not over until President Truman ended it on April 28, 1952.

Could It Happen Again?

There are never certainties in life, but a repeat is unlikely. Due in great measure to the correction of faults in the structure of the national economy, the nation now has safeguards to head off a calamity of the extent of the 1929 crash. Today's stock markets, and the nation's fiscal and monetary systems, are more strictly run, and monitored.

The U.S. economy has shifted from one in which farms were mostly family businesses. We've gone from the heavy industries of labor-intensive pre-Depression America to the era of automation, to a computer-based "information age," and the "service economy." Our people are better educated.

Should someone lose a job, there are "safety nets" that did not exist when the bottom fell out of everything and everywhere in the 1930s. Unemployment insurance, Social Security, Medicare, "welfare" and "work fare," children's services, and many other institutions ensure that no American has to go hungry, homeless, with no help, and, worst of all, without hope.

How to sum up the years of the Great Depression? Try the words of the author who put his mark on it, and captured it in *The Grapes of Wrath*, published in 1940. For *Esquire* in 1960, John Steinbeck wrote, "Looking back, the decade seems to have been as carefully designed as a play. It had a beginning, middle and end."

In that great drama, the United States was changed, lives were remolded, and the government was forced into functions, duties, and responsibilities that it never had before, and now could never turn its back on.

The Least You Need to Know

◆ In 1940 President Franklin D. Roosevelt broke the "eight-year limit" precedent set by George Washington by winning a third term in a landslide.

◆ FDR's State of the Union message to Congress in 1942 set out the goal of securing the four freedoms: of speech, of religion, from want, and from the fear of war.

◆ Charles A. Lindbergh became a spokesman for isolationism that placed "America first."

◆ Following the Japanese attack at Pearl Harbor on December 7, 1941, America's entry into World War II brought an end to the worst and longest economic depression in American history.

Great Depression Chronology

The Roaring Twenties

1920

Prohibition begins.

The 19th Amendment grants women the right to vote.

Widespread disobedience to Prohibition leads to the rise of the "speakeasy" and bootlegging.

The age of the gangster is born.

Radio stations begin broadcasting music into homes.

Harding elected president; Coolidge, vice president. They defeat the Democratic ticket of James M. Cox and Franklin D. Roosevelt.

F. Scott Fitzgerald publishes *This Side of Paradise*.

Sinclair Lewis publishes *Main Street*.

1921

Glutted inventories contribute to a recession.

Veterans Bureau established to provide aid to men who served in the "Great War."

1923

Harding dies, Coolidge becomes president; he declares, "The business of America is business."

Congress approves Soldiers' Bonus Act.

1924

Harding administration corruption revealed. Scandal is known as "Teapot Dome."

Coolidge elected president.

The nation enjoys "Coolidge Prosperity."

1927

Charles A. Lindbergh flies solo across the Atlantic, becomes national hero.

Coolidge declines to run for re-election.

1928

Herbert Hoover defeats Democrat Alfred E. Smith.

Amelia Earhart is first woman to fly the Atlantic solo.

1929

Agricultural Market Act provides price supports for farmers.

Real estate boom in California and Florida.

Maldistribution of wealth brings credit-buying, known as "the installment plan."

Rampant speculation and "buying on margin" sends the stock market to new heights.

On October 29, stock market crashes, triggering the Panic of 1929.

The Great Depression begins.

The Hoover Years

1930

Hoover leaves Depression relief measures to the states and local authorities.

Increased U.S. tariffs trigger drop in world trade.

1931

Veterans demand a speed-up in payment of bonuses.

Empire State Building opens in New York City; because of the Depression, offices are mostly unoccupied.

Chicago gangster Al Capone convicted of tax evasion.

1932

Nazis come to power in Germany.

Federal Reconstruction Finance Corporation provides emergency assistance to financial institutions.

Federal Home Loan Bank established to reduce bank foreclosures on homes.

Charles Lindbergh's baby is kidnapped and murdered.

Army breaks up veterans' "Bonus March" in Washington.

Franklin D. Roosevelt defeats Hoover in a landslide.

The New Deal

1933

In face of a run on banks, FDR declares a national "bank holiday"; most re-open in a few days.

In "the first 100 days" of FDR and his "Brain Trust Advisors," Congress passes:

- ◆ Civilian Conservation Corps (CCC)
- ◆ Federal Emergency Relief Act (FERA)
- ◆ Agricultural Adjustment Act (AAA)
- ◆ Tennessee Valley Authority (TVA)
- ◆ Federal Securities Act
- ◆ National Employment System Act
- ◆ Home Owners Refinancing Act
- ◆ Farm Credit Act
- ◆ National Recovery Act (NRA), establishing the Public Works Administration (PWA)

Civil Works Administration (CWA) created to provide emergency unemployment relief.

Fiorello La Guardia elected mayor of New York.

Prohibition amendment repealed.

Chicago World's Fair.

1934

U.S. government abandons the Gold Standard.

Works Progress Administration (WPA) formed.

Securities and Exchange Commission (SEC) created.

Communications Act establishes Federal Communications Commission (FCC) to regulate broadcasting.

National Labor Relations Board created.

National Housing Act creates Federal Housing Authority.

Democrats gain seats in the House and Senate.

John Dillinger killed by FBI agents in Chicago.

Art Deco and streamlining dominate in the designs of buildings, cars, trains, planes, and household goods.

Jean Harlow and Clark Gable are the top movie stars.

The Second New Deal

1935

FDR calls for measures to secure the livelihood of Americans, old-age insurance, and housing improvements.

Beginning of Federal Theater Project, Federal Writers' Project, Federal Music Project, and other programs to assist and employ people in the arts.

Father Coughlin, the Townsend old-age assistance plan, Huey Long's "Every Man a King Movement," the Silver Shirts, and other groups gain millions of followers.

The Communist Party sees an opportunity to foment a "Red" revolution in the United States.

Poor land management and drought in the Midwest result in creation of the "Dust Bowl" and mass migration of farmers to California.

Soil Conservation Act creates the Soil Conservation Service.

Rural Electrification Administration formed to bring electricity to isolated rural areas.

FDR issues an executive order to create the National Youth Administration (NYA) to provide work and schooling for persons between 16 and 25.

The Liberty League forms to oppose the New Deal.

U.S. Senator Huey "Kingfish" Long assassinated.

Congress passes the Social Security Act.

Labor leader John L. Lewis spearheads the formation of the Congress of Industrial Organizations (CIO).

Automakers are hit with "sit-down strikes."

Humorist Will Rogers and aviation pioneer Wiley Post die in plane crash in Alaska.

1936

U.S. Supreme Court delivers a blow to the New Deal by striking down the AAA as unconstitutional.

Americans of the Abraham Lincoln Brigade fight against fascists in the Spanish Civil War.

Margaret Mitchell's *Gone with the Wind* becomes a runaway best-seller.

New York District Attorney Thomas E. Dewey topples Charles "Lucky" Luciano.

Lindbergh flees the United States for privacy and becomes the darling of the Nazis in Germany.

Britain's King Edward VIII abdicates for "the woman I love," American divorcée Wallis Warfield Simpson.

FDR re-elected; Republican opponent Alfred M. Landon carries only Maine and Vermont.

FDR's Second Term

1937

Supreme Court invalidates the NRA; FDR calls the Court "nine old men" and demands that Congress expand the Court from 9 to 15 justices. The plan to "pack the Court" fails.

National Housing Act creates U.S. Housing Authority to build low-rent housing projects; the first opens in New York City.

The nation's businesses suffer a sharp reversal, called the "Roosevelt Recession."

Nazi dirigible Hindenburg explodes while landing at Lakehurst, New Jersey, ending dream of "lighter than air" travel.

Amelia Earhart vanishes in the Pacific on a round-the-world flight.

1938

FDR calls for measures to "keep ourselves adequately strong in self-defense."

Congress authorizes Rep. Martin Dies to form a House committee to investigate "Un-American Activities;" its chairman, J. Parnell Thomas, targets communists and "Red" influence in New Deal programs and agencies.

National minimum wage established by law.

Republicans make big gains in seats in the House and Senate.

England and France pursue a policy of appeasement in dealing with Nazi Germany; at the Munich Conference, Hitler is allowed to take a portion of Czechoslovakia. Federal Theater Project provides stages for leftist productions.

Orson Welles's *The War of the Worlds* radio production fools thousands of Americans into believing Earth has been invaded by Martians.

1939

For the first time, FDR's annual message to Congress asks for no new government assistance programs.

Opponents of a proposed Administrative Reorganization Act accuse FDR of seeking dictatorial powers. On his own, he forms the Executive Office of the White House.

New York World's Fair; San Francisco "World's Fair of the West."

Congress slashes federal-aid funding, forcing an end to the Federal Theater Project and eliminating jobs in the WPA.

The New Deal is pronounced dead.

Germany invades Poland; Britain and France declare war.

In a year of destined-to-be-classics movies, including *The Wizard of Oz*, David O. Selznick's *Gone with the Wind* sweeps the Academy Awards.

John Steinbeck publishes *The Grapes of Wrath*.

World War II Ends the Great Depression

1940

Roosevelt requests billions of dollars for defense and war aid to Britain.

First peacetime draft begins.

Republicans nominate Wall Street lawyer Wendell Willkie for president.

Promising to keep the United States out of the war, FDR wins an unprecedented third term.

1941

Roosevelt's annual message to Congress enunciates the "Four Freedoms."

FDR and Britain's Prime Minister Winston Churchill meet secretly to forge an Anglo-American alliance to beat the dictatorships and secure a lasting peace.

Congress approves "Lend-Lease" to provide military aid to Britain and France.

Germany invades Russia; United States grants USSR aid.

Charles A. Lindbergh opposes U.S. intervention in the war in Europe and is major voice for "America First."

FDR declares an unlimited national emergency.

As American industries convert to wartime production, millions of jobs are created.

Japan's sneak attack on U.S. bases in Hawaii plunges the country into the Second World War.

The Great Depression ends.

Roosevelt's Fireside Chats in the 1930s

1933

Sunday, March 12	On the bank crisis
Sunday, May 7	Outlining the New Deal program
Monday, October 22	On the currency situation

1934

Thursday, June 28	Review of achievements of 73rd Congress
Sunday, September 30	On moving forward to greater freedom and greater security

1935

Sunday, April 28	On the Works Relief Program

1936

Sunday, September 6	On drought conditions

1937

Tuesday, March 9	On reorganizing the judiciary
Tuesday, October 12	Legislative recommendations to the special session of Congress
Sunday, November 14	On unemployment census

1938

Thursday, April 14	On economic conditions

1939

Friday, June 24	On party primaries

Great Depression Glossary

Abraham Lincoln Brigade   American volunteers who fought in the Spanish Civil War (1936–1939).

America First   A movement opposed to U.S. intervention in the Second World War whose main spokesman was Charles Lindbergh.

Art Deco   Ultra-modern style of design introduced at the Paris design exposition in 1925.

bank holiday   The closing of banks by the federal government in March 1933 to prevent panicky people from withdrawing funds. It lasted from one to eight days.

bear market   When stock prices fall; a period of selling.

bearish   A stock owner who's in a mood to sell, usually out of lack of optimism about the state of the economy.

B.E.F.   Bonus Expeditionary Force. Veterans of World War I who marched to Washington, D.C., in 1932 to demand accelerated payment of a government bonus. Also known as the Bonus Army.

Blue Eagle   Symbol of the National Recovery Administration (NRA).

boondoggle   A job (usually government) that is seen as a waste of money and pointless. The original meaning of boondoggle was a useless leather strap that was worn decoratively.

bootlegging   The selling of illegal liquor.

Brain Trust   President Roosevelt's unofficial advisors at the start of the New Deal. Also the Brains (plural) Trust.

bull market   Stock prices rise.

bullish   Being optimistic about the economy.

Bund   American Nazis.

CCC   Civilian Conservation Corps. A New Deal youth program for reforestation and other conservation projects.

consumer confidence   When people are optimistic about economic conditions. Without it, they don't buy things and the times turn bad.

Coolidge Prosperity   A period of economic boom during Calvin Coolidge's administration (1923–1928).

Copperhead   FDR's term for Democrats in government who opposed the New Deal. He tried to purge them from the Democratic Party but failed.

cost of living   The price of maintaining a standard of living in terms of the cost of good and services.

deficit spending   The government knowingly spends money that it doesn't have.

disposable income   What's left over from one's income after taxes and the basic necessities.

Dow Jones Industrial Average   A measure of stock market worth determined by averaging the prices of specified companies; in the 1930s they were heavy industries, such as steel.

dry   A person in favor of Prohibition.

Dust Bowl   Area of prolonged drought and wind storms in prairie states.

economic growth   The increase in the gross national product.

fireside chats   Informal addresses to the nation by way of radio by President Roosevelt. Between 1933 and 1945 he made 30.

first 100 days   The period of rapid legislative action in which numerous New Deal programs were created. Also known as "the 100 days."

flappers   Youth of the 1920s, especially women, who wore opened galoshes that flapped when they walked and danced.

flivver   The Model T Ford. Henry Ford said people could have it any color, as long as it was black. Sold cheaply, the flivver put the average American on wheels.

Fordissmus   Name given to Henry Ford's system of mass production on an assembly line.

Forgotten Man   Unemployed veteran of World War I.

gold standard   Basing the value of currency on the price of gold. The United States went off the gold standard in 1933.

gross national product   The total value of the nation's goods and services. Today it's GDP (gross domestic product).

Hooverville   A shantytown built by homeless people in the early 1930s; named after President Hoover, whom people blamed for the Depression.

husbandry   Management of domestic resources, such as farming.

installment plan   Buying on credit with a portion of the cost of the item "put down" and the balance paid over time; it was introduced in the 1920s.

interregnum   The period between a new president's election and his inauguration. Prior to 1936, it was four months. Today, it's about two and a half months.

jawboning   A political and propaganda technique intended to gain support for a policy or program.

John Barleycorn   Synonym for whiskey.

Keynesianism   A policy of federal government deficit spending, pump priming, public works, direct relief payments, and a planned economy to bring about recovery and to institute continuing government welfare programs. Named after British economist John Maynard Keynes.

Kingfish   Nickname adopted by Huey Long, taken from the name of a character on the radio show *Amos 'n' Andy*.

maldistribution of wealth   The rich are rich, the poor are poor, and never the twain shall meet; a major cause of the 1929 Crash and the Great Depression.

Middletown   Fictitious name for Muncie, Indiana, in a sociological study conducted in the 1920s by Robert S. and Helen Merrel Lynd of changing attitudes, morals, and social status.

muckraker   A journalist who stirs up trouble for governments.

New Deal   Policies and programs of President Roosevelt's first two terms.

New Woman   The socially and morally liberated woman of the 1920s.

nine old men   Roosevelt's term for the elderly justices of the U.S. Supreme Court who invalidated parts of the New Deal.

normalcy   A return to peace and prosperity after World War I, as promised by Republican presidential candidate Warren G. Harding in 1920.

NRA   National Recovery Administration. The foundation of the New Deal, it was meant to enlist private enterprise in efforts to attain economic recovery; later declared unconstitutional.

Okies   A term for Dust Bowl migrants from Oklahoma that came to mean anyone left homeless who took to the roads looking for jobs, particularly in California.

on margin   Buying stocks on credit, with the stocks used as collateral.

paper loss   When wealth in the form of financial instruments such as stocks declines, but the stocks are held in the hope that their value will recover.

planned economy   Control and regulation of all aspects of the economy by a strong federal government. Keynesianism.

Prohibition   The banning of the sale and use of alcoholic beverages by the 18th Amendment to the U.S. Constitution; the years between 1920 and 1933.

pump priming   Use of government funds to stimulate an economic recovery from a recession or depression.

radio priest   Father Charles E. Loughlin. Roman Catholic priest who garnered millions of followers by radio for his right-wing National Union for Social Justice.

recession   Slowing down of the economy, resulting in job loss. Whether the country is in a recession is determined by the number of calendar quarters in which gross national product had been negative or very small. Also called "contraction."

recovery   Pulling out of a recession or depression.

redistribution of wealth   Taxing wealth and passing it on to the nonwealthy through government programs.

repeal   The ending of Prohibition (1933).

Roaring Twenties   Synonym for the 1920s, also known as the Jazz Age and the Flapper Era.

Share the Wealth   Program of redistribution of wealth advocated by Huey Long.

Silver Shirts   Right-wing organization ("Protestant Militia of America") identifiable by their silver shirts and hatred of Jews, Roman Catholics, and democracy.

sit-down strike   A strike by workers who remain at the places where they work, rather than form picket lines.

Social Security   Federal system of payments to retired people, disabled, and others. Enacted in 1935.

soup kitchen   A place that dispenses free food to the needy.

speculation   Buying for a quick profit on the stock market and in real estate. A cause of the Great Depression.

sticky prices, sticky wages   A point at which prices and wages remain at a certain level, resulting in recession.

streamlining   Design of machinery, cars, trains, planes, ships, furniture, and household appliances in which form followed function.

stock   Shares of ownership in a company.

Swing   An outgrowth of jazz popularized by dance orchestras.

Teapot Dome   A scandal of the Harding presidency involving the illegal leasing of U.S. oil reserves.

Technocracy   A government run by scientists and other experts on technical matters. It was the idea of a New York City eccentric named Howard Scott.

Temperance Movement   People against drinking liquor.

Townsend Plan   Proposed by California Dr. Francis Townsend, it was a precursor of Social Security.

Wets   People who opposed Prohibition and sought its repeal.

WPA   Works Progress Administration. A New Deal program to put people to work on government construction jobs.

Yellow Dog Contract   An employee agrees (or is forced by his employer) not to join a union. Outlawed in 1932.

Appendix D

Further Reading

Allen, Frederick Lewis. *Only Yesterday: An Informal History of the 1920s*. New York: Harper & Row, 1931.

———. *Since Yesterday: The Nineteen-Thirties in America, September 3, 1929–September 3, 1939*. New York: Harper & Row, 1940.

Badger, Anthony J. *The New Deal: The Depression Years, 1933–1940*. New York: Hill & Wang, 1989.

Barnouw, Eric. *A History of Broadcasting in the United States. Vol. 1: A Tower in Babel, to 1933*. New York: Oxford University Press, 1966.

Bergman, Andrew. *We're in the Money: Depression America and Its Films*. New York: New York University Press, 1971.

Bernstein, Irving. *A Caring Society: The New Deal, the Worker, and the Great Depression*. Boston: Houghton Mifflin, 1960.

Bird, Caroline. *The Invisible Scar*. New York: David McKay, 1966.

Brinkley, Alan. *Voices of Protest: Huey Long, Father Coughlin, and the Great Depression*. New York: Alfred A. Knopf, 1982.

Carter, John F. *The New Dealers*. New York: Literary Guild, 1939.

Case, Brian, and Stan Britt. *The Illustrated Encyclopedia of Jazz*. New York: Harmony Books, 1978.

Chandler, Lester V. *America's Greatest Depression, 1929–1941*. New York: Harper & Row. 1970.

Colmer, Michael. *Pinball: An Illustrated History*. New York: New American Library, 1976.

Condon, Don, ed. *The Thirties: A Time to Remember*. New York: Simon & Schuster, 1962.

Conklin, Paul K. *The New Deal*. New York: Crowell, 1967.

Consumer Guide. *Cars of the '30s*. New York: Beekman House, 1980.

Cowley, Malcolm. *The Dream of the Golden Mountain: Remembering the 1930s*. New York: Viking, 1980.

Dallek, Robert. *Franklin D. Roosevelt and American Foreign Policy, 1932–1945*. New York: Oxford University Press, 1979.

Daniel, Cletus E. *Bitter Harvest: A History of California Farm Workers, 1870–1941*. Berkeley: University of California Press, 1981.

Daniels, Jonathan. *The Time Between the Wars: Armistice to Pearl Harbor*. Garden City, NY: Doubleday & Co., 1966.

Dooley, Roger. *From Scarface to Scarlett: American Films in the 1930s*. New York: Harcourt Brace Jovanovich, 1979.

Dubofsky, Melvin, and Stephen Burnwood, eds. *Women and Minorities During the Great Depression*. New York: Garland, 1990.

Dunning, John. *On the Air: The Encyclopedia of Old-Time Radio*. New York: Oxford University Press, 1998.

Ellis, Edward Rabb. *A Nation in Torment: The Great American Depression, 1929–1939*. New York: Capricorn Books, 1971.

————. *The Epic of New York: A Narrative History*. New York: Old Town Books, 1966.

Fast, Howard. *The Naked God: The Writer and the Communist Party*. New York: Praeger, 1957.

Filler, Louis, ed. *The Anxious Years: America in the Nineteen Thirties—A Collection of Contemporary Writings*. New York: G.P. Putnam's Sons, 1963.

Fitzgerald, F. Scott. *This Side of Paradise*. New York: Charles Scribner's Sons, 1920.

————. *The Great Gatsby*. New York: Charles Scribner's Sons, 1925.

Friedman, Milton, and Anna Jacobson Schwartz. *The Great Contraction, 1929–1933*. Princeton, NJ: Princeton University Press, 1965.

Furnas, J. C. *Stormy Weather: Crosslights on the Nineteen Thirties: An Informal History of the United States, 1929–1941*. New York: G.P. Putnam's Sons, 1977.

Gabree, John. *Gangsters: From Little Caesar to the Godfather*. New York: Gallahad Books, 1973.

Galbraith, John Kenneth. *The Great Crash, 1929*. Boston: Houghton Mifflin, 1955.

Gornick, Vivian. *The Romance of American Communism*. New York: Basic Books, 1977.

Gottlieb, William P. *The Golden Age of Jazz*. New York: Simon & Schuster, 1979.

Gregory, James N. *American Exodus: The Dust Bowl Migration and Okie Culture in California*. New York: Oxford University Press, 1989.

Hamm, Charles. *Yesterdays: Popular Song in America*. New York: W.W. Norton & Company, 1979.

Harkness, John. *The Academy Awards Handbook*. New York: Pinnacle, 1994.

Harrod, R. F. *The Life of John Maynard Keynes*. New York: Avon Books, 1971.

Heide, Robert, and John Gilman. *Dime-Store Dream Parade: Popular Culture, 1925–1955*. New York: E.P. Dutton. 1979.

Higham, Charles. *American Swastika*. Garden City, NY: Doubleday & Co., 1985.

Horan, James D. *The Desperate Years: A Pictorial History of the Thirties*. New York: Bonanza Books, 1962.

Hudson, Lois Phillips. *Reapers of the Dust: A Prairie Chronicle*. Boston: Little, Brown & Co., 1964

Jeffers, H. Paul. *Napoleon of New York: Mayor Fiorello La Guardia*. New York: John Wiley & Sons, 2002.

Jellison, Charles A. *Tomatoes Were Cheaper: Tales from the Thirties*. Syracuse, NY: Syracuse University Press, 1977.

Kessner, Thomas. *Fiorello H. La Guardia and the Making of Modern New York*. New York: McGraw-Hill Publishing Co., 1989.

Klehr, Harvey. *The Heyday of American Communism: The Depression Decade*. New York: Basic Books, 1984.

Kyvig, David E., ed. *FDR's America, 1933–1945*. St. Charles, MO: Forum Press, 1976.

Lacy, Leslie Alexander. *The Soil Soldiers: The Civilian Conservation Corps in the Great Depression*. Radnor, PA: Chilton Book Co., 1976.

Lash, Joseph P. *Dealers and Dreamers: A New Look at the New Deal*. New York: Doubleday, 1988.

Leighton, Isabel, ed. *The Aspirin Age: 1919–1941*. New York: Simon & Schuster, 1949.

Leuchtenburg, William. *Franklin D. Roosevelt and the New Deal*. New York: Harper, 1963.

Lewis, Tom. *Empire of the Air: The Men Who Made Radio*. New York: HarperCollins, 1991.

Long, Huey. *Every Man a King: The Autobiography of Huey Long*. New Orleans: National Book Co., Inc., 1933.

Lynd, Robert S., and Helen Merrel. *Middletown: A Study in Modern American Culture*. New York: Harcourt, Brace & Co., 1929.

Lyons, Eugene. *The Red Decade: The Stalinist Penetration of America.* New York: The Bobbs-Merrill Company, 1941.

Mangione, Jerre. *The Dream and the Deal: The Federal Writers' Project, 1935–1943.* Philadelphia: University of Pennsylvania Press, 1983.

Marquis, Alice G. *Hopes and Ashes: The Birth of Modern Times, 1929–1939.* New York: Fress Press, 1986.

McElvaine, Robert S., ed. *Down and Out in the Great Depression: Letters from the "Forgotten Man."* Chapel Hill: University of North Carolina Press, 1983.

———. *The Great Depression: America, 1929–1941.* New York: Times Books, 1984.

Meltzer, Milton. *Brother, Can You Spare a Dime? The Great Depression, 1929–1933.* New York: New American Library, 1977.

Miller, Nathan. *F.D.R.: An Intimate History.* New York: Doubleday & Co., 1983.

Moley, Raymond. *The First New Deal.* New York: Harcourt, 1966.

Parish, Michael E. *A Vision Shared: A Classic Portrait of America in Prosperity and Depression, 1920–1941.* New York: W.W. Norton, 1992.

Peeler, David P. *Hope Among Us Yet: Social Criticism and Social Solace in Depression America.* Chicago: University of Chicago Press, 1987.

Perrett, Geoffrey. *America in the Twenties: A History.* New York: Simon & Schuster, 1982.

Schlesinger, Arthur A. Jr. *The Coming of the New Deal.* Boston: Houghton Mifflin Co., 1958.

Seldes, Gilbert. *The Years of the Locust (America, 1929–1932).* Boston: Little, Brown & Co., 1933.

Shachtman, Tom. *The Day America Crashed.* New York: G.P. Putnam's Sons, 1929.

Shannon, David A. *Between the Wars: America 1919–1941*. Boston: Houghton Mifflin Co., 1979

Skolnik, Peter L., with Laura Torbet and Nikkie Smith. *Fads: America's Crazes, Fevers and Fancies From the 1890s to the 1970s*. New York: Thomas Y. Crowell Company, 1978.

Sloat, Warren. *1929: America Before the Crash*. New York: Macmillan Publishing Co., 1979.

Smith, Jean. *The Shattered Dream: Herbert Hoover and the Great Depression*. New York: William Morrow, 1970.

Stein, Walter J. *California and the Dustbowl Migration*. Westport, CT: Greenwood Press, 1973.

Steinbeck, John. *The Grapes of Wrath*. New York: Alfred P. Knopf, Everyman's Library Edition, 1993. First edition: 1940.

Sterling, Kittross. *Stay Tuned: A Concise History of American Broadcasting*. Belmont, CA: Wadsworth, 1990.

Terkel, Studs. *Hard Times: An Oral History of the Great Depression*. New York: Random House, 1980.

Thomas, Gordon, and Max Morgan-Witts. *The Day the Bubble Burst: A Social History of the Wall Street Crash of 1929*. Garden City, NY: Doubleday & Co., 1979.

Tugwell, R. G. *The Brain Trust*. New York: Viking Press, 1968.

Warren, Frank. *Liberals and Communism: The "Red Decade" Revisited*. Indianapolis: Indiana University Press, 1966.

Warren, Harris Gaylord. *Herbert Hoover and the Great Depression*. New York: Oxford University Press, 1959.

Watkins, T. H. *The Great Depression: America in the 1930s*. Boston: Little, Brown, 1993.

———. *The Hungry Years: A Narrative History of the Great Depression in America*. New York: Henry Holt and Company, 1999.

Wecter, Dixon. *The Age of the Great Depression, 1929–1941*. Chicago: Quadrangle Books, 1971.

Wilson, Edmund. *The American Earthquake: A Documentary of the Twenties and Thirties*. Garden City, NY: Doubleday & Co., 1958.

Wiltz, John E. *From Isolation to War, 1931–1941*. New York: Thomas Y. Crowell Co., 1968.

Winslow, Susan. *Brother, Can You Spare a Dime? America from the Wall Street Crash to Pearl Harbor: An Illustrated Documentary*. New York: Paddington Press, 1979.

White, William Allen. *Forty Years on Main Street*. New York: Farrar & Rhinehart. Inc., 1937.

Works Progress Administration. *The WPA Guide to California*. New York: Hastings House, 1939.

———. *The WPA Guide to Louisiana*. New York: Random House, 1939.

———. *The WPA Guide to Massachusetts*. New York: Random House, 1939.

———. *The WPA Guide to New York City*. New York: Random House, 1939.

Worster, Donald. *Dust Bowl: The Southern Plains in the 1930s*. New York: Oxford University Press, 1979.

Index

B

X–Y

Z

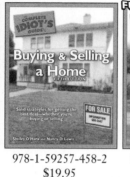

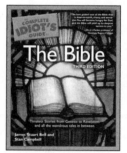
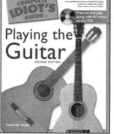